Greta Garbage's Outrageous Bathroom Book

Greta Garbage's Outrageous Bathroom Book

by Greta Garbage

Ten Speed Press

Berkeley   Toronto

Ten Speed Press
PO Box 7123
Berkeley, California 94707
www.tenspeed.com

Distributed in Australia by Simon and Schuster Australia, in Canada by Ten Speed Press Canada, in New Zealand by Southern Publishers Group, in South Africa by Real Books, in Southeast Asia by Berkeley Books, and in the United Kingdom and Europe by Airlift Book Company.

Library of Congress Cataloging-in-Publication Data

Garbage, Greta, 1942–
  Greta Garbage's outrageous bathroom book / Greta Garbage.
      p. cm.
Includes bibliographical references and index.
  ISBN 1-58008-286-6
  1. Entertainers—Miscellanea. 2. Celebrities—Miscellanea.
3. Curiosities and wonders—Miscellanea. I. Title: Outrageous
bathroom book. II. Title.
  PN2285 .G29 2001
  791'.092'2—dc21

                            2001002797

Cover design by Victor Mingovits, NYC
Interior design by Victor Mingovits, NYC, based on an design by Jeff Brandenburg/Image Comp

First printing, 2001
Printed in Canada

1 2 3 4 5 6 7 8 9 10 — 05 04 03 02 01

Dedicated to Albert Podell, my friend, counselor, and editor, who spent many hours grunting over this one and helping it all come out smoothly.

Contents

ALCOHOL AND DRUGS

SPORTS

ANIMALS

INTERNET

ARTSY-FARTSY STUFF

MONEY

PEOPLE: MANIPULATING THEM FOR FUN AND PROFIT

INTERESTING PEOPLE, PLACES, AND THINGS

LOVE AND MARRIAGE

LEGAL LOONYISM

POLITICS

BODY AND SOUL

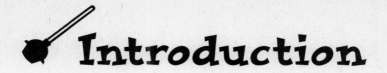 Introduction

Move over Uncle John—this is an edgier and far more interesting bathroom book, filled with shorter and more shocking stories about celebrities, sex (plus celebrities and sex!), drugs, computers, pornography, strange people, famous people, psychics, crime, sports, movies, television, dogs, cats, politics, money, cars, and much more.

Some bathroom readers are for constipated people; this one, with sexier and shorter articles, is for people on the run. To be read a few pages at a time while on the john, it contains more than 1,000 shocking stories, fascinating facts, titillating bits of trivia, hilarious pieces of humor, bizarre news stories, and quirky quotes on more than fifty different topics. These items range from just-plain-interesting topics (celebrity sex secrets, kinky sex, sports trivia, disgusting presidents, etc.) to practical advice you rarely find elsewhere (and never all in one place!), like how to get off jury duty, clone your dog or cat, be a movie extra, get a raise, get revenge, be a sperm donor, cure hemorrhoids, stop smoking, win lotteries and radio contests, tell if someone's lying, slip out of traffic tickets, beat car salesmen at their own game, and catch a cheating partner.

So, thanks for buying this toilet book—I'm flushed with excitement that you'll soon be reading it.

Greta Garbage
GretaGarbage@aol.com
www.GretaGarbage.com

NOTE: I attempted to give attribution as much as possible, but some of the material comes from the Internet, where sourcing (especially for humor and trivia) is scarce. If you know who wrote something, and I haven't listed them at the bottom of the section or in the additional sources at the end of the book, please e-mail me at GretaGarbage@aol.com and let me know. I will add the name of the author to the next edition of this book.

Also, some Web sites may not work because the Web changes so quickly. Try searching for the term (on a search engine like Google.com) to see if the site has moved or if someone has created a similar site.

# Celebrities

SHOCKING BEHAVIORS OF THE STARS

Joe Eszterhas, in his deliciously gossip-filled book *American Rhapsody*, claims that **Farrah Fawcett** once had to go to the bathroom so badly that she did so—right on the lawn of the hostess's house at a Hollywood party. Guests watched her in horror from the windows during the party.

Charlie Sheen once admitted that he **beat a neighbor's peacock to death** with a broomstick because "it kept shitting all over my basketball court."

Have They No Shame?

Madonna has said some pretty bad things about Catholicism—not to mention all the things she has *done* that were hardly in keeping with church doctrine, and what her persona has done to the image of the *real* Madonna. Despite this, according to *Movieline*, she had the nerve to ask the pope to personally christen her daughter (who was born out of wedlock) Lourdes!

Watch out for **Sophia Loren**. Jeannette Walls of MSNBC.com reported that after Walter Matthau died, there were "conflicting reports" as to how Loren obtained his watch.

"She took it off Walter's body during a viewing" says one appalled source. "When it happened, Walter's widow asked her what she was doing. Sophia said she wanted a memento, so Walter's wife said, 'Oh go ahead and take it.'" Loren's spokeswoman said that **Matthau's wife presented it to her as a memento.**

Here's a little story to make you privy to celebrity lifestyles. Cary Grant was once on a train in France when he decided to check a painful hemorrhoid by standing on a toilet so he could see in the mirror, and then spreading his cheeks apart. He forgot to lock the door and someone walked in.

Nancy Sinatra reportedly stayed home and watched the final episode of *Seinfeld* instead of going to the hospital to see her father when he was dying. Afterward, she was quoted as saying, "I guess I could have taped it."

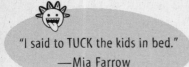

Anna Nicole Smith wanted $800 million for only fourteen months of marriage to a man who was **sixty years older than she was.** That came out to close to $2 million a day for putting up with gramps.

Linda Ronstadt admitted that "My big fantasy has been to **seduce a priest.**"

According to *Movie Stars Do the Dumbest Things,* when Sonny died in a ski accident **Cher** acted grief stricken, saying things like, "I never stopped loving him." This caused one person who knew her well to comment, "Can everyone else have forgotten how much **she hated his guts?**"

Hard to Believe

Less than a month before the Simpson-Goldman murders, **O. J. Simpson** made a television pilot for a series called *The Frogmen.* NBC has never shown it, partially because there's a scene of him as a Navy SEAL, holding a blade to the throat of a friend's daughter. (Some think he was wearing that SEAL outfit the final night he visited Nicole.) Military commandos who were brought to the set taught him this **"silent kill" knife technique.**

The elegant movie star **Joan Crawford** once challenged a twenty-one-year-old director to a **burping contest**—and she helped teach him how to do it. The director was Steven Spielberg.

Were They Criminal?

According to *Celebrities: Jokes, Quotes, and Anecdotes 2001 Calendar,* long before **Oprah Winfrey** became famous, she saw Aretha Franklin emerging from a limo, ran over to her, and told her that she had been abandoned and needed money. Aretha gave her $100—which she used not for food but to stay in a hotel.

> When Kevin and Cindy Costner were first married, and desperately broke, they took a honeymoon to Mexico—and skipped out on their hotel bill.

Old-time star **Lou Costello,** of the comedy team Abbott & Costello, was **a raging kleptomaniac.** He stole items from the studio, sometimes even before finishing the filming of a movie. One director had to plead with him to "lend" him back a clock he had lifted since they needed it to redo a scene. **SEE "CELEBS ON DRUGS," PAGE 26.**

One Star's Death Obsession

Angelina Jolie has shocked people with her statements about her brother and their ambiguous relationship, including (at the Oscars), **"I'm in love with my brother."** SEE "THE OSCARS," PAGE 54.

Apparently that was only part of her weirdness. It seems that on her wedding day to her first husband, she wrote his name on her shirt—**using her own blood.** When she married uber-weird Billy Bob Thornton, both wore a small vial of each other's blood around their necks.

She also told *US Weekly* of Thornton, "You know when you love someone so much you can almost kill them? We nearly kill each other . . . I nearly was killed last night." (She was apparently well matched with weirdo Thornton because he responded by saying, "I was looking at her sleep and I had to restrain myself from literally squeezing her to death.")

Her **obsession with death** is also apparent from the following bizarre facts:

- She wanted to be a mortician when she grew up.
- She has a collection of daggers.
- She's obsessed with Vlad the Impaler.
- The Japanese word for death is tattooed on her shoulder.
- She sleeps with knives.

CELEBRITY MAFIA NICKNAMES
- Mark "Marky Three Legs" Wahlberg
- Robert "Three Strikes" Downey Jr.
- Whitney "Bongwater" Houston
- Charlie "STD" Sheen

SOURCE: TOPFIVE.COM

Jack Nicholson's Least-Shining Moments

In a few incidents that have come to light, **Jack Nicholson** acted like his character in *The Shining*—except that in one situation he used a golf club instead of an axe. In a more recent case, his problem was with a different kind of hooker than the kind you use for golf.

First, a 1994 lawsuit from a man who unwisely cut off the pugnacious star while driving alleged that Nicholson went berserk and **took a golf club to his windshield.** A judge later dismissed assault and vandalism charges against Nicholson and he settled the civil suit.

Jack Nicholson's toilet seat has a rattlesnake embedded in it.

More recently, a lawsuit filed against Hollywood's famed naughty boy was for behavior between the sheets rather than behind the wheel. A woman claimed that Nicholson offered her and a friend $1,000 for **three-way sex.** But when she tried to collect afterward, he began slapping her around, dragging her by the hair, pounding her head on the floor, and threatening to kill her.

In the latest salacious incident, *another* woman accused Nicholson of **bursting her breast implants** during an attack at a small dinner party at his home.

None of the defendants fared badly financially from their alleged ordeals. The golf club incident involved a substantial cash settlement. The sexual encounter woman settled out of court for $32,500, and the breast implant lady offered her story to the *National Enquirer* for $100,000.

Odd Celebrity Pet Stories

James Ulmer's *Hollywood Hot List* includes the outrageous story of **Kirstie Alley's** weird pet possum, which she took with her during a promotional trip for one of her movie bombs, *Sibling Rivalry.*

When she tried to bottle-feed the bottom-nosed creature and failed, she insisted that the studio send over a lactating woman to **wet-nurse the possum** as soon as possible!

They thought she was kidding, but she threatened to fly home and skip doing promotional work for the picture if they didn't comply at once. As it turned out, she probably should have.

Jim Carrey has a **pet iguana**—and a special chef to make food for it. The chef goes with Jim when he's filming a movie, and of course, so does the lizard.

Drew Barrymore is so crazy about her cat that she has been quoted as saying that if she died before him, she wanted her ashes put in his food "so I can live inside him."

Britney Spears confessed that when she was young and living in the south, she and friends would engage in **cowtipping,** approaching sleeping cows and tipping them over.

Mike Tyson has a tiger fetish. His Las Vegas home is filled with bright gold tiger paintings. He keeps a pet tiger and feeds it the legs of old horses that have to be put to sleep. The tiger got its revenge one day, according to the *New York Post*, by pinning Tyson to the ground while they were wrestling. "The tiger's foot was on his head," says a friend who witnessed the gladiator-style near execution at Tyson's pad. Mike "had to pet it for three or four hours before it got bored and got off of him."

Stars Who Insist That Others Don't Look at Them

It is against the law to stare at the mayor of Paris, but there's no law in America against staring at a movie star. Some stars act as if they are the Mayor of Paris, insisting that those around them don't look at them at all. And maybe what will happen one day is that people *will* stop looking at them—or start looking at them like they're crazy—which they may deserve.

When **Julia Roberts** moved into a ritzy apartment complex in Hollywood, all the tenants received notices telling them not to make eye contact with her if they saw her in the halls or lobbies.

Looking at it from another standpoint, being stared at ain't no fun either. Rush & Malloy in the *Daily News* quoted **Jack Nicholson** as saying, "One of the toughest things is going to an art museum where you're standing looking at a Van Gogh and going, 'Wow,' and you turn around and here's eight people looking at you!"

"No Eye Contact" Edicts Are Contagious!

- At Sylvester Stallone's Miami residence, workers were told not to look at Stallone.

- Backstage workers at Neil Diamond's concerts were told not to look directly at him.

- Tom Cruise was said to have issued a "don't look" order during the filming of *Eyes Wide Shut*. ("Don't look" is what people wisely did about that movie as well.)

- David Letterman not only doesn't want anyone looking at him as he walks from his office to the stage to start his show, but one of his employees goes through the area first to make sure no one is peeking.

- Jennifer Lopez, who is known to make a lot of expensive backstage demands, has another one, according to Jeannette Walls. "Some guy had to go in advance of Jennifer and clear out the hallways. . . . What's worse, he had to tell everyone that they were not to make eye contact. That under no circumstances was anyone to look at Ms. Lopez."

- People were told not to talk to, photograph, or look at John Travolta.

Other Prima Donna Behavior

Star magazine reported that **Cameron Diaz** has become "such a demanding diva that when she needs her **underarm hair shaved,** she makes her personal assistant do it." In one instance, instead of going back to her trailer to shave her pits, she had her assistant shave them in front of two hundred extras. This happened while she was filming *The Sweetest Thing,* but to further prove that the movie wasn't titled after her, she would also make her assistant take off her boots for her in between takes.

❧

Not only has it come out that **Renee Zellweger** doesn't want people looking at her, but a man was fired for "giving" something to her. Last year, her limousine driver in California was a man who set up a Web site that was going to charge people $5 to **watch a young girl lose her virginity.**

This driver, a father with three children, had written a movie about his (extremely interesting) life and asked if he could "give" her a script instead of taking a tip for the ride. The next day he was fired for it.

❧

Sigourney Weaver insisted that no one use the treadmill next to her at her health club.

❧

Richard Gere made dozens of important people wait while he insisted on having a forty-person elevator all to himself at the New York Film Critics Awards. Wrote Richard Johnson of the Buddhist actor, "Oneness with the Universe is one thing, but oneness in an elevator may be too much."

❧

Jeannette Walls, who writes the Scoop column for MSNBC.com, gave a **"Peel Me a Grape Award"** to **Mariah Carey,** "For her entourage of handlers, one of whom sticks out his hand to retrieve the singer's used chewing gum." (God knows what he has to do when she gives someone a Lewinsky.)

Celebs from Hell

PR Week asked publicity people to name the worst people they ever had the displeasure of working with. The "winners" were:

Mike Tyson	Dr. Laura Schlessinger
Eminem	Dennis Rodman
Kathie Lee Gifford	Woody Allen
Martha Stewart	Sean "Puffy" Combs

SEX SECRETS OF THE STARS
Bad Sexual Behavior

Although some say this story is an urban legend, **Sly Stallone,** while making the movie *Judge Dredd,* had sex with an extra, forgetting that he was still wearing his microphone. The whole crew supposedly heard him telling the girl, **"Slap my butt."**

To add to his humiliation, the cast had T-shirts made up and wore them the next day. They said, "Slap My Butt."

Mel Gibson is a notorious practical joker. Indeed, he's known to give his leading ladies **a dead rat,** which they no doubt find hilarious. When he was working on the set of *Lethal Weapon 4,* he put one of Joe Pesci's cigars in the, ahem, wrong end. He didn't let Pesci know about it until after he had smoked it.

The Day John Died revealed that **JFK Jr.** was into porn flicks—so much so that he hung onto them for reviewing and had to pay close to $1,000 in late fees to one video store for all his **overdue adult videos. SEE "PORNOGRAPHY," PAGE 141.**

GOOD SEXUAL BEHAVIOR

If you believe it, Madonna once said, "Everyone thinks I'm a raving nymphomaniac and that I have an insatiable sexual appetite. The truth is, I'd rather stay home and read a book."

Milton Berle, once the biggest name in television, was accused a few years ago of ruining a thirty-three-year-old bellman's sex life by grabbing him in the crotch and squeezing. The bellman at the Taj Mahal Hotel in Atlantic City says that he told Uncle Miltie, "You look terrific for your age," which may have irritated him because of the mention of his age. He said Berle then **"lunged for his crotch and squeezed,"** necessitating later hospital visits.

Berle decided to fight the suit, saying he was suspicious that it took the bellman two years to institute the suit. He added: "I'm nearly eighty-eight years old. I have better things to do in my life than go around grabbing some guy's crotch. Hell, at my age, I'm lucky if I can find my *own* crotch."

Old-time swashbuckling movie star **Errol Flynn** once masturbated on the front door of old-time gossip columnist Hedda Hopper. Afterward, he asked her, "Will you invite me to come here again?"

Jim Carrey says it thrills him to know his fans are getting excited watching him talk out of his butt. (He also says the only thing he won't do for a laugh is have sex with an animal.)

Marlon Brando wants to be filmed above the waist only because he's gotten so fat. So to make sure no one films him down below, he has shown up on the set of his movies with **no pants on underneath his coat.**

Who's Hung in Hollywood?

If you're interested in the size of **celebrities at full monty,** check out Internet newsgroups (such as alt.showbiz.gossip and alt.gossip.celebrities), books *(Penis Size and Enlargement),* tabloids (such as *Star,* which ran a story on genitalia), and newsletters (an amazing one by Chuck Thomspon is filled with stories about celebrity penises).

Are they accurate? Most come from people who have seen (in person or videos or movies) or sampled the product themselves. Some are just rumors, but they are probably based on fact. Here are some secrets about who really measures up—and who doesn't.

Very hung men in Hollywood have been called **"Hollywood loaves"** (and women who go after large men "size queens"). No one disputes that some men who belong to this coveted club are:

- **Liam Neeson:** According to an article in *Penthouse,* actress Dana Delany once said that if Liam Neeson, James Woods, and Ed Begley Jr., were placed in the same room, there wouldn't be room for anyone else.
- **James Woods:** See above. By the way, he was once kneed in the groin by a girlfriend and he filed assault charges against her. Photos of him had to be taken, which ended up being circulated.
- **Bruce Willis:** He has said that he wants to be nude in a film, and in fact, was exposed in *The Color of Night.* According to Chuck Thompson's newsletter, in the director's cut, one can still "ogle Bruce's big thick circumcised shlong. . . . There's almost more hair down there than on his head. . . . Keep it coming! We want to die hard."
- **Sean Connery:** When he was young, he posed nude in art classes— and supposedly caused at least one artist to drop her pencil.
- **David Letterman:** One of his fans has created a Web site called "Dave's Basket," consisting of various shots of Dave "stretching out" his jeans.

- **Warren Beatty:** According to a fascinating book, *Penis Size and Enlargement*, Shirley MacLaine, Warren Beatty's sister, once said that she wanted to be in a movie with her brother so she could see what all the fuss was about.
- **Don Johnson:** He's said to be as big around as a beer can.

Others with a mountain of evidence stacked up against them:

Patrick Stewart	Peter Lawford
Brendan Fraser	Rob Lowe
Harrison Ford	Ryan O'Neal
David Duchovny	Alex Baldwin
Charles Bronson	Jack Nicholson
Jason Priestly	James Caan
Jim Carrey	Matt Dillon
Woody Harrelson	Tommy Lee Jones
Lyle Lovett	Bruce Jenner
Jason Patric	Robert Redford
Jimmy Smits	Christopher Reeve
Kiefer Sutherland	Steve Martin
Michael Caine	Dolph Lundgren
Sean Penn	Dick Cavett

The Legend Lives On

Did **Elvis** belong to the "National Endowment of the Arts?" He used to refer to his pole as "Little Elvis," but also once described Little Elvis as "a big ole ugly Hillbilly pecker."

John Wayne was probably more of a duchess than a duke. Photos of him in women's clothes, complete with pocketbook, appeared in the tabloids. **SEE "FAMOUS CROSS-DRESSERS," PAGE 89.**

Frank Sinatra was so endowed that one of his wives, famous actress Ava Gardner, said of him, "He only weighs 120, but **100 pounds is cock.**"

Clark Gable was called the King of Hollywood, but an old-time movie star once said that he was so small, he was practically the **Queen of Hollywood.**

Errol Flynn entertained Hollywood partygoers by playing "You Are My Sunshine" on the piano—using only his organ.

A few other well-endowed old-timers:

- **Charlie Chaplin's** tool was referred to as "the eighth wonder of the world."
- **Gary Cooper** was supposedly "hung like a horse."
- **Ernest Hemingway** was "like a 30-30 rifle shell."
- **Roddy McDowall** was not only endowed but flexible, and supposedly performed self-fellatio in front of others as a "party trick."

Tiny Meat or Hamster Hung?

Marky Mark (Mark Wahlberg) revealed in an interview that Leonardo DiCaprio was originally the one being considered for the lead role in *Boogie Nights*. But Wahlberg, who has claimed to be average or smaller, said he got the coveted part when he told the director that he had an inch on Leonardo—and then proved it.

Tom Jones once boasted on Howard Stern's television show that when he is at the gym, "Even men admire me." Old-time movie star Mamie Van Doren deflated his image by saying, "He must have **socks stuffed down there** because his penis is very, very small."

There's a lot of controversy about **Arnold Schwarzenegger,** and some of it has to do with his joystick. There are reports that have him at nine inches, but as one person wrote on the Internet, "I saw a picture of a flaccid Arnold in *Spy.* If that dinky thing grows into nine inches, then the Amazing Kreskin must be involved."

Kevin Costner once said that audiences would be "hurt" if they didn't see him in the nude in *For the Love of the Game.* Perhaps he should have kept his mouth shut—and his pants on. An article by Julie Keller revealed, "A clipped shower scene featuring Costner's, um, full monty, inspired laughter at a Scottsdale, Arizona, screening. 'The audience laughed at Kevin's penis,' one exec told *New York Magazine.*"

Another Kevin was revealed to have fallen short in certain areas in an *Examiner* article titled "**Kevin Bacon's** Bits Are Too Little." There, they told the story of a digital image made of him for a movie—and his sex organs were supposedly too small to show up!

Robert Downey Jr. is quoted in *Movie Stars Do the Dumbest Things* as saying that he would do a nude scene but hoped he wouldn't have an erection because "Maybe it's not as big as I want it to be."

The *New York Post* reported a few years ago that one of the top plastic surgeons in Los Angeles had a lawsuit filed against him by former employees. It was claimed in the lawsuit that he had poked fun at the penises of Don Johnson and **Michael Jackson**, even supposedly exposing and obscenely manipulating Michael Jackson's penis while thoroughly scrutinizing it. On another occasion, while examining Michael Jackson's penis, he had allegedly said something to the effect that Jackson had never used it!

After they split, Roseanne was glad to tell people secrets about Tom Arnold: "In lovemaking, what he lacked in size, he made up for in speed." But he got back at her by saying, "Even a 747 looks small when it lands in the Grand Canyon."

While **Don Johnson,** believed to be one of the most well-endowed men in Hollywood, was recovering from liposuction, his doctor supposedly pointed to Don's exposed genitals and said, "Why would Melanie Griffith settle for that?"

A semi-porn film called *Italian Stallion,* made early in **Sylvester Stallone**'s career, obviously didn't refer to him. As one person who saw it said: "Poor thing is so small **you need a magnifying glass to see it.**"

Brad Pitt may also be the pits in this area. He was measured last year in the bathroom of the Howard Stern Studio and came out the second largest of the male staff in the room. He was approximately six inches.

Wayne Newton may be the current King of Las Vegas, but he may be more like a queen in other areas: He was described as being **"hung like a gnat."**

As told in *That's Disgusting: An Adult Guide to What's Gross, Tasteless, Rude, Crude, and Lewd,* when **Montgomery Clift** *(Suddenly Last Summer, A Place in the Sun,* etc.) died, his autopsy was performed by the chief medical examiner of New York.

Afterward, the doctor's wife, a famous psychiatrist, was said to have discussed Monty's dick at dinner parties, telling people that she had seen it at the autopsy and that it was **small and shriveled.**

She also claimed that she had flicked it, which she would then proceed to demonstrate. Such revelations, when they hit the newspapers, did nothing for either doctors' career or reputation—but it did get them invited to a lot of dinner parties.

Stars Who Have Admitted to Masturbation

Whoopi Goldberg admitted, "When I was younger I tried to go down on myself with some success." She says she was able to reach her desired goal, but "I couldn't do much down there."

By the way, this "hobby" is much more common among men than women, and Masters & Johnson said that .003 percent of all men were able to perform **self-fellatio.** Some need help to do it. It has been said—and it probably isn't true—that **Marilyn Manson** had two of his ribs removed so that he could easily bend down to give himself oral sex.

It's better not to try to picture her taking a whack at this one: The eighty-nine-year-old co-star of the *Titanic,* **Gloria Stuart,** admitted in her autobiography, "I am devoted to masturbation." (Still?)

"Don't knock masturbation. It's sex with someone I love."
—Woody Allen

Howard Stern said that he spanks the monkey so much he's in "danger of being arrested for animal cruelty." He said that when he was young, his mother kept asking, "What happened to all the Kleenex?" and he had to make believe he had a cold.

Sock It to Them

Esquire gave a Dubious Achievement Award to **Kelsey Grammer,** star of *Frasier,* after a thirty-three-year-old nursing student claimed that only an hour and a half after they met, he began **sucking her toes and moaning,** "Feed me. Feed me." Instead she gave him the boot.

May God have mercy on his sole: **Charlie Sheen** is rumored to be a foot fetishist. (He's also a tattoo fetishist, with more than a dozen of them on his body, including one that looks like a memo pad with the message, "Back in 15 Minutes.") **SEE "THE SMELL OF DE-FEET," PAGE 65.**

"It took about a minute and a half—and that includes my buying the dress."
—Joan Rivers, on her first sexual experience

Underage Virginity Losses

Dustin Hoffman told an Australian publication that he lost his virginity at fifteen by making believe he was his brother when he was in a darkened room. According to the Page Six column of the *New York Post,* the young woman wanted to make love to his older brother, and when she asked Dustin if he was the brother, Dustin said yes in his brother's voice—so he could get laid. Afterward, when the woman saw his face and realized what happened, she screamed.

A few other admitted virginity losses:
- **Cher** claimed she lost her virginity to **Warren Beatty** when she was sixteen—and she said he wasn't so hot as a lover.
- **Sean Connery** lost his virginity at eight.
- **Gillian Anderson** *(X-Files)* lost her virginity at thirteen.

MEMORABLE THOUGHTS ON VIRGINITY

- "I remember the first time I had sex . . . I still have the receipt."—Groucho Marx

- "I knew her before she was a virgin."—Groucho Marx, about Doris Day

- "I'm as pure as the driven slush."—Tallulah Bankhead

- "I used to be Snow White but I drifted."—Mae West

Sniffing Out a Hollywood Pervert

Talk about the pits. A kiss-and-tell—or in this case, a sniff-and-tell—exposé writer recently dated a guy she called merely "Mr. Movie Star" and revealed his secret fetish: **armpit sniffing!** Get a whiff of that!

Now, as Hollywood perversions go, this is pretty penny-ante stuff compared to the genuinely astonishing range of creepy and weird sex that pampered Hollywood stars have been known to engage in, and unlike Jack Nicholson's brutal streak, at least it isn't illegal or fattening.

Despite this, the exposé set off a guessing contest to identify the armpit bandit. The writer mentioned he was in the movie *The Thin Red Line,* which pretty much narrowed it down. **George Clooney** got fingered and angrily denied it. That still left: **Woody Harrelson** (more known for inhaling reefer smoke than armpits), **Sean Penn, Jared Leto,** and **John Cusack.**

Then the *National Enquirer,* with their implacable army of reporters, managed to sniff out the truth: They say the guilty party is John Cusack. His current girlfriend, Neve Campbell, denied it, but for obvious reasons she would.

Promiscuous Celebrities (Or, Does Tom Cruise?)

He doth protest too much. After it was reported in a man's magazine that **George Clooney** had slept with a thousand women, he said, "Of course, it's not true. And if it were, nobody would really claim that." (Really?)

Frank Sinatra once said, "If I had as many love affairs as I have been given credit for, I would now be speaking to you from a jar at Harvard Medical School."

Do They or Don't They? They Do.

- ℮ Wilt Chamberlain claimed to have had sex with twenty thousand women.

- ℮ Charlie Sheen claimed that he had sex with five thousand—giving him the name "Machine."

- ℮ Marilyn Monroe was said to be "the original good time was had by all," according to Bette Davis.

"Madonna just bought a home with nine bedrooms. That means 'no waiting.'"
—Jay Leno

Others rumored to be bad boys (at one time, if not now):

Jack Nicholson	Warren Beatty
Dennis Rodman	Geraldo Rivera
Leonardo DiCaprio	Ryan O'Neal
Prince	Tommy Lee
Scott Baio	David Duchovny
Led Zeppelin	

Old-time oversexed stars:

Errol Flynn (leading to the expression "In Like Flynn")
Clark Gable
Marilyn Monroe
Rock Hudson
Steve McQueen
Anthony Quinn

CELEBRITY BODIES
Take It *All* Off

Julia Roberts has never done a nude scene before the cameras. In *Pretty Woman* she used a body double. She has implied that the reason is modesty, saying, "I just don't feel that my algebra teacher should ever know what my butt looks like."

But the real reason may be that she isn't such a pretty woman below her neck. One man on the Internet whose friend worked in costuming said that was true—that Julia hadn't done any nude scenes because the executives (not she) wanted it that way. He posited that her body was "**a little goofy looking in the buff.** . . . She appeared somewhat knock-kneed . . . her body droopy and hairy . . . her hips and butt were supposedly not that great. Her big feet . . . everyone saw those gun boats in her bath scenes with Mr. Gerbil. . . . She will probably remain clothed."

Sharon Stone once said, "I can't put a sentence together so thank God I can take my clothes off." But she now claims she was tricked into that infamous pantyless shot. She claims that the director told her to **remove her panties** because they reflected too much light.

Sure. As her friend Joe Eszterhas explained it, it would have been impossible for Sharon Stone not to know exactly what was going to be filmed. He wrote, "The shot had to be lighted, and the hair and makeup people were between her legs most of the morning." Saying she didn't realize what was going to happen was "Sharon's way of saying that she didn't inhale."

"Sarah Jessica Parker has a no-nudity clause in her next movie contract. I have a no-nudity clause too. If there's a movie without nudity, I don't see it."
—Jay Leno

Not everyone wants to see stars naked. Ananova.com did a survey asking people which stars they would pay to keep their clothes on. **Mariah Carey** was one of the winners: "The woman looks like **a human sausage** in those trailer-trash outfits of hers. We certainly don't need to see what she looks like naked," wrote one of the voters. And someone wrote of **Liam Gallagher,** another winner: "I have been told he has a bum that could rival an orangutan."

Helena Bonham Carter had a no-nipple clause in her contract for *Fight Club,* which made the nude scene she did with Brad Pitt difficult to film.

Keanu Reeves fought to get a particular part of a bathtub sex scene between himself and Charlize Theron put back into *Sweet November.* The studio left the two of them in the bubble bath (covered in bubbles so you couldn't see much anyway), but they deleted the part of the clip where Reeves went underwater.

Even though all women would have universally wanted to see it, Universal cut the shot of **Kevin Costner's penis** in *For the Love of the Game.*

Roseanne did a nude scene, not for a film, but for the offbeat magazine *Gear.* Afterward, she said, seemingly seriously, "I am hot, and I know that I am as sexy as any of those twenty-year-olds."

According to IMDB.com, since playing the well-hung porn star Dirk Diggler *(Boogie Nights),* **Mark Wahlberg** finds that whenever he goes into men's bathrooms, others surreptitiously look at him to see what the real story is. "Guys keep checking me out. It's become a bit of a pain actually," he complained.

The Truth about Celebrity Bodies

How about the **two biggest puckers** in Hollywood, Melanie Griffith and Angelina Jolie. Are those lips for real?

- **Melanie Griffith,** whose lips keep getting bigger and bigger, says on her Web site, "Yes, I used to put collagen in my lips but not anymore. That is the straight story from me to you."
- Some think that the reason she isn't using collagen anymore is that she now has a permanent implant. "You can tell it's an implant because there are sharp edges around the corners of her mouth," said one person, who is not a fan of her weird-looking muzzles.
- As for **Angelina Jolie,** she contends that her lips are real. "When I was born, they said I was a pair of lips and [had] this very small head, and I had the same size mouth when I was a baby [as I do now]. If I have to kiss someone with a very small mouth, I seem to devour them and it's quite disgusting."

Someone posted on the Internet that **Tom Cruise** has "the dreaded sloping shoulders syndrome." Movies camouflage this problem, usually by having him wear jackets with "impossibly padded shoulders."

When *Vanity Fair* ran a photo spread of him, all the pictures showed his body in profile and his face either turned toward the camera or shown only from the side so you wouldn't see the truth.

According to Amy Reiter of Salon.com, a popular celebrity game is **"Knob Touch,"** in which men take out their penis at a big party and walk around seeing how many celebrities they can touch with their organ.

Reiter also wrote that **Jennifer Love Hewitt** was said to have named her breasts Thelma and Louise, but Hewitt later denied it.

Michelle Pfeiffer wasn't chicken about admitting in an interview that although everyone else thinks she is beautiful, she personally thinks she looks like a duck. (Maybe someone was goosing her at the time.)

Dolly Parton once lost a Dolly Parton look-alike contest. (For her, "parton" was such sweet sorrow.)

Richard Gere portrayed a gynecologist in *Dr. T and the Women*. His costar, Liv Tyler, complained afterward that she was "uncomfortable to have Richard Gere looking between my legs all day."

And speaking of Richard Gere, next time you see his hands close-up, they may not be his. They supposedly have to use hand models for close-ups in his movies because his fingers are so short and his hands so unsexy.

Behind the Celebrity Behinds

America may be obsessed with breasts, but it often seems as if celebrities are more concerned about what's behind them.

"My butt is fascinating to me. I like it so much that whenever I dance, I'm always looking at it," said **Tori Spelling**. *Star* magazine also reported that Tori said she **doesn't wear underwear** because "She didn't want a visible panty line spoiling what she believes is the best-looking backside in Hollywood." She said she's been working out and now "I'm really proud of my butt. . . . I always notice that women in magazines never show their butt. But I get a guy interested in me by walking away from them. . . . You talk, show them that you're intelligent, then you say, 'I have to go to the bathroom.'"

After her famous scene in *Basic Instinct,* **Sharon Stone** put no-nudity clauses in her contracts, and told others she wouldn't take her clothes off in a film because "My ass hangs half way down to my knees." (No one noticed because they were too busy trying to look up the *front* of her skirt.)

In the book *Movie Stars Do the Dumbest Things,* they quoted **Will Smith** explaining why he did his own underwear scenes for *Enemy of the State.* "I have a special butt. It has special curves and it kinda has its own attitude. I think the audience can feel that, and if I were to try to put someone else's butt in that place, the audience would feel cheated and emotionally insulted."

Elizabeth Hurley tries to keep her glutes at their maximus with the following odd ritual: Every morning after she showers, she says she sandpapers her behind in order to keep it smooth.

Mel Gibson's rear end was shaved for his role in *Lethal Weapon 2.* (This behind-the-scenes fact shows up a lot, so we know that Mel doesn't have a swell-looking ass.)

George Clooney is notorious for his practical jokes. (Such tales can't all be told here. If you want to see those kinds of celebrity stories, read *That's Disgusting: An Adult Guide to What's Gross, Tasteless, Rude, Crude, and Lewd.*)

For example, Jeannette Walls of MSNBC.com revealed that when Clooney was on a boat with friends in the south of France, he took one of his friends' cameras when he wasn't looking, dropped his pants, **mooned the camera,** and said nothing about it afterward—no doubt reveling in the thought of his friend's jaw-dropping reaction when he developed his film.

Said **Joan Rivers**'s daughter, Melissa Joan Hart, "If your butt looks good, your outfit looks good." (She might have added, "If your *tits* show, no one notices your outfit anyway.")

"If they show my butt in a movie, it better be a wide shot," said Jennifer Lopez. Indeed. As Cindy Crawford said about J-Lo's famous can, "I don't know if I would have the guts to walk around with that butt."

Christie Brinkley said, "I wish my butt did not go sideways, but I guess I have to face that." (If she's facing her ass, then she's got a *real* problem.)

"I admit I do have a very nice butt. Some say my career was built on it," said Jean-Claude Van Damme, who has indeed had the career of an ass.

"I have no butt. Everyone tells me that. It's tiny, and not even rock climbing helps," claims **Ricky Martin**.

Bad (and Good) Hair Days of the Stars

When he viewed the scenes in his movie *Striking Distance,* **Bruce Willis** thought his toupee was too obvious so he insisted on the scenes that displeased him being redone—at a cost of $750,000 to the studio. Studio honchos probably flipped their wigs when they saw that bill.

Star Trek skipper **Patrick Stewart** claims that being bald helps him because he can be used for two roles for the price of one by wearing a toupee. But he wasn't so cheerful about his shine when he went **bald at the age of nineteen.**

When **George Clooney** was making *O Brother, Where Art Thou?* they put a lot of pomade in his hair, made from whatever grease they could get. Not only did "it take a lifetime to get that stuff out of my hair," he told the *Daily News* of Los Angeles, "but you can imagine, being in Jackson, Mississippi, in July with the stuff scraped off the top of a canned ham piled in my hair. My hair was collecting bugs for weeks," he said.

And **Julia Roberts** says she hated hers to such a degree that she can't watch herself in movies that she did before the early '90s, when she started plucking her eyebrows. (With that mouth, it's unlikely anyone but Julia noticed her eyebrows.)

A marketing survey of which movies help sell products found the following startling fact: When a Kevin Costner movie was shown at a mall theater, there was an almost 10 percent increase in sales of hair-care products for men. His thinning hair seems to wig men out, reminding them that they had better do something fast before their hair ended up looking like his.

And hair are some more facts:

- **John Travolta** has someone color in his bald spot.
- **Whoopi Goldberg**'s receding hairline was probably caused by the tight cornrow braids she wore.
- Someone once said of **Martha Stewart**: "All that money, and her hair is still in her eyes."
- **Samuel L. Jackson** keeps two very expensive hairdressers with him on his set at all times—although his head is shaved.
- "My hair will probably outlive the human race," said **Burt Reynolds** on his hair transplant—which later didn't take.
- **Sharon Stone** said she doesn't know what her natural hair color is because she hasn't seen it since she was fourteen years old
- **Louella Parsons** once said of Joan Collins, "She looks like she combs her hair with an eggbeater."

Heavily balding stars who hide it:

- Charlie Sheen
- Emilio Estevez
- Woody Harrelson (sometimes)
- Ted Danson (sometimes)
- Dolly Parton
- Whitney Houston (whose wigs cost thousands of dollars)

CELEBRITY FREAKS

And the winner is . . .

When **Andy Garcia** was born in Cuba in 1956, he had an undeveloped twin about the size of a tennis ball on his shoulder. It has since been removed and Garcia has received the *Guinness Book of Records* dubious distinction of being "the most successful co-joined twin."

IN A CATEGORY ALL ITS OWN
Elvis had webbing between the toes of his right foot!
SEE "THE KING," PAGE 42.

Second place:

Hollywood actor **Mark Wahlberg** (also known as Marky Mark, and most famous for his role in *Boogie Nights*) has **three nipples**. The third nipple is about the size of a quarter and is below his regular nipple. It had to be airbrushed out of his famous Calvin Klein ads.

Runners-up:
- When **Sylvester Stallone** was born, his lips, chin, and half of his tongue were partially paralyzed because the forceps that helped deliver him injured a nerve in his face.
- **Dudley Moore** was born with club feet.
- **Damon Wayans** also had club feet.
- **Marilyn Monroe** may have had an extra toe on her foot.
- **Liam Gallagher** of Oasis may have an extra toe on each foot.
- **Alfred Hitchcock** was missing his belly button after abdominal surgery covered it up.
- **James Dean** had no front teeth.

Keep an Eye out for These People

Most famous person with a glass eye: **Peter Falk,** who lost his eye as a child because of a malignant tumor.

One-eyed old-timers not around anymore:
- Rex Harrison (Professor Higgins in *My Fair Lady*, etc.)
- Sammy Davis Jr. (lost his eye in a car crash)
- Sandy Duncan (lost her eye from a tumor at age twenty-five)

Famous one-eyed people in history:
- John Milton (seventeenth-century poet)
- Lord Nelson (famous English war leader)
- Guglielmo Marconi (developed the wireless telegraph)
- James Thurber (American writer)

High Fours for Missing Fingers!

- Daryl Hannah, star of *Splash,* and long-time girlfriend of JFK Jr. before his marriage, is missing one finger. A door slammed on it when she was a child and she wears a fake one in her movies.
- James Doohan (*Star Trek*'s Lieutenant Commander Montgomery Scott, who allegedly says "Beam me up, Scotty.")
- Telly Savalas
- Jerry Garcia
- Mickey Mouse

Bad Plastic Surgery

This is a subject forever discussed on newsgroups like alt.gossip.celebrities and alt.showbiz.gossip. Here are some of the top candidates for worst plastic surgery awards:

Mary Tyler Moore
Bruce Jenner
Joan Rivers
Tony Curtis
Latoya Jackson
Tori Spelling
Florence Henderson
Dyan Cannon
Linda Evans
Michael Douglas
Jack Lemmon
Sylvester Stallone

Michael Jackson
Carol Burnett
Mickey Rourke
Eddie Fisher
Melanie Griffith
Richard Chamberlain
Helen Gurley Brown
Sally Jessy Raphael
Julia Louis-Dreyfus
Dick Clark
Faye Dunaway
Kathie Lee Gifford

SEE "JACKO IS WACKO," PAGE 39.

"Lisa Marie has filed for divorce.
According to her attorney, she's going to make
Michael Jackson pay through his noses."
—Conan O'Brien

THE TRUTH ABOUT YOUR FAVORITE STARS
Stars Who Stink—Literally

You can't call it "body odor" anymore because that's politically incorrect. It's now **"discretionary fragrance."** Whatever you call it, here are some famous names who have been said to have enough "discretionary fragrance" to make others around them turn up their nose in disgust.

A long-time maid at Graceland revealed that **Elvis** had bad body odor. She said that no matter how bad Elvis smelled, though, he just splashed on more cologne. Even so, she said his smell didn't seem to affect women wanting to sleep with him.

According to *Elvis: Unknown Stories Behind the Legend*, his feet also smelled to high heaven, and he threw his unwashed socks into his suitcase when he was on tour. Then he gave the stinky suitcase to his mother to clean when he got home; the contents were supposedly so odiferous that she had to **put on a mask and rubber gloves to wash them.**

When the Spice Girls were all together, the other girls used to try to overcome the bad breath of **Spice Girl Geri Halliwell** by offering her some gum. "Does anyone want some chewie?" they'd hint strongly when her breath left them breathless.

According to **Wendy Goldman Rohm,** who interviewed Bill Gates before he became famous, Gates had bad breath and wouldn't bathe for days.

Donald Trump said of **Daryl Hannah,** "I have seen Daryl Hannah on many occasions and she is simply in need of a shower or bath."

Reporters who were with him while he was campaigning said that **Senator John McCain** (best known for losing in the primaries to George W. Bush) had bad breath.

According to Corsinet.com's Brain Candy celebrity insults section, Donald Trump once said to **Larry King,** "Do you mind if I sit back a little? Because your breath is very bad."

"Elizabeth Taylor's new fragrance, Black Pearls, is being boycotted by upscale department stores. Presumably it smells too much like Larry Fortensky."
—Will Durst, *That's Funny*

Clark Gable, best known for his role as Rhett Butler in *Gone With the Wind,* had halitosis so fiery he could have burned down Atlanta with one breath. Vivien Leigh, who played Scarlett O'Hara in the movie, said, "His dentures smelled something awful."

Sting supposedly doesn't use deodorant. In fact, when he gave an interview before a concert, the journalists couldn't stand to be around him and nicknamed him "Stink."

Rosie O'Donnell admitted that when she obtained her newborn son Parker, she didn't shower for a few days before so he could get used to her smell when he slept with her.

Celebs on Drugs—Stories You Didn't Know

There were rumors and stories in the tabloids about whether **Julia Roberts** was on drugs around the time she was making *Hook.* An Internet posting said that someone who worked at the gym Julia frequents reported that she showed up "**with hairy armpits, matted hair, very bad BO,** and an odorously noticeable lack of feminine hygiene. She was so ratty and stoned out looking that people barely recognized her."

"Cocaine isn't habit-forming darling. I should know. I've been taking it for years."
—Tallulah Bankhead,
famous actress of the '30s and '40s

Bruce Willis was walking down a street in New Jersey drinking a beer when a policeman stopped him. The cop noticed that Willis had something cigarette-shaped in back of his ear. The cop checked—and Willis was arrested for pot possession.

According to *Movieline,* **Bill Murray** was a pre-med student when he was arrested at Chicago's O'Hare Airport with marijuana. As a result, he left his pre-med courses. SEE "SMART STARS," PAGE 44.

Movie Stars Do the Dumbest Things revealed that in *Five Easy Pieces* **Jack Nicholson** supposedly took a snort of coke after every five takes—and because they did thirty takes on his campfire scene alone, he must have really been flying. He also supposedly **smoked 155 joints** while filming the campfire scene in *Easy Rider.*

Tim Allen spent more than two years in jail after being arrested for attempted drug dealing.

Woody Harrelson admits to being addicted to pot and says he breaks down in tears if he doesn't get his daily dose.

"Say no to drugs. That'll bring the price down."
—Geechy Guy

LSD has been tried by many famous people, especially back in the '60s and '70s, when there was less stigma attached to it. **Cary Grant** and movie producer Otto Preminger both admitted to experimenting with it.

One famous person gave LSD to someone else without their knowledge. Movie producer **Oliver Stone** (*Platoon, Wall Street, Born on the Fourth of July, JFK, Natural Born Killers*, etc.) had a fight with his father when he was young; he retaliated by **dropping LSD into his drink**. Oliver's father ended up hanging onto a tree limb.

Baird Jones of the *New York Post* reported that socialite (and Barry Diller's wife) **Diane von Furstenberg** developed cancer of the mouth from smoking marijuana. She said she never smoked cigarettes "so I think I must have gotten cancer because I smoked so much pot."

New York Post columnist Cindy Adams revealed that **Kim Delaney** once smuggled ganja for her friends after she went to the Caribbean. **SEE "WERE THEY CRIMINAL?", PAGE 4.**

Johnny Depp, who played in the true-story drug movie *Blow*, said of his own experience with cocaine, "Of course I tried it. I did my share of it, but it was never really my favorite." (And what is his favorite?)

How Old Are They Really?

Milton Berle 90+

Art Carney 80+

Ed McMahon 75+

Marlon Brando 75+

Bo Diddley 70+

Eddie Fisher 70+

Eartha Kitt 70+

Joan Collins 65+

Marlo Thomas 60+

Paul Newman 70+

Jon Voight 60+

Richard Gere 50+

Bryant Gumbel 50+

Bernadette Peters 50+

Phyllis Diller 80+

Lauren Bacall 75+

Esther Williams 75+

Dick Clark 70+

Fats Domino 70+

Hugh Hefner 70+

Pat Boone 65+

Kim Novak 65+

Robert Redford 60+

Warren Beatty 60+

Cher 55+

George Wendt 50+

Olivia Newton-John 50+

Steven Wright 50+

"Happy Birthday to Keith Richards. He turns fifty-seven today. Too bad he wasn't alive to see it."
—Craig Kilborn

"Former Beatle Paul McCartney is fifty-five today. I remember him when he was dead."
—Jay Leno

How Old Would They Be in 2002 If They Had Lived?

Charlie Chaplin 113

Clark Gable 98

Martin Luther King 74

Marilyn Monroe 76

Phil Hartman 64

JFK 85

John Lennon 62

Humphrey Bogart 103

John Wayne 95

Rock Hudson 77

James Dean 71

Elvis 67

Cary Grant 98

Montgomery Clift 82

How Tall Are Your Favorite Stars?

Women:

Bette Midler 5'1"	Joan Rivers 5'2"
Kellie Martin 5'3"	Bo Derek 5'3"
Drew Barrymore 5'4"	Cheryl Ladd 5'5"
Kate Moss 5'6"	Jennifer Lopez 5'6"
Lauren Holly 5'7"	Ashley Judd 5'7"
Shelley Hack 5'7"	Queen Latifah 5'8"
Cameron Diaz 5'9"	Nicole Kidman 5'10"
Brooke Sheilds 5'11"	Kristen Johnston 6'
Sigourney Weaver 6'	Brigitte Nielsen 6'
Geena Davis 6'	

Men:

Danny DeVito 5'	Michael J. Fox 5'4"
Dustin Hoffman 5'6"	Marlon Brando 5'8"
Robert De Niro 5'9"	Jack Nicholson 5'9"
Paul Newman 5'11"	Rick Schroeder 5'11"
John Travolta 6'	Kevin Costner 6'1"
Michael Caine 6'1"	Sean Connery 6'2"
Charlton Heston 6'2"	David Letterman 6'2"
James Garner 6'3"	Jimmy Smits 6'3"
Peter O'Toole 6'3"	Clint Eastwood 6'4"
Tom Selleck 6'4"	Christopher Reeve 6'4"

SOURCES: *National Enquirer, Globe*

Just Short of the Truth

e Russell Crowe is much shorter than he admits and wears elevator shoes with big boots. He may only be around 5'5".

e Despite his press releases, Mel Gibson is only around 5'6", and stood on a box for some scenes with 5'11" co-star Sigourney Weaver in *The Year of Living Dangerously*.

e Tom Cruise claims to be 5'9", but some reports have him as short as 5'4", although generally around 5'7".

e Eddie Murphy says he's 5'10"—no way, say those close to him.

e Robert Redford's "official" height is 5'10". He may be closer to 5'8".

e Al Pacino's "official" height is 5'7". Some say he's about 5'5".

e Sly Stallone's "official" height is 5'10", but he may actually be 5'7".

> Tim Allen is 6'5" (leading Jon Stewart to say that he's a dyslexic version of him).

CELEBRITY BACKGROUNDS

Most famous people have had to take some odd jobs while they were waiting for their big breaks. Here are a few of them.

Weird Work

- Rick Rockwell, the millionaire who got married on the Fox television show, *Who Wants to Marry a Millionaire?* was a Tampax salesman.
- Brad Pitt was a chauffeur for a delivery strip service.
- Warren Beatty scared away rats outside the National Theater in Washington.
- Sylvester Stallone swept out lion cages at the Bronx Zoo.
- Brad Pitt was a giant chicken at a Mexican restaurant.
- Sean Connery polished coffins.
- Dr. Ruth Westheimer was a trained sniper in Israel.
- James Cagney *(You Dirty Rat)* was a chorus girl.
- Jodie Foster was in Coppertone commercials as a child.

President George W. Bush sold sporting goods at Sears for a summer.

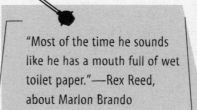

"Most of the time he sounds like he has a mouth full of wet toilet paper."—Rex Reed, about Marlon Brando

Those Who Worked for the Famous or at Famous Places

- Richard Hatch (winner of *Survivor*) was a chauffeur for Steve Rubel when he ran Studio 54.
- Diane Sawyer worked for Richard Nixon.
- Alec Baldwin was a doorman at Studio 54.
- Steve Martin worked at Disneyland, selling maps and guidebooks.
- Arnold Schwarzenegger modeled underwear for Frederick's of Hollywood.
- Andie MacDowell worked at McDonald's and Pizza Hut.

Interesting Work If You Can Get It

- Martin Sheen was a professional caddy.
- Matthew Perry was the number two junior tennis player in Ottawa when he was thirteen.
- Kathy Bates was a singing waitress.
- Whoopi Goldberg was a bricklayer, Sheetrock installer, mortuary cosmetician, and she also worked in a strip joint, although she didn't take off any clothes.

> Danny DeVito was "Mr. Danny" when he worked at his sister's beauty parlor.

- Oprah Winfrey was once Miss Fire Prevention.
- Goldie Hawn was a professional go-go dancer who danced in a cage.
- Mark Wahlberg was a shoplifter who robbed liquor stores and cars when he was young and on drugs.
- George Clooney once tried out for the Cincinnati Reds.
- Mickey Rourke was an ice cream man and bouncer in a transvestite club (and in 1991 he became a professional boxer).
- Geena Davis was a widow dresser.
- Jerry Hall shoveled manure in stables.
- Rod Stewart was a grave digger.
- Jenny Jones was a back-up singer for Wayne Newton.
- Pee-Wee Herman was a Fuller Brush salesman.
- Cindy Lauper cleaned dog kennels.
- Sylvester Stallone bounced outsiders at a dorm.

> Marilyn Monroe allegedly exchanged sexual favors for food. In 1946, she became the world's first Miss Artichoke.

Boring Work If You Have to Do It

- Don Johnson was a butcher.
- Julia Roberts was a soda jerk.
- Jay Leno waxed cars.
- Keanu Reeves managed a pasta shop in Toronto.
- Joan Rivers was an office temp.
- Dustin Hoffman typed names into Yellow Pages directories.
- Phil Donahue was a bank check-sorter.
- Rock Hudson and Dan Akroyd were mailmen.
- Arnold Schwarzenegger started a bricklaying business.
- Luciano Pavarotti was an elementary school teacher.
- Joe Pesci was a barber.
- Annette Bening was a cook.
- Jon Bon Jovi was a floor sweeper.
- Harrison Ford was a carpenter.
- Al Pacino was a mailman.
- Warren Beatty was a dishwasher.
- Tom Clancy was an insurance agent.
- Marlon Brando was an elevator operator.
- Jerry Seinfeld was a telemarketer, selling light bulbs.
- Tony Danza was a furniture mover and car wash operator.
- Michael Douglas was a gas station attendant.
- Hugh Hefner was an editor at Children's Activities magazine.

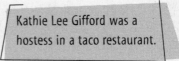

Kathie Lee Gifford was a hostess in a taco restaurant.

Michelle Pfieffer was a grocery cashier.

And finally, some interesting talk show host backgrounds from an article in the *National Enquirer*:

- **David Letterman** was a television weatherman who started making jokes, such as inventing disasters in fictitious cities. It took off . . . and so did he.
- **Geraldo Rivera** spent two years in the merchant marines, got a law degree, and tried fifty cases.
- **Sally Jessy Raphael** was fired eighteen times in show business before she hit it. During that time, she ran a perfume factory and an art gallery.

SOURCES: *Movie Stars Do the Dumbest Things, Movieline, The Instant Genius,* USELESSFACTS.NET, *National Enquirer*

Strange Ways They Began Their Careers

- **Mel Gibson** really wanted to be a chef, but went to drama school after his sister secretly sent in an application and entry fee for him.
- **David Duchovny** was going for his doctorate, writing a dissertation on magic and technology in fiction, when he got an acting job—in a beer commercial.
- **Ted Danson** was a student at Stanford University when he spotted a stunning waitress, followed her to an audition—and got a role.
- **Tom Cruise** tried to compensate for being short and dyslexic by being outstanding in sports. Once, when he was injured and unable to play, he took up acting to occupy himself and realized he was better at that.
- **Bruce Willis** stuttered as a child. He joined a drama club in high school and discovered (as have many stutterers) that when he was performing in front of an audience his stutter vanished.

> Ben Stiller, a nerdy-looking kid, began making movies at the age of ten about getting revenge on bullies who were tormenting him.

Real Names of the Famous

- Meg Ryan grew up as Peggy Hyra.
- Sigourney Weaver's real name is Susan—Sigourney comes from a character in *The Great Gatsby*.

> Kirk Douglas was Issur Danielovitch.

- Kevin Spacey's full name is Kevin Spacey Fowler.
- Jay Greenspan became Jason Alexander, famous for *Seinfeld*.
- Tim Dick became Tim Allen (Dick's middle name was Allen).
- James Garner was James Bumgarner.

> The man who played Charmin's "Mr. Whipple," is now eighty-two years old. He received a lifetime supply of Charmin as part of his payment. (And yes, he says he really does squeeze it.)

- Alice Cooper was Vincent Furnier.
- Ellen Burstyn was Edna Rae Gilhooley.
- Hulk Hogan was Terry Bollea.
- Jane Seymour was Joyce Frankenberg.
- David Copperfield was David Kotkin.
- Slash was Saul Hudson.
- Elton John was Reginald Kenneth Dwight.
- Billy Idol was William Broad.
- Ralph Lauren was Ralph Lifshitz.
- Tammy Wynette was Virginia Pugh.
- Soupy Sales was Milton Hines.
- Michael Crawford was Michael Dumbell-Smith.
- Bo Diddley was Elias Bates.
- Danny DeVito was Daniel Michaeli.
- Rodney Dangerfield was Jacob Cohen.
- Larry King was Lawrence Harvey Zeiger.
- Cher was Cherilyn Sarkisian.

Charles Bronson was Charles Buchinshky.

Michael Keaton is really Michael Douglas—Keaton was his middle name and he took that for his last because there was already a famous Michael Douglas.

More Famous Name Changes

- Allen Stewart Konigsberg is Heywood Allen, better known as Woody Allen.
- Tony Curtis was once Bernard Schwartz.
- Tom Cruise was Thomas Mappother.
- Michael Caine was Maurice Mickelwhite.
- Engelbert Humperdinck was Arnold Dorsey.
- Kathie Lee Gifford was Kathie Epstein.
- Alan Alda was Alfonso D'abruzzo Jr.
- Whoopie Goldberg was Caryn Johnson.
- Doris Day was Doris Kappellhoff.
- John Wayne was Marion Morrison.
- Natalie Wood was Natasha Gurdin.
- Mickey Rooney was Joe Yule Jr.

Celebrity Causes

Richard Roeper of the *Sun-Times* put together a long list of causes the celebrities espouse. The following are a few of the more interesting ones:

- **Naomi Campbell** appeared almost nude in ads saying, "I'd rather go naked than wear fur."
- **Madonna** wrapped herself in the American flag and said, "If you don't vote, you're going to get a spanky."
- **John Cleese,** trading on his famous "Dead Parrot" sketch from *Monty Python,* made a video supporting a campaign to save the wild parrots.
- When **Alec Baldwin and Kim Basinger** were married, their cause was saving carriage-pulling horses in Manhattan.
- **Goldie Hawn** is against the use of elephants in the circus.

> "I was asked to do a benefit for babies born addicted to crack. And I said, 'OK . . . but I think we both know what they're gonna spend it on.'"
> —Laura Kightlinger

- **Jimmy Buffett** became involved with a "Save the Manatee" club.
- **Meryl Streep** fought against chemicals in apples.
- **Elizabeth Hurley**'s cause, believe it or not, is **drug-addicted monkeys.** According to the *Scottish Daily Record,* the actress and model has come to the defense of the monkeys on Spider Island, who have supposedly been drugged with heroin to make them tourist-friendly. Furthermore, she's angry about the occasional tourist monkey who's placed on roller skates because some of his toes have been cut off to fit the skates!

All in the (Celebrity) Family

- Although there's no evidence she ever tuned in, turned on, and dropped out, **Winona Ryder**'s godfather was famed LSD Guru, **Timothy Leary,** and **Uma Thurman**'s mother was once married to Timothy Leary.
- **Julianna Margulies**'s father was in advertising, and he wrote that obnoxious Alka Seltzer jingle "Plop plop, fizz fizz. Oh what a relief it is."
- **Jennifer Aniston**'s godfather was **Telly Savalas.**

The Odd Background of Mel Gibson

- The British absolutely hate **Mel Gibson** for his British-bashing role in *The Patriot*. So the *Mirror* dug up some interesting facts on this man, whose full name is Mel Columcille Gerard Gibson.

- He was born in New York, but his parents didn't want him to be drafted for the Vietnam War. After they won on the quiz show Jeopardy, they used the money to move to Australia.

- Mel was subjected to strict Catholic discipline at his Australian school . . . and set the unwanted record for **the most strappings in one week:** twenty-seven.

- The night before his audition for *Mad Max*, which got him started in movies, Mel was beaten up in a bar fight so badly he had a face "like a busted grapefruit," he admitted. He still got the job.

- Two priests approved Mel's role in *Lethal Weapon* before he agreed to make the movie. They gave him the go-ahead because even though there's a lot of violence in the film, he ultimately triumphs over evil.

- He was such a drunk (he's now in AA) that while shooting the movie he was having **beer before breakfast** and tequila slammers with whiskey chasers after work.

- Mel's neighbors in Greenwich, Connecticut, dislike him because he built a sheep barn only thirty feet from the local river. The manure from the sheep has been blamed for polluting their local beach so badly that they had to shut it down.

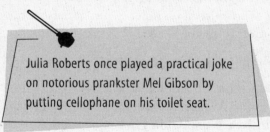

Julia Roberts once played a practical joke on notorious prankster Mel Gibson by putting cellophane on his toilet seat.

Celebrities Who Hate Their Moms

New York Post columnist Cindy Adams did a Mother's Day column called "Stars Who Don't Celebrate Mother's Day," a subject which has also been covered in the tabloids and *USA Today*. Here are a few stories about them.

Oprah Winfrey may not celebrate Mother's *or* Father's Day. In an interview with *Ebony* she questioned whether Vernon Winfrey, who brought her up (although he wasn't married to her mother), **was really her father.** She added that her mother "carried her in shame."

Oprah's mother retaliated by giving an interview to the *National Enquirer,* expressing shock and sorrow that Oprah would say these things. Her mother added: "Since she's gotten into all that money, she's let it turn her head. Now she just says things for publicity. But she doesn't need publicity that much."

The Star claimed that when Jennifer Aniston's mother was "stricken with life-threatening double pneumonia," not only did her famous daughter refuse to help her, but she let her mother "seek medical attention at a dingy public clinic that treats the homeless and destitute." The problem between them supposedly stems from her mother having talked to a tabloid television show.

Marcia Clark, the prosecutor who gained fame from the O. J. Simpson case, not only doesn't talk to her mother and father, but she once filed **a restraining order** to keep them away from her.

The cause of the problem? Her parents supported her ex-husband during a bitter divorce and custody battle. (Her first husband, by the way, a professional gambler, was later murdered.)

Demi Moore was furious at her mother for selling gossip about her to the tabloids. It may not have helped that her mother also had an arrest record for drunk driving and arson, and had posed nude for *High Society.* But Demi and her mother patched things up when her mother was near death from a brain tumor. Demi even tried to help by getting her a psychic healer.

Brook Shields's mother, Teri, was the poster mother for pushy managers years ago, but the two appear to be estranged even now.

Roseanne (who also doesn't celebrate Father's Day) not only charged her mother with psychological and physical abuse but also claimed she was regularly molested by her father, a charge he vigorously denies.

Indeed, her family filed a $70-million lawsuit against her, and her mother said, "I will own up to any responsibility that I have to. But not incest and molesting."

Others pissed off at their mothers (and/or vice versa) include:

- LeAnn Rimes (she's suing her parents)
- Soon-Yi Previn Allen (the daughter of Mia Farrow, and now married to her stepfather, Woody Allen)
- Meg Ryan (she's mad at her mother for leaving her family to pursue her own career)
- Dolly Parton (she and her siblings sued to have their mother declared incompetent)

CRAZY CELEBS
Is Nolte Nuts?

Nick Nolte walks around with a dirty-looking yellowing bathrobe over his business suits—even while he's in public places like New York's ritzy Park Avenue. According to the Globe and an interview he did with Larry King Live, he also:

- Spends times in **a hyperbaric chamber** pumping oxygen into his body.
- Takes **growth hormones** that are usually used by dwarves.
- Puts a cranial electronic stimulator on his forehead to zap his brain with mild **electric jolts.**
- Takes vitamins and hormones by intravenous drip, which he administers to himself.
- Takes **ozone injections.**
- Studies his own blood under a microscope.

Is Clooney Looney?

Compared to Nolte anyone sounds pretty sane. But how normal is it to try out for the part of Dracula as if you were a **Kentucky hillbilly?** That's what **George Clooney** did when he auditioned for *Three Kings*. The producer, Francis Ford Coppola, thought he was so nuts that he called Clooney's agent to ask if he had any mental problems.

COLOR THEM CRAZY
Robert Redford sometimes wears pink ski boots, seemingly to shock people. Billy Bob Thornton eats only orange-colored foods, and Claudia Schiffer likes all the purple candies removed from her Skittles.

Jacko Is Wacko

No question: Michael Jackson beats them all. Elizabeth Taylor may be the only person who thinks that he is normal. "He's the least weird man I've ever known." (What kind of people does she know?) Here's proof that she's wrong:

- When Liz married construction worker Larry Fortensky (which was pretty weird, too), Michael Jackson wanted his **giraffes to be dressed in tuxedos** and to serve as attendants at the wedding.
- Jackson also wanted his "best friend," who turned out to be a chimpanzee, to serve as bridesmaid, dressed in a tuxedo designed by Valentino.
- Jackson walks around in public wearing a face mask with his nose falling off as a result of numerous plastic surgeries undertaken to try to turn himself into **a white Diana Ross.**
- In fact, he may have kept **his original nose as a souvenir.** A biographer of Jackson's wrote that one of his housekeepers found a jar in a cupboard with part of a human nose and a date on it that corresponded to his first nose job.
- He once slept in a hyperbaric chamber saying it would help him live to be 150. He had photos taken of himself and gave them to the *National Enquirer* to run under the condition that they use the word "bizarre" to describe him. (Easy enough.) After the story came out, he denounced it.

"With his womanly voice, stark white skin, and Medusa hair, his gash of red lipstick, heavy eyeliner, almost nonexistent nose, and lopsided face, Jackson was making his television appearance in order to scotch all rumors that he is not quite normal."
—*Times of London*

Other indications of Michael Jackson's weirdness:
- Jackson tried to buy the elephant man's bones.
- He keeps a coffin in his home.
- **He likes to watch brain surgery**—and was reported in one instance to have smiled throughout the gory operation.
- He once tore up $100,000.
- He has **a shrine to Elizabeth Taylor** in his home and has proposed to her even though she's more than twenty-five years his senior.
- He had **facial electrolysis,** and may now have had hair implanted in his chin to make his ghostly white features more realistic.

Other Nutty Star Behavior

- **Mel Gibson** has spent hundreds of dollars a week on Chinese herbs—including crushed deer antler—to improve his sex life.
- **Woody Allen** takes his temperature every two hours (except when he's sleeping).
- **Adam Sandler** likes to disguise his voice as a woman's, then call pizza take-out places and joke around with them.
- **Johnny Depp** is afraid of clowns.

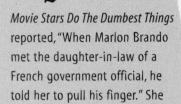

Movie Stars Do The Dumbest Things reported, "When Marlon Brando met the daughter-in-law of a French government official, he told her to pull his finger." She did, and then Brando, "let out a Wagnerian fart."

SEE "STARS WHO INSIST THAT OTHERS DON'T LOOK AT THEM," PAGE 7.

GREAT CELEBRITY QUOTES
Too True

- "It was never my intention to 'market' my son as some have cynically claimed in the press . . . all the projects we have turned down because they were not the right sort of exposure for him."—Kathie Lee Gifford, in her autobiography
- "I'm a great liar."—O. J. Simpson, 1996
- "Michael loves to have children around him."—Michael Jackson's wife

Duh . . .

- "Sure I've slapped her . . . and there have been times when I punched her without thinking, but I never beat her."—Ike Turner, denying charges that he had abused Tina Turner
- There's an annual United Kingdom "Foot in Mouth" Award, which was presented this year to Alicia Silverstone for the following incomprehensible comment: "I think that Clueless was very deep. I think it was deep in the way that it was very light. I think lightness has to come from a very deep place if it's true lightness."
- "I don't care if people think I'm an overactor. People who think that would call van Gogh an overpainter."—Jim Carrey
- "I've been planted here to be a vessel for acting, you know what I mean?"—Leonardo DiCaprio
- "Nuclear war would certainly set back cable."—Ted Turner

SOURCE: *Stupid Celebrities*

Celebrity Putdowns

- "[Joan Crawford's] slept with every male on the MGM lot except Lassie."
- "The only man who thinks she's a ten is her shoe salesman."—Bob Hope, about Phyllis Diller
- **"Her only flair is in her nostrils."**—Pauline Kael, about Katharine Hepburn
- "He drools a lot. He has such active glands."—Mamie Van Doren, about Warren Beatty
- **"She's a vacuum with nipples."**—Otto Preminger, about Marilyn Monroe
- "James Woods . . . working with him is like being pregnant. In the beginning you're so happy and excited. And then in the middle you're thinking, 'I might have made the biggest mistake of my life.' And by the end you just want it over with."—Melanie Griffith
- "John Travolta's performance: **William Shatner's hairpiece is more convincing."**—Rita Kempley
- "Jennifer Lopez only fakes being a Latina. . . . When she has to be Latin, she's Latin. But she doesn't know how to do it well."—Salma Hayek
- "Kevin Costner has personality minus."—Madonna
- "Politically, **Mel Gibson is somewhere to the right of Attila the Hun.** Beautiful, but only on the outside."—Susan Sarandon

What Zsa Zsa Said

- "Personally I know nothing about sex because I've always been married."
- "I want a man who's kind and understanding. Is that too much to ask of a millionaire?"
- "How many husbands have I had? You mean apart from my own?"
- "I'm a great housekeeper. Whenever I get divorced, I keep the house."

What Others Said about Zsa Zsa

- "She's been married so many times she has rice marks on her face."—Henny Youngman
- "She has discovered the secret of perpetual middle age."—Oscar Levant
- "She's the only person who ever left the Iron Curtain wearing it."
- "One more face-lift and she'll have pubic hair on her chin."—Virginia Graham
- "You can calculate her age by the rings on her fingers."

- "Brando? I do not enjoy actors who seek to commune with their armpits."—Greer Garson
- "She ran the whole gamut of emotions from A to B."—Dorothy Parker, about Katharine Hepburn

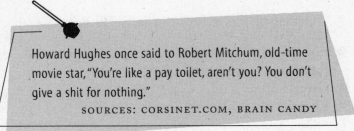

Howard Hughes once said to Robert Mitchum, old-time movie star, "You're like a pay toilet, aren't you? You don't give a shit for nothing."

SOURCES: CORSINET.COM, BRAIN CANDY

"I have more talent in my smallest fart than she has in her whole body."
—Walter Matthau, about Barbra Streisand

Bette Davis once said of Joan Crawford, "I wouldn't sit on her toilet."

Can We Bitch?

Here are a few zingers from **Joan Rivers:**

- "Elizabeth Taylor's so fat, she puts mayonnaise on aspirin."
- "Madonna's so hairy, when she lifted up her arm, I thought it was Tina Turner in her armpit."
- "If I found [Yoko Ono] floating in my pool, I'd punish my dog."
- "Boy George is all England needs—another queen who can't dress."

SOURCES: *Star,* CORSINET.COM'S BRAIN CANDY, *Stupid Celebrities*

THE KING

And now for some amazing Elvis facts to get you all shook up:

- When he was young, Elvis had a lot of work done on his face to make him so handsome. His nose was straightened and slimmed. His acne-scarred skin was smoothed out. He had **implants put in his chin** (which gave him that marvelous chiseled-chin look). And his hair was really a light reddish blonde but he dyed it black.

- Elvis refused to wear blue jeans because it reminded him of when his father was in jail.
- The people who decide whose faces should go on U.S. postage stamps continually postponed issuing an Elvis stamp, possibly because of his drug usage. Or perhaps it was because you have to be dead to qualify, and like the readers of the *Weekly World News*, the postal service had some questions about that.
- Elvis once said "Caucasian? It was on my army draft card. I **thought it meant circumcised."**
- Graceland earns more profit than Elvis earned while he was alive.
- Elvis's middle name, Aaron, is **misspelled on his tombstone.**
- When Elvis was at his peak, he earned so much money that one year he was the largest individual taxpayer in America.
- More people saw Elvis's Hawaii special than saw Neil Armstrong walk on the moon.

"I find it hard to believe that Elvis Presley faked his death because he died on the can. If I was going to fake my death, I wouldn't be pounding one out."
—Bobcat Goldthwait

They Didn't All Love Him Tender

Not everybody loved Elvis. According to the *Whole Pop Catalog*, an Elvis fan club president once complained to **Groucho Marx,** "You haven't mentioned Elvis Presley."

Groucho Marx replied, "I seldom do unless I stub my toe."

Before Elvis's appearance on his show, **Ed Sullivan** firmly said, "I wouldn't have Presley on my show at any time."

Steve Allen said, "The fact that someone with so little ability became the most popular singer in history says something significant about our cultural standards."

The King was on the throne when he died, reading a book on the Shroud of Turin. Elvis had become so addicted to reading in the bathroom (and suffered such constipation from the drugs he took) that he had a special chair in the bathroom just for reading.

And Elvis Didn't Love Everyone Else Tender Either

According to British writer Anthony Burgess, Presley **hated the Beatles,** or the Fab Four, as they were called, partially because "they dethroned him, musically."

He suspected the long-haired Englishmen might be communists and homosexuals, and publicly referred to them as the "Fag Four."

Most people would have let it go at that. But not the King. He wrote to the former head of the F.B.I., his good friend **J. Edgar Hoover,** and offered to get "dirt" on the Beatles for him.

SMART STARS

"In show business, you've got a pretty good chance of being the smartest person in the room," said Michael J. Fox. But not all stars are dumb.

- **Sharon Stone** belongs to Mensa, the organization of people with high IQs.
- **James Woods** once scored 800 on the verbal part of the SATs and 799 on the math section. "Who gives a shit?" was his response to this.
- **Cindy Crawford** was the valedictorian in her high school and briefly went to Northwestern University on a chemical engineering scholarship.
- **Kevin Spacey** was co-valedictorian in his high school.
- **Jodie Foster** graduated from Yale.
- **Tommy Lee Jones** went to Harvard and was the roommate of former vice president and presidential apirant **Al Gore.**
- **Mick Jagger** attended the London School of Economics.

"It's like, you know, I have no verbal skills, none . . . nothing, I mean, hey. Really, OK. Jeez. Understand?"
—Diane Keaton

"I'm a meathead. I can't help it, man. You've got smart people and you've got dumb people."
—Keanu Reeves

Close But No Diploma

- **Jason Alexander** got kicked out of Boston University a year before graduation.
- **David Duchovny** was a dissertation away from a Ph.D. in English Lit at Yale.
- **Elizabeth Shue** dropped out of Harvard with only one semester to go.

Smart Comedians, Bad Grades

- **Jim Carrey** dropped out of school.
- **Adam Sandler** said, "If you don't get the best grades, don't fret—I didn't do too well in school and I'm a multimillionaire."
- **Michael Richards,** *Seinfeld*'s Kramer, couldn't get into college.
- **Robin Williams** was voted least likely to succeed in high school.

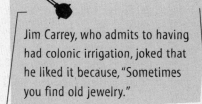

Jim Carrey, who admits to having had colonic irrigation, joked that he liked it because, "Sometimes you find old jewelry."

Stars Who Didn't Graduate from High School

According to the *Book of Lists*, these people surprisingly didn't even graduate from high school:

Cary Grant	Peter Jennings
Billy Joel	Herman Melville
Charles Dickens	Thomas Edison
Mark Twain	Noel Coward
Charlie Chaplin	

Celebrity Career Mistakes

Imagine how different these movies would have been if the stars who were originally offered the roles had taken them:

- **Billy Crudup** turned down Leonardo DiCaprio's role in *Titanic*.
- **Mel Gibson** turned down the role of James Bond.
- **Elvis Presley** turned down the role played by Jon Voigt (Angelina Jolie's father) in *Midnight Cowboy*, and opposite Barbra Streisand in *A Star Is Born*.

John Travolta turned down Sly Stallone's role in *Rambo: First Blood* as well as Richard Gere's roles in *American Gigolo* and *An Officer and a Gentleman*.

- Marlon Brando turned down Peter O'Toole's role in *Lawrence of Arabia.*
- Montgomery Clift turned down Marlon Brando's role in *On the Waterfront.*
- Harrison Ford turned down Tom Hanks's role in *Saving Private Ryan.*
- Julia Roberts turned down Meg Ryan's role in *Sleepless in Seattle.*
- Sissy Spacek turned down Carrie Fisher's role in *Star Wars.*
- Carrie Fisher turned down Sissy Spacek's role in *Carrie.*
- Michelle Pfeiffer turned down Jodie Foster's part in *Silence of the Lambs.*
- Bette Davis turned down the role of Scarlett O'Hara in *Gone With the Wind* because she didn't want to play opposite Errol Flynn, who was originally supposed to play Clark Gable's role.
- Bob Hope, Danny Kaye, and Mitzi Gaynor were originally supposed to play the lead roles in *Some Like It Hot* instead of Marilyn Monroe, Tony Curtis, and Jack Lemmon.
- Lisa Kudrow, of *Friends,* briefly played the role of Roz on the pilot for *Frasier* but was fired.

SOURCE: ALT.GOSSIP.CELEBRITIES MOVIE MISTAKES LIST

OUT OF THIS WORLD
Psychic Believers

- **Barbra Streisand** says she visited a psychic to help her contact her dead father.
- **Rosie O'Donnell** contacted her mother—who died when she was ten—through a famous medium.
- **Demi Moore** held a séance when she lived in Idaho.
- **Liza Minnelli** has tried to contact the late Halston, a famous clothing designer, not to ask him what to wear, but because they were old friends.

PSYCHIC CONNECTIONS

- The sister of John Belushi is a practicing psychic who started out as a hairdresser.
- Billy Bob Thornton's mother is a psychic.
- Dan Aykroyd's mother is a psychic researcher.

Weird Past Lives

- **Shirley MacLaine,** best known as a past-life nut, says she was many different people in her past lives, including **a gypsy who had an affair with Charlemagne.**
- **Fergie,** former wife of Prince Andrew, claims to have been in psychic contact with Queen Victoria, who she says guided her while she was researching a book on her.
- **Montel Williams** and his former wife say they've had more than fifty past lives together.
- **Sean Connery** believes that before this life he was a railroad builder in Africa with a drinking problem that ultimately killed him.
- According to Hollywood and the Supernatural, singer **Loretta Lynn** has already lived three times, once as a Cherokee princess, once as an American housewife, and once as an Irish woman.
- **Willie Nelson** believes he's lived many times before, including once as a Native American.
- **Billy Bob Thornton**'s mother is a psychic, and he's also a firm believer in past lives, thinking he may have been **Ben Franklin.**

> Drew Barrymore says she was saved from drowning by her guardian angel, who was wearing "hot pink shorts."

- **Joan Rivers** was quoted as saying that she came to believe in spirits when she visited a haunted house and was **slapped on the butt by Edgar Allen Poe's ghost.** (After reading that, one should quote the maven, nevermore.)
- **Jim Carrey** visits psychics, including one who told him to get different kinds of ribbons to find the colors of his aura.
- **Jean-Claude Van Damme** claims to have seen the ghost of a man who killed himself a few years earlier in a hotel room he was staying in.
- **Linda Evans,** of Dynasty fame, now follows the three-thousand-year-old "Ramtha." Even though Ramtha has been repeatedly discredited, Evans lives with her and her followers in a commune-type situation.

Close Encounters

Twenty-five million Americans claim they've seen UFOs, and that includes many well-known people. According to *The Odd Index*:

- **Muhammad Ali** claims to have seen an unidentified flying object in Central Park, and another one over the New Jersey Turnpike.
- **Jackie Gleason** said he saw two UFOs.
- Former President **Jimmy Carter** said that he saw a UFO as large as the moon (some think he saw the planet Venus).
- **Jamie Farr,** of M.A.S.H., claims he saw a UFO in Arizona.
- Comedian **Dick Gregory** believes he saw three UFOs one night.
- **William Shatner** says he not only saw a UFO but received a telepathic message from it.
- **Glenn Ford** claims he saw "two disks" that looked like UFOs.

Charlie Sheen says he was buzzed by a UFO when he was eleven.

Movies and Television

BEHIND THE MOVIE SCENES

Here are a few interesting facts about the notorious shower scene (in which Janet Leigh is murdered) in *Psycho:*

- The scene lasted less than a minute but it took a week to shoot.
- **Chocolate syrup** was used for blood.
- The woman whose hand was used as Norman Bates's mother's was **strangled to death** years later by a handyman and caretaker, just as Janet Leigh was in the movie.

The Exorcist was based on a true story, although it was actually a boy and not a girl, who was demonically possessed. It all started in 1949 in Maryland, and it took several attempts to successfully exorcise the lad. At no time did his head whirl around, although he may have vomited—especially if he saw the movie later.

Battlefield Earth probably received the worst reviews of any movie ever. *The Providence Daily Journal* said in their review, "Whenever we glimpse sunlight, the screen goes all stale yellow, as though someone had urinated on the print. This, by the way, is not such a bad idea."

How did the *Wizard of Oz* get the name "Oz"? Supposedly the author was looking at his filing cabinet, which was divided A–N and O–Z, and upon seeing O–Z, it hit him. . . .

A well-known fact (whispered for years) is that "Rosebud," Charles Foster Kane's last word in the movie *Citizen Kane,* was supposedly the pet name William Randolph Hearst used for his mistress Marion Davies's **sexual organs.**

Marilyn Monroe developed her distinctively sexy sashaying style of walk by removing the heel of one of her shoes and then practicing walking.

Speaking of Ms. Monroe, actor **Tony Curtis,** who starred with her in *Some Like It Hot,* was widely quoted as saying that kissing Marilyn was **"like kissing Hitler."** He later denied it, admitting that they were actually having an affair throughout the filming.

Peter O'Toole wants his epitaph to say what was once printed on his dry cleaning receipt: "It distresses us to return work that is not perfect."

Peter Fonda wears bulletproof trifocals.

Mark Wahlberg was sick fifty-two times during the making of *The Perfect Storm.*

The movie *Roman Holiday* was shot on location in Rome, inside real Italian palaces and mansions. But the filmmakers had to use some very unusual camera angles so the nude statues and paintings wouldn't appear on screen.

The Graduate Was the Ultimate Revenge

Here's getting back at your mother-in-law. Mrs. Robinson, in *The Graduate,* was based on the book's author Charles Web's mother-in-law, who was a real Connecticut prep school teacher. The mother-in-law, the real "Mrs. Robinson," thought the young author wasn't good enough to marry her daughter, Eve, and she tried unsuccessfully to keep the high school sweethearts apart. Years later, after they were married, he got back at her by making her look like **a cunning drunk who'd sleep with anyone,** even a young kid who was her son's friend.

According to the *Globe,* although both the author and his wife were wealthy at one time, they lost their money and divorced. Eve has shaved her head, and now calls herself "Fred." Stay tuned to see how this situation graduates.

Original Movie Titles

Pretty Woman was *3000*
E.T. the Extra-Terrestrial was *A Boy's Life*
No Way Out was *Finished with Engines*
Clueless was *I Was a Teenage Teenager*
Field of Dreams was *Shoeless Joe*

Hey, have you heard about Woody Allen's new movie: *Honey, I Molested the Kids!*

HOW TO BE A MOVIE EXTRA

Perhaps you want to be a movie extra, those people who walk along the sidewalk or sip imaginary cocktails in movie backgrounds because the stars would look silly sitting in an empty restaurant. Lots of people want to do this in our entertainment-saturated society, especially because it takes no talent. It's even possible to get a job as a real actor by doing this. It probably even happened. Once. Maybe. Here are a few tricks of the trade.

Get a Guide

How to Be a Working Actor: The Insider's Guide to Finding Jobs in Theatre, Film and Television by Mari Lyn Henry and Lynne Rogers is the bible for hopefuls. It has useful tips and lists casting directors and agencies, including those who specialize in extras. Reading it will also teach you some words and terms to make you sound more professional. For example, a "walla walla scene" is where extras pretend to be talking in the background. When they say "walla walla" it looks like they are speaking.

Register with a Casting Agency

If you're in an entertainment center like Hollywood, casting agencies can be found right in your local Yellow Pages. They will usually charge a small fee (around $25, if they ask for much more than that it's probably a scam) and this will get your photo in a directory.

These companies often try to make extra money by selling you professional services, such as headshots done by professional photographers.

"You may recognize me from the movies. I go a few times a week."
—Wayne Federman

Yes, they probably get a kickback on it. This doesn't mean they're a total scam, just that they may run a few money-grubbing businesses on the side. A good agency will actually try to get you work.

Interview Days

Ask the agency when they will have a call for possible extras. When you go, they'll take an instant photo of you, plus information like your height, weight, and other statistics. You should:

- Be nice and professional.
- Be ready to show up on a day's notice.
- Always show up fifteen minutes early.
- Bring several changes of clothing in case they're low budget, have very big crowd scenes, or want you to have a different look.

Proper Behavior

- Immediately fill out all paperwork.
- Don't try to stand out by asking dumb questions.
- Don't bother anyone.
- Stay in the area restricted to extras.
- Wait all day, no matter how bored you get, to see if you will possibly be called. (Bring a non-pornographic book to pass the time.)
- Be friendly to anyone you meet. Not only is it nice, and right, but more importantly, they might be important.
- Whether or not you are used, thank them and ask to come back.

Definite No-Nos

- Do not hassle the stars for autographs.
- Do not bother anyone.
- Do not leap in front of the camera.
- Do not disrupt the set.
- Do not try to get extra attention.
- Do not trip over the electrical cords.
- Do not mess with the equipment.
- Do not be a pest to the director, crew, or actors.
- If you do any of these things, you will not win any Oscars, except for an Exit Award

Movie Stars Who Are Real Cut-Ups (or Cut-Outs)

Think those extras you see in a movie are a bit stiff? Well, in expensive movies they may have been digitally added. And in others, those people may actually be **cardboard cut-outs,** that is, extras made out of cardboard, which should give stiff acting Keanu Reeves a run for his money.

The idea of creating cardboard extras was started by a company called Gonzo Bros., which began by printing full-sized photographs of four of their friends. Then, they created more "extras" by adding beards, glasses, wigs, and changing their hair coloring.

Now it's a big business. If someone is making a film with a Cecil B. DeMille–style crowd scene—where hundreds or even thousands of people are necessary to flesh out a crowd, they may slip in a few of these cardboard cuties to save a few dollars. Why not? Real flesh and blood extras have to be paid union wages at about $250 a piece, while these lightweights cost a mere $5 a day. Furthermore, they don't bug the stars for autographs, complain if they are left to sit all day while the producer and director wrangle over details, or have to go to the bathroom in the middle of a take.

MOVIE RATING SYSTEMS EXPLAINED
G = Nobody gets the girl.
PG = The good guy gets the girl.
R = The bad guy gets the girl.
NC-17 = Everybody gets the girl.
XXX = Everybody gets the girl and her cocker spaniel.

I hate sex in the movies. Tried it once and the seat folded up.

"If you suck a tit you're given an X rating, but if you cut it off with a sword it's PG."
—Jack Nicholson

THE OSCARS

No one knows exactly how that little gold man with "no genitalia and holding a sword," as Dustin Hoffman described the Oscar, got his name. The most colorful explanation comes from **Bette Davis,** who won two of them. She claimed she named the statue as such because the nude figure—especially the butt—looked just like the rear end of her first husband (Harmon Oscar Nelson).

According to MSNBC.com, which compared the three theories, in private Bette Davis used to say that the real "point of resemblance to Oscar was the huge sword on the front."

The Big Nipple

Was it a foreigner's mispronunciation, a slip, or an accuracy? Director Bernardo Bertolucci, when receiving an award for *The Last Emperor,* called Hollywood **"The Big Nipple."**

Bette Midler, while presenting an Oscar to someone else, lamented that she had never received one herself. "I've been waiting two years for the Academy to tell me they made a mistake. But do I bear a grudge? No. I have decided to rise to the occasion," she said. And with that, she lifted her breasts with her hands.

Losers

Shirley MacLaine was bitter when she lost the Academy Award to **Elizabeth Taylor** for *Butterfield 8* because it was generally suspected that Liz received the votes out of sympathy. That year she had almost died from pneumonia and needed emergency thoracic surgery. "I lost to a tracheotomy," said MacLaine, after the ceremony.

Jim Carrey talked out of his butt in front of two billion people. And then he complained when he didn't receive an Academy Award later. "I think of [the academy members] as hardworking, conscientious individuals who are trying to destroy me," he said, after being snubbed for an Oscar for *Man on the Moon.*

Vivien Leigh, who played Scarlett O'Hara in *Gone With The Wind,* used one of her Oscars as a doorstop. She used another one as a toilet-paper holder.

Marlon Brando once sent a friend who he believed to be Native American, Sacheen Littlefeather, to accept his Oscar. Later, the press found out that her real name was Maria Cruz, she was not the Apache she claimed to be, and she had once won the **Miss American Vampire contest.**

David Letterman said that hosting the Academy Awards was like being married to Larry King: "You know that it's going to be painful, but it will be over in about three hours."

In 1977, **Vanessa Redgrave** was so unpopular they had to sneak her and her bodyguards into the Academy Awards ceremony in a fake ambulance. After accepting her Oscar for Best Supporting Actress in *Julia,* she further alienated her peers and fans when she went on a freakishly bizarre rant in support of PLO terrorists. Afterward, one host commented to thunderous applause: "A simple 'thank-you' would have sufficed."

FUNNIEST OSCAR ACCEPTANCE LINE
Accepting for *The Producers,* Mel Brooks said, "I'll just say what's in my heart: ba-bump, ba-bump, ba-bump."

A you-really-like-me moment— almost. Director **Frank Capra** was so certain he would win the oscar for *Lady for a Day,* he started to walk toward the dais after Will Rogers announced "Frank" as the winner. To his embarrassment, though, when Rogers was finished it was another Frank.

More losers and losing speeches:
- Catherine Zeta-Jones ended a love affair on her way to the Oscars by kicking her boyfriend out of the limo.
- Debbie Reynolds asked during her presentation, "Who wrote this drivel?"
- **Kevin Costner** said of an Academy Award ceremony that he attended, **"The Oscars made my pits wet."**
- James Dean was nominated for two Oscars in two different years—both after his death in a car crash—and lost both.
- Eileen Heckart got an Oscar for Best Supporting Actress in 1972 for *Butterflies Are Free.* The next day she collected unemployment.
- Spencer Tracy's Best Actor Oscar (for *Captains Courageous*) accidentally read "Dick Tracy."

Winners

A dog was once nominated for an Oscar—and no one knew it. Robert Towne, of *Lord of the Apes*, spent eight years on a screenplay and ended up having to share the credit, along with other indignities. He was so disgusted that he replaced his own screen credit with the name of his Hungarian sheepdog (P. H. Vasak).

More winners:

- Besides the obvious publicity, presenters receive **more than $5,000 worth of goodies,** like designer watches and gold charms.

> When Chevy Chase hosted the Oscars in 1987, he opened by saying, "Good Evening Hollywood Phonies." (This may be why he only hosted it once.)

- In 1937, someone accepted on behalf of the Best Supporting Actress, who was laid up with a broken ankle and couldn't attend the ceremony. The man who accepted the award was never seen again—nor was the Oscar.
- Someone once won an Oscar without saying a word. John Mills won Best Supporting Actor for his performance as a deaf mute in *Ryan's Daughter*.
- People have been nominated and won for Oscar performances of fewer than ten minutes. Dame **Judi Dench** was onscreen in *Shakespeare in Love* for eight minutes, and Sylvia Miles was nominated for a memorable six-minute role in *Midnight Cowboy*.
- **Irving Berlin** once gave an Oscar to himself.

"I guess this proves there are as many nuts in the Academy as anywhere else,"
—Jack Nicholson,
when accepting the Best Actor Oscar for *One Flew Over the Cuckoo's Nest* in 1975

MOVIE AND TELEVISION CLICHÉS

Have you ever wondered why nobody on television has time to watch television? Or why women in the movies are always beautiful, but men are allowed to be ugly? That's just the way it is in the idealized onscreen world. Here are some other movie and television fantasies.

- **Bathrooms** are made for sex, murder, and drugs. No one ever uses them for their real purposes.
- **Houses** are immaculate, although no one is ever seen cleaning them (unless someone has killed or been killed in one).
- Sinister things are found in **basements,** and incredible things are found in **attics.**
- When someone **coughs,** he or she will be dead by the end of the movie.
- All people of Asian descent know **karate.**
- Everyone wins in **Las Vegas** (unless it's a movie about a dying, drunken loser, like *Leaving Las Vegas*).

Sex

- Two total strangers will invariably and inevitably reach an immediate, **simultaneous orgasm**—on the first try.
- No one ever needs or uses Kleenex or a towel after sex.
- No one needs or uses condoms during sex.
- Nobody has to sleep on **the wet spot.**
- No one ever sweats during sex.
- Women always come every time.
- Lovemaking never leads to pregnancy or venereal disease.
- It's never called "lovemaking."
- Teenagers who have sex will **die in horrible ways.**

Cars

- Cars will always start immediately (especially if you're being chased), unless they stall, in which case the person will climb out and sprint faster than the person chasing him.

COMPUTERS CLICHÉS

- Printers never run out of paper.
- Computers never crash.
- You don't have to save your files; just turn off the computer.
- Computers boot up immediately.

- Whenever a car hits something it will **instantly explode.** If it does not explode, it will always crash into a fruit stand.
- Nobody ever gets pulled over for speeding no matter how fast they are going or in which (wrong) direction they're traveling.
- In a car chase, someone can drive straight through a crowd of women and children and not hit a single one.
- The police never stop a car unless it is filled with drugs or guns—or there's **a dead body in the trunk.**

> All bad guys who capture a good guy will tell him their plans for world domination before killing him. Then, the bad guy will accidentally let the good guy go on to foil those plans.

Bad Guys versus Good Guys

- Bad guys come from England, except for Nazis, who come from Germany, but speak with English accents.
- All **insane murderers** are soft-spoken, highly educated geniuses.
- When shooting, no bad guy can hit the broad side of a barn.
- All cops are good guys, and they never go a day without a shootout.
- Good guys always have **perfect hair** and never need to brush it.
- A good guy is always white, but his best friend is always black.
- Racial profiling doesn't exist, but all drug dealers are black or Puerto Rican.
- In a James Bond movie, the bad girl always dies, but only after **sleeping with Bond.**
- A woman never fights, unless it's to hit a bad guy over the head with something when his back is turned.

SOURCES: MOVIE.COM CLICHÉS, ROB CLARK

BEHIND THE TELEVISION SCENES
Could You Win on *Who Wants to Be a Millionaire?*

Here are a few questions that were correctly answered on the television show—for $1 million!

Which of these U.S. presidents appeared on the television series *Laugh-In?*
- A. Lyndon Johnson
- B. Richard Nixon
- C. Jimmy Carter
- D. Gerald Ford

(The correct answer is B, and an IRS agent won the money.)

The earth is approximately how many miles from the sun?
- A. 9.3 million
- B. 39 million
- C. 93 million
- D. 193 million

(The correct answer is C, and a lawyer won the money.)

What insect shorted out an early supercomputer and inspired the term *computer bug?*
- A. moth
- B. roach
- C. fly
- D. japanese beetle

(The correct answer is A, and a teacher won the money.)

Which of the following men does not have a chemical element named after him?
- A. Albert Einstein
- B. Niels Bohr
- C. Isaac Newton
- D. Enrico Fermi

(The correct answer is C, and a service rep won the money.)

Could you have won the £1 million prize in England, where this show originated and is still popular? They've had very few winners there. The first, a fifty-eight-year-old garden designer and sometimes bereavement counselor, who is also distantly related to Prince Charles's mistress, Camilla Parker-Bowles, correctly answered the following question for £1 million (see the next page for answer):

Which king was married to Eleanor of Aquitaine?

> What did President and Mrs. Bush want to know about life on the first Survivor island? Salon.com's Amy Reiter reported that the winner of the first $1 million prize, Richard Hatch, revealed that when he met them, the Bushes wanted to know what he ate—and how he went to the bathroom.

(The answer, which of course you knew, was Henry II.)

Inside.com looked at *Who Wants to Be a Millionaire?* and found that three-quarters of the questions were taken from well-known reference books, such as *World Book Encyclopedia.*

Those who think the questions on this show are dumb may be smart. If a question refers to something that's too obscure, it comes back to the developers with a note on it saying WGAS (Who Gives a Shit).

On the subject of game shows, Salon.com ran a story about the real original Survivor, a Swedish show called Expedition Robinson. Here are a few differences:

- The winner took home only $33,000, instead of *Survivor's* $1 million.
- There were forty-eight contestants versus sixteen on *Survivor.*
- *Survivor's* losers have been better sports. A jilted player from their show threw himself in front of a train. (For a lousy $33,000!)

> When Regis Philbin goes to the bathroom before he goes on the air for *Who Wants to Be a Millionaire?*, a staffer makes sure his clip-on mic isn't still on, so the studio audience doesn't hear any embarrassing sounds from him.

Original Names of Popular Television Shows

- *Today* was *The Rise and Shine Revue.*
- *Charlie's Angels* was *The Alley Cats.*
- *Different Strokes* was *45 Minutes from Harlem.*
- *The Brady Bunch* was *The Brady Brood.*
- *Dallas* was *Houston.*

SOURCE: *The People Register*

Money Paid and Money Made

Years ago, Paragon Cable in New York tried cutting off service to dead-beats who didn't pay their bills. But they did much better when they instead filled every single one of their channels with C-SPAN—the deadly dull show containing hot-air proceedings from Congress, and other less than thrilling public affair outlets.

People soon called Paragon *begging* to have the opportunity to pay up and get their programs back.

Writers who wrote the classic movies and television shows prior to 1960—for example, *I Love Lucy*—along with the actors and actresses who played in them, collect nothing from the television and video sales of their work.

> When ABC decided to place billboards above urinals to advertise one of their shows, they poked fun at their competitor's NBC "Must-See TV" slogan. Their headline was "Must-Pee TV."

Most Popular Springer Shows

Maybe you don't watchthe *Jerry Springer Show* (or maybe you do!), but here are five of the most popular programs they've done, according to *Jerry Springer's Wildest Shows Ever:*

- "I Broke the World's Sex Record"
- "It's Your Mother or Me"
- "I've Been Keeping a Secret"
- "Stripper Wars"
- "I Have a Bizarre Sex Life"

"If you're looking to save the whales, call *Oprah*. If you're sleeping with a whale, call us."
—Richard Dominick, executive producer for *Jerry Springer*

"Talk-show hosts never seem to have any idea how much time is left in the show.... They're always looking off camera. 'Do we have time?'... You never see Magnum P.I. go, 'Should I strangle this guy or are we gonna take a break here? Can you stay for another beating?'"
—Jerry Seinfeld, *Sein Language*

Sex

KINKY PEOPLE
Weirdo Turn-Ons

There's no accounting for people's tastes ... or what they like to taste. Here are a few weird activities that turned some people on:

A dutchman in England would get on a bus, climb under the seat, and **stick his tongue through the gap in the cushions.** (This was atypical because Dutchmen are better known for putting their thumbs into dykes.) He might have gotten away with his actions—there probably were *some* women who didn't complain—but he stuck to the same route each time and was easy to catch.

A man with a hang up for big breasts got the names of women who had just had babies from birth announcements. Then he made harassing calls to them, inquiring about their **breast growth.**

A mugger would steal glasses from people on the street and wear them in bed, getting **sexually aroused by wearing glasses** that had just been stolen.

A man spent his time at libraries crawling under the tables searching for women wearing sandals. When he found them, he stabbed their feet.

A nineteen-year-old male in Atlanta, Georgia, made believe he was a music video producer and was going to put girls in his upcoming video. He got them to go off with him in his car, and he'd stop the car and threaten to kill them unless . . . **they bit his belly button.**

In Japan a man called women and asked them **to turn over their underwear** to him for inspection. They did.

Almost one-third of people who admitted to making love in unusual places said that they had made love on a toilet seat. And the most popular type of toilet was the kind made for the disabled, since the stalls are larger.

You know the old joke that goes, "I always hold my wife's hand. If I let go, she goes shopping." Well, one man, whenever he went out without his wife, would go to the supermarket and squeeze and poke bread. He was fined $8,000 for the cost of the goods he damaged—that's a lot of dough for squeezing a lot of dough. His sentence was to have his wife with him whenever he went shopping.

United Press International reported on a man in Nebraska who police called the "Big Bonnet" because he wore one, along with other baby clothes. He'd appear in public, bend over a bench—and paddle himself.

A man in Edinburgh got women to let him cut their hair by posing as a hairdresser. (If he'd been any good, the story would probably never have come out.)

A female manager at McDonald's received a phone call from a police impersonator claiming that they had to conduct a strip search because money had been stolen from the restaurant. He ordered her to take off her clothes—and she did.

A shoe advertisement claimed that 37 percent of all women preferred shoe shopping to sex.
SEE "SEX SECRETS OF THE STARS," PAGE 9.

The Associated Press reported the case of a man in New Jersey who robbed a dozen urologists' offices because he was angry with them for refusing to give him a prostate exam that he didn't need. He apparently just enjoyed receiving them.

A man called women and told them he was their husband's psychologist and that the women were too rigid and they should make love with the first man they saw. Then he called them back and got details—except in one case where the woman called the police.

The Smell of De-Feet

There are more nerve endings on the feet than almost any other part of the body, which may explain why people have eroticized feet throughout the centuries. Some fetishists are turned on by certain toes, the arch, **"toe cleavage"** (that crack between the toes), or all of the above, because feet are the number-one fetish in the country.

In many cultures, women would sooner show their sex organs than their tootsies. Roman women even put weights in their togas so their feet wouldn't accidentally show. (Even so, they couldn't escape their men's "roman" hands.)

Columnist Dick Morris lost his political job when it came out that he was into **sucking the toes of prostitutes.**

Instead of putting his foot in his own mouth, a Tory minister in England got caught putting someone *else's* foot in his mouth. When he was dismissed, one tabloid gleefully crowed, "Toe Job, No Job."

Fergie, the former Duchess of York, a.k.a. Duchess of Pork, and spokeswoman for Weight Watchers, inadvertently helped bring this kink out in the open when her boyfriend was photographed fondling her toes. So a publisher is now taking advantage of all this great free publicity by coming out with a book titled *Footsie with Fergie: How to 'Properly' Make Love with Your Toes.* No, it's not written by Fergie but by a couple calling themselves "The Duke and Duchess of Delirium."

One of the world's weirdest serious sentences was penned by Nancy Friday, who became famous for writing about sexual fantasies: "Sooner or later, **the shoe, the vagina, and the penis** are going to have to sit down and have it out."

Unusual Sexual Terms

- **Acarophilia:** Affinity for itching
- **Acomoclitic:** Preference for hairless genitals
- **Actirasty:** To become aroused from exposure to the sun's rays
- **Adamitism:** Going naked for God
- **Alvinolagnia:** Stomach fetish
- **Anasteemaphilia:** Attraction to a person because of a difference in height

- **Antiophilia:** Fondness for floods
- **Avering:** A boy's begging in the nude to arouse sympathy
- **Botulinonia:** Sex with a sausage
- **Dacryphilia:** Arousal from seeing tears in the eyes of a partner
- **Furtling:** Getting aroused by putting fingers underneath the genital areas of cut-outs.
- **Psellismophilia:** Becoming aroused by stuttering
- **Sacofricosis:** Cutting a hole in one's pants pocket to masturbate while in public

SOURCE: SEXUALRECORDS.COM

Are You a Sexual Compulsive?

Al Cooper, who did a study on people with a compulsion to visit porn sites, developed a "sexual compulsive quiz." To see if you have a problem, answer these questions (honestly), which come from the test:

- Is there secrecy, shame, or guilt around your preferred sexual activity?
- Are their times when you fear your sexual urges are controlling you?
- Do you spend an excessive amount of time in this sexual activity or thinking about it?
- Is sexual satisfaction short-lived and are you driven to have sex again and again within a short period of time?

"I saw a phone-sex line, 970-PEEE, for people who want other people to urinate on them during sex. It's $1.50 for the first minute, 95 cents for each additional minute. Who can pee longer than a minute? Wouldn't you get suspicious after half an hour? Are you guys running the faucets?"
—Jon Stewart

HOW TO CATCH A CHEATING PARTNER

First, here are some ways to determine if your partner is indeed having an affair:

- She loses interest in sex with you.
  She becomes more interested in sex.
- Suddenly he can't look you in the eyes.
  Suddenly, he can.
- She starts finding fault with everything you do, in an attempt to distract from her own guilt.
  She starts telling you how great everything you do is because she feels guilty.
- He comes home smelling of perfume or cologne, or has lipstick stains on his handkerchiefs.
  He comes home with no unusual smells (extra shower at her place) without a handkerchief. (He may have gotten lipstick on it and thrown it away.)
- She starts saying wonderful things about the person, say, her new office assistant. (Some people are so enamored of their new lover that they can't stop talking about that person, even to their own spouse.)
  She says terrible things about him, so you won't suspect she cares.
- He becomes irrationally jealous, and accuses you of cheating.
  He suddenly couldn't care less if you're cheating.
- She stops calling as often during the day.
  She calls more often during the day.

Odd Phone Behavior

If the above doesn't satify your suspicions, here are a few cleaner-cut ways to tell from your partner's behavior if he or she is cheating:

- There are a lot of calls and hang-ups or wrong numbers.
- She hangs up the phone when you walk in the room.
- He goes into another room to make calls.
- She suddenly goes out of her way to allay suspicion about the person she's speaking to. "Sure, BOB! I'll be right back to you on that, BOB! Bye, BOB!"

Check the last phone number called. Say your spouse abruptly hangs up the phone when you walk into the room. Either use *69 to find out what number he just called or hit the old "redial" button and see who picks up. Princess Di used this latter trick to find out if Charles was faithful. If you use it, and Camilla Parker-Bowles answers, hang up.

Check other numbers. Cheaters often leave a paper trail, so you may find phone numbers (and odd credit card charges) that you don't recognize on bills. (Or the phone bills may disappear because the cheating partner grabs them so you won't find suspicious numbers.)

Also, check cell phone records for the first number your spouse calls when leaving your house, and also the number called right after work, or right before he or she gets home in the evening.

Other Behavior Changes

- He suddenly starts checking his e-mail a lot.
- She spends a lot of time online when you're not around.
- He starts having a lot of errands to do.
- She stays at "work" late at night way too often, especially if her paycheck doesn't show it. (Check her paycheck stubs for claimed overtime.)
- He frequently doesn't show up when expected.
- She's always coming home late, often with a series of incredibly lame excuses. "The dog ate my car."

The Underwear Test

There's a spray that reveals if people have semen on their underwear, which is a pretty good gauge of infidelity if it turns up positive on a woman's underpants and she hasn't been making love with her husband. (If she has, one company that tests for semen will then also test for DNA to see if the sample is the husband's or some other man's.)

Actually, though, this product is meant for wives to spray on their *husband's* jockey shorts. So, if semen shows up, he may have spilled his seed in the commission of an adulterous act. (True, there are other ways it could have happened, and for other reasons, but try to tell that to a woman who finds some.)

Finally, if *you're* the one who **wants to cheat,** there's an "alibi service" that answers the phone as if they were a hotel operator. They provide clients with phony dinner and taxi receipts (to support their stories) and send phony invitations to nonexistent conferences in other cities so cheaters can make up a story about a business meeting. At the moment they're only in Europe, but an evil idea like this is bound to spread.

TALKING DIRTY
The Worst Sexual Description

Who do you think won an award for bad writing? (No, not me.) Hard to believe that it was none other than the famous writer John Updike. The following sentence, from Updike's *Gertrude and Claudius,* won a Literary Review contest for the worst description of sex, which it deserved:

> *She would have lain down in the warm mud for him, even the mud of the pigsty, to enter the exaltation she found in his brute love.*

First prize was captured by Sean Thomas, who wrote:

> *Shall I compare thee to a Sony Walkman. She is his own Toshiba, his dinky little JVC, his sweet Aiwa . . . Aiwa, aiwa aiwa aiwa aiwa aiwa aiwa aiwa aiwa aiwa aiwaaaaaaaaaahhhhhhhhh.*

Sexy Cities and Towns

"Fancy telling people that you live in these places?" asked the "Friday humour" mailing list out of the United Kingdom.

- Brown Willy (Cornwall, UK)
- Seymen (Turkey)
- Fuku (Shensi, China)
- Comdom (France)
- Wanks River (Nicaragua)
- Shag Island (Indian Ocean)
- Sexmoan (Luzon, Philippines)
- Wet Beaver Creek (Australia)
- Pis Pis River (Nicaragua)
- Tittybong (Australia)
- Bastard (Norway)
- Dikshit (India)
- Muff (Northern Ireland)
- Wankie (Zimbabwe)
- Dildo (Newfoundland, Canada)
- Twatt (Shetland and also Orkney, UK)
- Lickey End (West Midlands, UK)
- Squaw Teat Creek (Renamed East Rattlesnake Creek)

SEX IN THE STATES

- Shafter (California)
- Climax (Colorado)
- Colon (Michigan)
- Climax (Michigan)
- Butte (Montana)
- Intercourse (Pennsylvania)
- Fairyland (Tennessee)

Made-Up Sex Words

Someone with far too much time on their hands decided to put an "s" in front of all words beginning with "ex." Many of these words are so useful that they should become part of our vocabulary.

sexaggerate	sexamine
sexceed	sexcellent
sexceptional	sexchange
sexchangeable	sexclusive
sexcommunicate	sexcuses
sexhaustion	sexhibition
sexhilarate	sexpedite
sexpensive	sexperience
sexperiment	sexpert
sexpiration	sexpletive
sexplore	sexpression
sexquisite	sextemporaneous
sextracurricular	sextralegal
sextraterrestial	sextraordinary
sextreme	sextrovert

Naughty Word Alert

Is your boss spying on you, (the bastard)? Supposedly 30 percent of all companies *do* monitor their employees' e-mail in various ways. *Wired* magazine reported that if your company uses Cameo software to search for **"inappropriate activity,"** the following are some of the words that will be flagged.

If they seem an odd choice, not only are they indicative that you're viewing sex sites, but also that you're looking for a new job (which you may need if these words come up.) Or that **you may be planning to blow up your workplace** (which you may want to do when you realize that your boss is monitoring your private e-mail).

Bimbo	Résumé
Fondle	Job offer
Ammonium nitrate	Reefer
I'll show him/her	Signing bonus
Unfair	Performance review

Another company uses a different method. *Time* magazine reported on the **PORNsweeper,** which looks for "pink pixels," and also measures the ratio of skin color to other colors to see how much clothing the person is wearing (or not wearing). But what happens if you innocently send Grandma some baby pictures?

SEX ACTS
Sex Laws

The good city council of Clarksville, Tennessee, decided to pass an ordinance that said the operators of **the adult-only bookstore** in town could not have sex on the premises of their shop. But they left out the words "on the premises," so the law basically read that this poor couple who owned the shop couldn't have sex *anywhere!*

Ever wanted to wear **a penis costume?** Well, don't do it in Nevada if you're a member of their legislature because it's illegal to conduct official business wearing a penis costume during the time that the legislature is in session.

And if you're in Newcastle, Wyoming, don't have **sex inside a store's walk-in meat freezer** or they'll freeze you out.

Attention saleswomen in Liverpool, England—tropical fish stores are allowed to be topless.

In Colombia, the first time a couple has sex, her mother must be in the room as a witness.

No prostitutes in Sienna, Italy, can have the name *Mary.*

In Connorsville, Wisconsin, a man can't **shoot off a gun while his female partner is having an orgasm.**

In the state of Washington, there's a law against having sex with a virgin—even on the wedding night!

If there are any nude people in a house in Kentucky, they must be registered.

You can't have sex with a truck driver in a toll booth in Harrisburg, Pennsylvania.

All Systems Go

Cold hands could mean cold heart and cold other places too. If **vasoconstriction,** or narrowing of the blood vessels, is occurring in the hands, it's also in the genitals, meaning a woman is not well lubricated and a man is less likely to get an erection. Says Dr. Kevin Pezzi about this: "If people have cold hands when they're together, it means they're anxious and not psychologically ready for sex."

The first vibrators in the mid-1800s were made of steam. And although most today are battery operated, the larger ones that use electricity may emit harmful electrical fields, similar to electric blankets.

According to *Tailwinds,* in the 1500s, Saint Jerome forbade his nuns to eat beans in the belief that passing gas "tickled the genitals," as the wind passed by.

People who appear to be crazy in love may really be a bit crazy. Similarities have been noticed between people obsessing about their loved ones and obsessive-compulsive disorder. Instead of having to see if their stove is still on, or whatever their obsessive thought is, people in the early throes of love may have to keep thinking about their loved one.

Telling the person to get over it isn't going to help, because the cause is physiological. Both groups seem to have a lower than normal level of a brain chemical called serotonin.

Let's Misbehave

According to *Cosmopolitan* magazine, it would take the typical American couple, at the average rate that they make love, more than four years to try every one of the **529 positions in the Kama Sutra.**

Useless-sex.com reported on the following sex studies:

- People who are married spend almost ten minutes less on each sex act than those who are living together.
- Lesbians in one questionnaire said their last sex session lasted more than one hour.
- One in five women have multiple orgasms, while more than a third of lesbians do.
- Erotic sensations can move at **156 miles per hour,** which explains why you feel good so quickly when someone touches you.

Sexual Healing

If you think fantasies are a waste of time, try thinking of your favorite one next time you're in pain. In one experiment, people could keep their hands in ice water for three minutes when they thought of something sexual—and only one minute when they thought of something boring. (The only problem with this is that most people thinking of something sexual would rather have their hands somewhere else.)

> **SEX KILLS PAIN**
>
> - Sex has been shown to stop headaches because it causes the brain to release endorphins, which kill pain.
>
> - Having sex has been proven to relieve arthritis pain for up to six hours.

Kissing

- Some say that kissing started so that people could **smell and taste someone's face** to gauge their mood.
- Kissing can lead to wrinkles since puckering up uses facial muscles.
- The more passionate the kiss, the more muscles are used.
- Using Xs at the end of a letter for kisses started in the Middle Ages when people couldn't write and used crosses as signatures.
- Lipstick was used in Egyptian times by women who specialized in **oral sex,** to make their lips look exciting.

Could a Case of Venereal Disease Have Changed the World?

Every day in this world, one million people catch a sexually transmitted disease. But just one of those could have lead to America, in the opinions of the authors of *Who's Had Who?* It is known that **Henry VIII** slept with a prostitute at sixteen, and that he probably contracted **syphilis.** This caused him to act crazy and irrationally, for example, divorcing Catherine of Aragon despite the political consequences.

His folly caused England to leave the Catholic Church, and ultimately this led to Puritanism, which was brought to America. Because we were affiliated with the English, we came into World War II on the English side. Their conclusions: Without this one sexual act, "There would be no Church of England, no English-speaking America, and no free Europe."

BREASTS
Oh, Go Ahead and Stare

According to BizarreNews.com, *The New England Journal of Medicine* printed a study showing that **men who ogle women's breasts** for ten minutes each day are healthier than those who don't have this, er, hobby.

In fact, breast-staring may be as good for the body as aerobic exercise—and a lot more fun. The reason is that staring at something extremely pleasurable increases the metabolism. So the man drooling over the aerobics video could end up healthier than the models in it.

> "If you're up against a girl with big boobs, bring her to the net and make her hit backhand volleys."
> —Billie Jean King

Real Sex related the story of erotic dancer Crystal Storm, who claimed that **her bust was 127 inches,** but it was really "only" fifty inches. When Philadelphia's Department of Licenses and Inspections cited her for deceptive advertising, she said she had given the figure in centimeters.

Best Bust Awards

Pink Ribbon magazine surveyed women about who they thought had the best breasts. **Spice Girl Geri Halliwell** came in first, **Jennifer Lopez** was second. The runners-up were:

Elizabeth Hurley   Elle MacPherson
Pamela Anderson   Britney Spears
Madonna

Saggies

A debate arose on a gossip newsgroup as to who had the saggiest breasts. Their award went to **Kathie Lee Gifford.** The award also went to **Laura San Giacomo,** from *Just Shoot Me* (and when Laura heard of her award, she probably wished they would).

Bras

Prince Charles may have wanted to be reincarnated as Camilla's tampax, but **Jesse Ventura** is obviously a "tit man" because he said he'd like to be reincarnated as a size 38DD bra.

In Russia, where cash-strapped companies often pay their employees in merchandise, an underwear factory **paid its employees in brassieres**—thirty-three to forty-two a month. (Their employees are probably better off than another Russian company that paid its workers in rubber dicks—perhaps a subtle way of telling them that they were getting screwed.)

An embarrassing typo occurred when the *New York Times* accidentally quoted Ivana Trump, Donald's former wife, as saying that she buys **six thousand bras** every six months. The correct figure, she said later, was six *dozen,* which is still ridiculous.

> "I was the first woman to burn my bra—it took the fire department four days to put it out."
> —Dolly Parton

Here are a few more titillating factoids about bras:
- The most popular bra size in America is 36C, according to the *New York Times.*
- The most popular size a decade ago was 34B. (Some joke that the growth is part of **the Clinton legacy.**)
- 70 to 85 percent of all American women are said to wear the wrong bra size.
- The size of requested implants has also increased.
- "Pick-up" type bras make up 10 percent off all purchases—and 15 percent at Victoria's Secret, according to the *New York Times.*
- To determine when a young woman needs to wear a bra, she should do **the "pencil" test,** which means placing a pencil under her breast. If she can hold it, she needs a bra.

Other Underwear Stories

As many as 10 percent of all people in the United Kingdom may put their **underwear in the refrigerator** to help them keep cool.

Bikini bathing suits and tight blue jeans may cause women to have urinary tract infections, says a prominent urologist. The clothing can push bacteria into a woman's organs.

A few companies are now selling jeweled and beaded thongs—called **Peeping Thongs**—and low-riding skirts, so that future Monica Lewinskys can more easily flash their thongs (and fat rears) at future presidents.

THE PENIS
Odd Stories in the News

People have tried everything to get around drug tests—even using **a false penis.** When one heroin addict tried this, though, he made a few mistakes:

- The pink color of the fake member didn't match the real organ.
- "Urine" from the fake member was squirting all over the place.
- It was **eight inches long** (and since only 2 percent of the population is that large when erect, it raised eyebrows).
- The "urine" was cold, whereas urine coming from the body is warm.
- And finally, the surest giveaway of all, when he pulled it out to offer a sample, **the man dropped and caught it** before it hit the ground. SEE "HE'LL PEE FOR YOU," PAGE 110.

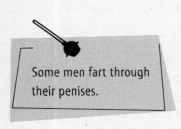

Some men fart through their penises.

A court ruled that a man who was running for office could walk down the street **dressed as a penis** because he was making a political statement by doing so. Others thought he was behaving in a lewd way so as to get more attention than his opponent, who he thought was—all together now—a prick.

An **eighteen-inch dildo** became an actual murder weapon. A Key West man raped a woman by trying to force the giant dildo into her. He perforated her colon, killing her.

An Australian charity golf tournament, which was organized by a cosmetic surgery outfit, offered penis (and breast) enlargements to the best players. (Talk about getting the shaft!)

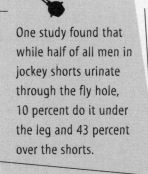

One study found that while half of all men in jockey shorts urinate through the fly hole, 10 percent do it under the leg and 43 percent over the shorts.

A Few Historical Factoids

- At one time, all popes were checked to see if they had penises because in the ninth century, a certain Pope "John" slipped through, and some think she may have been **Pope "Jane."**

- The word *testify* comes from men swearing on their testicles that something is true, which was done in Roman times.

- **Hitler was missing one testicle.** So was Napoleon.

The Small-Penis Rule

It is said that one way fiction writers avoid a lawsuit when describing someone who might be close to someone real is to write that he has an extremely small penis. This makes the person who the character is modeled after less likely to insist that it's him. SEE "WHO'S HUNG IN HOLLYWOOD?", PAGE 10.

Broken Hearts and Broken Ah . . .

In the United States, more than ten thousand people each year injure themselves—some actually **fracture their penises**—while trying out bizarre sexual positions. Other causes for broken penises include overly enthusiastic lovemaking, erratic movements during sex, (usually when the male accidentally strikes the woman's pelvis bone), or falling down (or off a bed) with an erection.

Because some of these breaks occur during masturbation, presumably these people become so preoccupied with what they're doing that they fall off the bed face first, but not necessarily on their face, while they have an erection.

In countries such as Iran, though, there is another reason for the frequent reports of fractured and injured penises. They have a habit of **slapping an unwanted erection** with their hands to make it go down.

"Pamela Lee said her husband [Tommy Lee] tattooed her name on his penis. Which explains why she changed her name from Anderson to Lee."
—Conan O'Brien

Incredible Shrinking Penises

Honey, I shrunk my . . . oh, shut up. Actually, people have been worried about this for a long time, so much so that there have been nationwide shrinking penis panics. These started with a few whispered admissions of **inexplicable shrinkage,** followed by unstoppable rumors, until mass hysteria took over.

In all these cases, thousands of people have been utterly certain that their penises were shrinking and would soon disappear. Men have gripped their favorite family member with their hands, string, clamps, or chopsticks, desperate to hold on to every fraction of an inch.

One bout of penis paranoia in northeast India in 1982 became so bad that the government sent out doctors with loud speakers to calm everyone. They also measured penises of nervous people to convince them that they were in no jeopardy.

Dr. Edell Dean, one of America's most popular "media doctors," who writes an interesting daily column in HealthCentral.com, has chronicled this phenomenon. He told of another panic two years later that lasted for a year. In that case, 5,000 Chinese in a backwater province claimed **evil penis-purloining ghosts** had visited them. They reported that when the "ghosts" arrived, they experienced a chilly sensation, followed by their willies shriveling up. (Of course, anyone who thinks they've seen a ghost might indeed suffer some shrinkage.)

There are no known cases of such mass hysteria in the United States, Canada, or Europe, and an uncharitable observer might believe that Asian men have a case of insecurity about the size of their male members, because studies have shown them to be slightly smaller than their Western neighbors. So the whole thing could have started with a glance at a Caucasian's member in a men's room . . . followed by panic.

VIAGRA SLOGANS AND SONGS

- Viagra: The quicker dicker upper.
- Get a piece of the rock.
- Strong enough for a man but made for a woman.
- Here's the beef.
- Suddenly.
- Hard day's night.
- I am a rock.
- Reach out and touch someone.
- We bring good things to life.
- This is your penis. This is your penis on drugs.

SEE "PRESIDENTIAL PENISES," PAGE 237;
"ANIMAL PENISES," PAGE 129;
AND "DEATH BY BRA—AND PENIS," PAGE 259.

How to Tell if Your Viagra Is Working

- You like to sleep on your back, so you had to remove the ceiling fan.
- Sunbathing nude, outside, lying down you look like a sundial.
- You always lose limbo contests.
- You can make drawings in the sand without having to find a stick.

SPERM AND FERTILITY
How to Be a Sperm Donor

Although you could make a lot of money donating your sperm to a fertility bank, you've probably let it all slip between your fingers! Each day, you produced enough new sperm cells to **double the population of the United States.** Someone asked *Playboy Advisor* how to become a sperm donor and they said that only one in twenty people who applied were accepted. To be one of those, you must be college educated, taller than 5'9", and healthy.

You'll be paid for your "time," not for your "output," at approximately $50 a pop. If that seems like a lot of money for doing what comes naturally, remember that bull semen goes for as much as $200 a pop, and stud fees for dogs and cats are often the pick of the litter—and a champion can sell for thousands.

How much would someone pay for sperm from one of the biggest newspaper publishers, video producers, entrepreneurs, or raconteurs in America? Four vials of cryogenically frozen sperm were **auctioned on Ebay for $25,000,** according to the *New York Post.* Who was the newspaper magnate donating his sperm? Al Goldstein. Whoever bought it didn't get screwed.

The Bobbitt Prayer

You all remember John Bobbitt—who could forget?—who was married to a manicurist who decided to cut more than just nails. Here's a prayer the ex-marine-husband-turned-occasional-porn-actor might make:

Now I lay me down to sleep,
I pray the Lord my shlong to keep.
And if I wake and it is gone,
I hope to find it on the lawn.
Much attention I must pay,
To assure I put the knives away.
The mower, chain saw, the hatchet too,
Why there's no telling what she'd do.
To rid me of my manly charm,
I must keep it safe, away from harm.
So I cross my fingers, as I close my eyes,
And I cross my legs to avoid surprise.

No Baby on Board

The chemicals in children's disposable diapers—so strong that they have been used to put out forest fires—may cause male infertility and testicular cancer later in life for those who wear them as children.

Pamela Anderson Lee, when asked if she would have more children with Tommy, said he had been "fixed actually. He has been neutered or spayed. What do you call it?" (Depends on whether he's a person or a dog.)

Absence not only makes the heart grow fonder, it may make it easier to have children. One analysis found that the longer a man is away from a woman, the more his sperm count leaps.

Other factors that could affect fatherhood:

- Staying seated for a long time (possibly explaining why professional drivers have lower than average sperm counts)
- Saunas, fever, or whatever causes high temperature
- Tight underwear

Maybe one reason there are so many people in India is that they use condoms for purposes other than for what they were intended. According to the *Jakarta Post*, about **five hundred million, or half the condoms distributed, are used to plug radiator leaks** in vehicles, or are dyed and sold as balloons.

In other countries, condoms are placed over the muzzle of rifles to protect them from sand if they're being used in deserts.

Sperm Smuggling

The latest trend in prison is not smuggling drugs or money *in* but **smuggling sperm *out*** so that prisoners' wives and girlfriends can have children while they're away. Two prisoners recently got caught after guards became suspicious when they realized that prisoners with long sentences had very young children coming to visit them along with their wives and girlfriends.

A forty-year-old Russian trucker was caught at the border with 28,000 condoms—and was allowed through when he said they were for his own personal use.

Is There a Sperm Bank for the Smart?

In yet another attempt to create a master race, the inventor of the shatter-proof eyeglass lens came up with the notorious **Nobel Prize Sperm Bank.** According to *Bigger Secrets,* all the semen available to those wanting children were supposed to have come from people who had won the Nobel Prize.

Instead of producing children, however, the plan has spawned controversy and criticism. Only one Nobel laureate admitted to having donated his sperm, and he's a racist fool whose sperm no one is likely to want anyway. Many other Nobel winners have publicly denounced the plan, calling it everything from "pretty silly," and "weird," to "snobbish." "The old-fashioned way [of having babies] still seems better to me," said one.

How can you tell if a sperm is happy? It's got egg on its face.

But that doesn't stop people from trying to be more selective. When **Jodie Foster** had a baby, she supposedly chose a scientist with a 160 IQ. One sperm bank said that they had received requests for **Brad Pitt's semen.** And those who argue for a sperm bank of this sort [Nobel Prize] have said that in a modern society, without natural selection, we would soon be overrun by genetic defectives and imbeciles.

Although some evidence may be seen for this (if you tune in to *Jerry Springer* or other talk shows), it doesn't yet seem that this is preventing intelligent people from being born.

BRAND-NAME CONDOMS

Nike condoms: Just do it.

Toyota condoms: Oh, what a feeling.

Pringles condoms: Once you pop, you can't stop.

Campbell's Soup condoms: M'm, m'm good.

Avis condoms: Trying harder than ever.

Kentucky Fried Chicken condoms: Finger-licking good.

AT&T condoms: Reach out and touch someone.

Bounty condoms: The quicker picker upper.

Energizer condoms: It keeps going and going and going.

Hallmark condoms: For when you care enough to give the very best.

FedEx condoms: When it absolutely, positively has to be there overnight.

Star Trek condoms: To boldly go where no man has gone before.

MASTURBATION
Master Your Domain the Mormon Way

These are excerpts from a famous document allegedly put out by the Mormon Church, which forbids masturbation because "it separates a person from God and defeats the gospel plan . . . [and] causes people to lose interest in prayer." Here are suggestions about what to do if **the urge to go blind** strikes you:

- **Pray fervently** and outloud when the temptations to masturbate are the strongest.
- Yell "stop" to those thoughts and **recite a prechosen scripture.**
- Set goals of abstinence . . . a week, a month, a year.
- Think of having to **bathe in a tub of worms** and eat several of them as you are thinking about engaging in the act.
- During your toilet and shower activities, leave the bathroom door or shower curtains partially open to discourage total privacy.
- Reduce the amount of spices and condiments in your food.
- Wear pajamas that are difficult to open, yet loose and not binding.
- Have a physical object to use . . . a book of Mormon prayer, firmly held in hand, even in bed at night.
- In very severe cases . . . **tie a hand to the bed frame** . . . so semi-sleep masturbating can be broken. This can also be accomplished by wearing several layers of clothing that would be difficult to remove while half-asleep.
- The Mormons end this section by reminding people that "**Satan never gives up.**"

Next comes guidelines on how to avoid even the slightest possibility that one might do the dirty deed:

- **Never touch the intimate parts** of your body except during normal toilet procedure.
- Break off friendships with people who masturbate.
- Don't look in the mirror when you bathe.
- **Don't stay in the bathroom** for more than five to six minutes.
- Dress yourself so securely you can't touch vital parts and so "by the time you started to **remove protective clothing,** you would have sufficiently controlled your thinking that the temptation would leave you."
- Pray—but not about this problem because "that will tend to keep the subject in your mind."

WANT TO IMPROVE YOUR SPERM?

Watch dirty videos. A Japanese study found that men with fertility problems who masturbated to exciting sexual material increased their sperm count along with the number of healthy sperm.

 Bone Up on Buzzwords for Masturbation

For men:

Burp the worm	Jerk the gerkin
Jackin' the beanstalk	Pocket pinball
Tickle your pickle	Keep the census down
Pounding your pomegranate	Tenderize the meat
Hand to gland combat	Doodle your noodle
One-handed clapping	Paint the pickle
Pamela Anderson Polka	Staff meeting
Slamming the salami	Tussle your muscle

For women:

Hit the slit	Pet the poodle
Tickle the taco	Fondle your fig
Beating the beaver	Beating around the bush
Fanning the fur	Jocelyn Eldering
Muffin buffin	Nulling the void
Pampering the pussy	Petting the petunia
Tiptoeing through the two lips	

SOURCE: HTTP://RAMPAGES.ONRAMP.NET /~STOOGE /MASTURBATION.HTML

"If God had intended us not to masturbate
he would have made our arms shorter."
—George Carlin

HOMOSEXUALITY
Some Celebs Who Have Come Out

Those who don't want their orientation known have every right to keep it private, so unless some story has already received play, you aren't going to read it here. As Johnny Depp said, "The real malice isn't in pointing out that someone homosexual is homosexual, but pretending that such people don't—or even worse—shouldn't exist." The more you know, the more you'll accept.

A Few Bisexual Admissions

According to the *Book of Lists,* **Winston Churchill,** famed British Prime Minister, admitted to novelist W. Somerset Maugham that he had had sex with a man once to "see what it was like." When Maugham asked what it was like, Churchill said "musical."

Robert Downey Jr. said: "I think everybody is bisexual. When no girls were around, my (male) best friend in high school and I would make out with each other as a last resort."

George Michael, who admitted to a British paper that he hadn't had sex with a woman in ten years, said his first choice would be Tom Cruise— "but I wouldn't kick Nicole Kidman out of bed" (although he'd most likely just want her to watch).

Gore Vidal, on whether his first sexual experience was with a man or a woman said, "I was too polite to ask."

Unlikely Couples

Marlon Brando was the "roommate" of the nerdy **Wally Cox,** who played the popular "Mr. Peepers" on television. He has admitted to other relationships with males but, according to a juicy quote book, *In or Out,* said he didn't consider himself to be homosexual. He told Truman Capote that some men were attracted to him and by having sex with them, "I just thought I was doing them a favor."

Rock Hudson married a woman after the studio found out about his affair with movie star **George Nader.** The studio also sold Nader's contract to a European studio to get him out of the country.

You Knew This All Along

Many in Great Britain believe that **Prince Edward** is gay and that he married Sophie Rhys-Jones to squelch rumors about his homosexuality. It didn't help when they started living separately about four minutes after the ceremony—nor did the rumors from years ago that he had been kicked out of the Marines because he allegedly had an affair with another recruit.

...But Maybe You Didn't Know This

According to *Movieline*, the father of **Ann Heche** (Ellen DeGeneres's one-time lover) was a choir director and closet homosexual who died at forty-five of AIDS.

As wonderful and famous an actor as he was, **Sir John Gielgud**'s knighthood was delayed for years because he had been arrested and fined once after being caught soliciting a man for sex.

> When Frank Sinatra married the young, anorexic looking Mia Farrow, Ava Gardner said, "I always knew Frank would end up in bed with a boy."

Funny Quotes about Homosexuality

- Better oral sex than Oral Roberts.
- "I remember when outing meant a family picnic."—Rodney Dangerfield
- Actor Nathan Lane, when asked if he was gay, said: "Look, I'm forty, I'm single, and I work in musical theater. You do the math."
- "Conservatives believe that genes determine everything except homosexuality. Liberals believe that genes determine nothing except homosexuality."—Slate.com's Chatterbox's "Law of Biological Determinism"
- "If it hadn't been Errol Flynn, I wouldn't have even remembered it."—Truman Capote
- "Martina was so far in the closet, she was in danger of being a garment bag."—Rita Mae Brown, about tennis player Martina Navratilova
- "People should be very free with sex; they should draw the line at goats."—Elton John

SOURCES: USELESS-SEX.COM, *In or Out*

Are They or Aren't They? Homosexual Controversies

> "Ever since I admitted in an interview that I was bisexual, it seems that twice as many people wave at me in the streets."
> —Elton John

A former male model and porn star sued **John Travolta,** saying he had been his lover for two years, and a detailed lawsuit of their alleged relationship was widely quoted in the tabloids. Travolta, when asked if he was concerned about rumors of his sexual predilections, stated: "Some people might look at it as lessening my reputation, others as heightening my reputation."

Jodie Foster and a girlfriend who was with her when her son was born wear matching wedding bands.

Kevin Spacey raised eyebrows as well as questions when he skirted around the question of his orientation in an *Esquire* interview. After that, someone who sure looked like him was all over some young man, an event someone captured in photos that appeared in the *Globe.*

So what's the answer? A researcher claimed that gays were likely to have shorter index fingers than their ring finger, because finger length is influenced by male hormones in the womb. Rush & Molloy in the *Daily News* quoted Nathan Lane as saying, "Kevin Spacey has been spotted shopping for mittens."

Neal Travis, in the *New York Post,* said that the newest way of outing Hollywood stars was to pose questions about them in fictional articles. For example, James Ellroy, writing in *GQ* magazine, questioned (in passing) whether **Raymond Burr**—whose love for young boys there was no question about—thought Robert Taylor, Dave Garroway, Adlai Stevenson, Burt Lancaster, Leonard Bernstein, Montgomery Clift, and Randolph Scott were "**rump wranglers.**"

There were also questions about one of **Elizabeth Taylor's husbands** (actually, several of them), namely Richard Burton. One biographer claimed Burton tried to seduce Eddie Fisher—another one of Liz's husbands—at the same time he was stealing Liz from him.

The book also hinted strongly that Burton may have had an affair with famed actor **Laurence Olivier.** Richard Burton's brother vehemently denied all rumors, telling a British tabloid, "If Richard was a homosexual, then I'm a nun."

Gay Historical Controversies

Lord Baden-Powell, who founded the Boy Scouts, was obsessed with looking at photos of young boys without any clothes on, although he created no known merit badges in that area.

Homophobes like to quote **the Bible** as proof that homosexuality is a sin. But King James (of the King James Bible) was said to "navigate the windward passage," as they said in those days, and he was buried beside his male lover.

There's been at least one probable **homosexual vice president** in American history—and possibly a president as well. William Rufus de Vane King, Franklin Pierce's vice president in the 1850s, was nicknamed "Miss Nancy" and was rumored to have had sex with some of the male slaves on his plantation.

> "So now we hear that Lincoln may have been homosexual. All along we thought he loved Mary Todd but it was really Mary *and* Todd."
> —David Brenner

The Complete Book of Sexual Trivia claims that **Horatio Alger,** whose name is synonymous with success, may have had to resign as a minister in Massachusetts after he admitted that he had had homosexual relationships with two parishioners' sons.

Other historical figures raising questions and reappraisals:

- George Washington (probably bisexual)
- James Buchanan (may have been gay)
- Alexander the Great (bisexual—and he decked his horse out in a lavender saddle and rhinestones)
- Lawrence of Arabia (insisted his camels be color-coordinated)
- Abraham Lincoln (may have had at least one long-term gay affair. He shared a bed with a man before he married Mary Todd.
- Daniel Boone
- Naval war hero John Paul Jones
- General Robert E. Lee
- King Richard the Lionhearted
- Leonardo da Vinci (bisexual)

Homosexuality in Animals

The great animal activist Cleveland Amory revealed that a lot of nature documentaries showing animals mating are actually scenes of *same*-**sex animals going at it.** Same-sex mating is a common situation among many animals, and a zoo director in Holland takes gays and lesbians on tours of homosexual activities in his zoo to show them that **homosexuality is a natural phenemenon** occuring throughout the animal world.

He does this to help gays and their families see, "They are not strange at all, they just belong to a minority. . . . Homosexual animals are not regarded with suspicion by their own species. There is absolutely no rejection of homosexual" activities or the animals engaging in it.

According to *Anonova* news service, the most popular zoo exhibits are:
- Male monkeys who go nuts for each other
- Geese who take part in "gay marriages"
- A lesbian chimpanzee
- Homosexual "orgies" among flamingos

"Not That There's Anything Wrong with It"

There's nothing wrong with whatever two people choose to do consensually so long as they don't hurt others—or as Marilyn Monroe put it, "No sex is wrong if there's love in it." But you can't convince a lot of bigots that someone else's sexual orientation and activities are none of their business and that they don't have a right to try to stop or change it. Here are some interesting stories related to prejudice.

Around the World

Wonder whatever happened to **the Greek Island of Lesbos?** People who live there were uncomfortable with the association (and jokes). They now call themselves by the name of their largest town, which is Mytilene (pronounced Mitilini).

> Even today, in such countries as Iran, Afghanistan, Saudi Arabia, Libya, and Sudan, homosexuality is punishable by death, and methods of execution are horrific. For example, in Afghanistan, homosexuals have been buried alive under the rubble of a stone wall felled on top of them by a battle tank. If they survive, they are spared.

Can't Hurt To Look

Reuters described **oil wrestling** as "a sport in which burly men covered in olive oil and wearing **leather trousers** wrestle [and] put a hand down the opponent's trousers to get a better grip."

When gay groups came to watch an oil-wrestling group in Turkey, *Curious Times* reported that the group objected, saying having gays watch them was "immoral."

A law passed in 1935 under Hitler against male homosexuals was so sweeping that it not only **outlawed homosexual acts,** but even homosexual *fantasies.* Incidentally, Hitler condemned homosexuality between men but lesbians were rarely sent to concentration camps.

In America

A Florida man **beat his wife's neutered, male poodle**–Yorkshire terrier to death because the dog repeatedly humped his Jack Russell terrier, and **he thought her dog was gay.** (Dogs mount each other as a sign of dominance, not just sexuality.)

When you call someone a fag, you're really calling them **a cigarette.** At the turn of the century, because it was believed that smoking was effeminate, the term was used to describe gays.

On a tombstone in a congressional cemetery is found the following inscription: "When I was in the military they gave me a medal for killing two men, and a discharge for loving one."

GENDER BENDERS
Famous Cross-Dressers

Billy Bob Thornton was quoted in IMDB.com as saying that he keeps his wife **Angelina Jolie** close to him by **wearing her underwear.** He was apparently serious about this because he confessed that he wore her underwear at the gym one day and someone there noticed. He stood up for the rights of cross-dressers everywhere by telling the shocked man, "I don't think it's strange at all."

Kelsey Grammer, whose name often comes up when discussing kinky activities, was said, by his former girlfriend, to enjoy wearing women's clothes around the house.

Old-time movie stars **Esther Williams and Jeff Chandler** were to marry until she walked in on him wearing her red wig, chiffon dress, and high heels.

J. Edgar Hoover, former head of the FBI, was spotted at one party in makeup (and false eyelashes) and was wearing a fluffy black dress, lace stockings, high heels, and a black curly wig. He was calling himself "Mary."

And the Marv Alpert Award goes to ...

Pamela Anderson Lee says she likes it when her boyfriend wears her underwear, bikinis, and dresses; she says it's sexy and proof that "he has a sense of humor." But she was quoted in *Movie Stars Do the Dumbest Things* as saying that she didn't want Tommy Lee wearing such garments outside to gamble in Las Vegas, because **"they were a little too short for him if you know what I mean."**

Faux Females

The second man in space wore women's underwear. According to *Moon*, a book about the space program, "Gus" Grissom had to wear a **woman's panty girdle** to hold in his urine.

Winona Ryder claimed that she was supposedly mistaken for a boy when she first entered junior high school and was beaten up by male students who thought she was one of them. (Now, instead of hitting her, men hit *on* her.)

Mickey Rourke once worked as a bouncer in a cross-dresser's club and said he was constantly being "hit on by transvestites."

Babe Ruth wore women's silk stockings underneath his uniform (they were up to his knees) in the belief that it would bring him good luck. (They seemed to have worked.)

"I was shocked that I wasn't more attractive," **Dustin Hoffman** said about his female role in *Tootsie.* (Actually, he shouldn't have been so shocked, since he's not that hot looking as a guy either.)

Odd News Stories

Who ever thought this one up? At the University of Vermont they have a freshman tradition called an "elephant walk." The incoming freshmen wear women's underwear and march in single file, **holding each other's genitals.**

Studs who were duds: A study of four hundred Americans and Australians who experimented in online interactive features found that almost half of them at one time made believe they were the opposite sex when they were online.

A woman in Greece had a nervous breakdown the night before her wedding when she found her future husband making love to the best man. That would never have made the news—except he was **wearing her wedding dress.**

And here's a truly horrible story. According to the *AP,* nine Saudi men were sentenced to five years in jail and repeated floggings for dressing in women's clothes and engaging in "deviant sexual behavior." These men will have to undergo the torture of having their floggings inflicted fifty-two times in fifty separate sessions, with fifteen days between each session to recover and worry about the next bout of torture.

A Famous Woman Who Was a "Man," and Vice Versa

King Edward VIII, who gave up his throne for the woman he loved, may have really given it up for a man. His love, divorced American Wallis Simpson, has been said to have suffered from Androgen Insensitivity Syndrome, a theory supported by her angular masculine looks.

Napoleon may have suffered from a glandular disease called the Zollinger-Ellison Syndrome, according to the *Reader's Digest Book of Facts.* After his death, it was noticed that he had **a feminine plumpness,** rounded breasts, white soft skin, and no hair. Not to mention only one testicle and **a penis that was only one inch long** when auctioned hundreds of years later. (No wonder he couldn't successfully penetrate Russia!)

"I don't remember any more beautiful guy that was a girl than me."
—Tony Curtis,
about *Some Like It Hot*

Noel Coward once said of Lawrence of Arabia, "If he'd been any prettier, he would have been Florence of Arabia."

Sex Changes

Remember the scandal a few years ago when **Eddie Murphy** picked up a **transexual hooker** in West Hollywood? (It was the same red-light district where Hugh Grant was caught with Miss Divine Brown.) As to what happened to the prostitute later, in a bizarre accident, she locked herself out of her high-rise apartment dressed only in a bra, pants, and a towel. Trying to swing on the towel from her deck to an open window next door, she missed, and fell five floors to her death.

New York State spends close to $1 million a year on estrogen for its almost one hundred male prison inmates who are waiting to become female. According to law, the prisoners must receive **free hormone treatments.** It is suspected that a few of these men may be deliberately committing crimes in order to get themselves incarcerated so they can afford their expensive hormone treatment.

Male and female fetuses are anatomically identical until the eighth week of gestation. By the third month, all internal and external sex organs are fully formed and differentiated. (By six months, while in the womb, the male child can have an erection.)

Torrin Polk, a University of Houston receiver said of his coach, "He treats us like men. He lets us wear earrings."

"A beauty queen in Thailand had to give up her crown because she turned out to be a man. Judges became suspicious when her talent was peeing standing up."
—Conan O'Brien

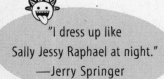

"I dress up like Sally Jessy Raphael at night."
—Jerry Springer

FUNNY SEX

 ## Things Men Shouldn't Say Out Loud
in Victoria's Secret

- "No thanks, just sniffing."
- "No need to wrap it. I'll eat it right here."
- "Does this come in children's sizes?"
- "I'll be in the dressing room going blind."
- "Mom will love this."
- "The size doesn't matter. She's inflatable."

Slogans Rejected by Motel 6

- We put the "ho" in hotel.
- As seen on *Cops*.
- We left off the "9" but you know it's there.
- Now with 40 pecent fewer cockroaches.
- Thirty-two days without an Ebola incident.
- Our staff is guaranteed to steal only small items.

Politically Correct Sex

- A bisexual person is "sexually non-preferential."

- A hooker is a "sexual care provider."

- Her breasts don't sag; they have "lost their vertical hold."

- She doesn't have big hooters; her "cups runneth over."

- She does not have a great butt; she is "gluteus to the maximus."

- She does not have great cleavage; her breasts are "centrally located."

- You don't ask her to dance; you request a "pre-coital experience" with her.

SEE POLITCALLY CORRECT "PETS," 128.

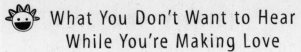

What You Don't Want to Hear While You're Making Love

- "Honey, I'm home."
- "Forget the archbishop."
- "I wanna refund."
- "I'm telling mommy."
- "The wrong hole?"
- "Where's the remote?"
- "You're still here?"
- "It's not infectious."
- "I'm a guy."
- "I'm almost twelve."
- "You in yet?"
- "Let's get married."
- "I hope you don't mind if I scream my own name."
- "It doesn't fit."
- "I'm Lorena Bobbitt."

Roseanne said of Don King: "His head looks like my crotch."

How to Be Coy

A Man's Life, a compendium of interesting items, reveals how a woman says common sexual terms.

ENGLISH	GIRL-TALK
Cock	It
Balls	Those
Tits	These
Cunt	There
Fuck	Dinner and a movie

Thoughts about Sex

- I wouldn't be caught dead with a necrophiliac.
- You'll never hear a woman say: "My, what an attractive scrotum."
- Why is bra singular and panties plural?
- If you don't believe in oral sex, keep your mouth shut.
- If sex is a pain in the ass, then you're doing it wrong.
- A woman never forgets the men she could have had; a man the women he couldn't.
- Sex is like air. It's not important unless you aren't getting any.

Sexual Slang

Breasts:
- Hand warmers
- Love bubbles
- Tamale toothers
- Twin peaks

Male genitals:
- Ladies lollipop
- Bush beater
- Hairy hot dog
- Lung disturber (in your dreams)
- One-eyed night crawler in a turtleneck sweater
- Pink pencil

Condom:
- Shower cap
- One-piece overcoat

Intercourse:
- Buzz the Brillo
- Horizontal hula
- Put four quarters in the spit

Murphy's Laws on Sex

- Sex is like snow. You never know how many inches you are going to get or how long it is going to last.
- Virginity can be cured.
- Sex is dirty only if it's done right.
- Thou shall not commit adultery . . . unless in the mood.

"Sex is hereditary. If your parents never had it, chances are you won't either."

10 Things Women Shouldn't Say After (or During) Sex

- "Please understand I'm only doing this for a raise."
- "They're not cracker crumbs; it's just a rash."
- "Have you ever seen *Fatal Attraction*?"
- "How long do you plan on being almost there?"
- "I bet you didn't know I work for the *National Enquirer*."
- "I think biting is romantic, don't you?"
- "I'll tell you who I'm fantasizing about if you tell me who you're thinking of."
- "Oprah had a show about men like you."
- "I've been getting these little blisters lately."
- "When would you like to meet my parents?"

10 Things Men Shouldn't Say After (or During) Sex

℮ "I was so horny tonight I would have taken a duck home."

℮ "You wanna do those dishes before you leave?"

℮ "What tampon?"

℮ "You're great in bed but your sister gives better blow jobs."

℮ "Next time I come over, don't bother with the underwear, OK?"

℮ "My first wife was prettier but you can screw a lot better."

℮ "Okay guys, it's a wrap. Cut and print it."

℮ "I'm not into relationships. Can't we just screw like every Tuesday night or something?"

℮ "What are you planning to make for breakfast?"

℮ "I really hate women who think sex means something."

> "We are powerless in cases of oral-genital intimacy unless it obstructs interstate commerce."
> —J. Edgar Hoover, about oral sex

The Dirty Mind Quiz

1. Men and women go down on me. All day long it's in and out. I discharge loads from my shaft. What am I?

2. This useful tool, about six inches long, is enjoyed by both sexes, and is usually found hung, dangling loosely, ready for instant action.

3. What's a four-letter word that ends in *k* and means the same as intercourse?

4. What is it that a cow has four of and a woman has only two of?

5. What can you find in a man's pants that is about six inches long, has a head on it, and women love so much they want to blow it?

6. What word starts with an *f* and ends with *uck*?

7. What four-letter word ends with *unt* and is always and only applied to a woman?

8. What does a dog do that you can step into?

9. I go in hard. I come out soft. You blow me hard. What am I?

Answers: (1) elevator (2) toothbrush (3) talk (4) legs (5) $20 bill (6) firetruck (7) aunt (8) pant (9) bubble gum

Sex Calorie Counter

Removing clothes:
    With partner's consent 10
    Without partner's consent 150

Getting into bed:
    Lifting partner 10
    Dragging partner along floor 150

Positions:
    Man on top, woman in kitchen (Italian position) 10
    Woman on top, man getting permission (Russian position) 15
    Both on top (American) 60

Achieving erection:
    Losing it 14
    Searching for it 114

Putting on condom:
    With erection 10
    Without erection 100

Pulling out:
    After orgasm 10
    A few minutes before orgasm 1,000

> What smells turn women on? According to the Smell and Taste Treatment Center, the smell of men's cologne actually turns women off slightly. The smell that most arouses women is a mixture of Good & Plenty candy and cucumber.

> "I've tried several varieties of sex. The conventional position makes me claustrophobic. And the others either give me a stiff neck or lockjaw."
> —Tallulah Bankhead

A Few Serious Facts about "Sexual Dieting"

- **Sex for one hour burns off a dozen Hershey's kisses.**
- Kissing someone uses up about nine calories, so if you average three kisses a day, you can burn almost 10,000 calories a year.
- Sex uses as much energy as climbing two flights of stairs.
- **There are five calories in a teaspoon of semen.**

> "It's a disgusting habit to put someone's thing where you put food . . . unless they put a piece of pie on it."
> —Roseanne, about oral sex

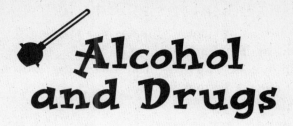

Alcohol and Drugs

LUSHIOUS FACTS ABOUT ALCOHOL

Alcohol really does **make sex better for women.** First, it raises their testosterone levels, which increases sexual excitement. If you're a male, you may want to set your watch: This libido increase occurs one or two hours after consumption—especially in women on the pill.

Alcohol also increases women's estrogen levels, and higher estrogen **"enhances the sensate qualities of the vagina."** In other words, alcohol makes women's senses feel better, according to *Fascinating Health Secrets* by Dr. Kevin Pezzi.

When rats were given alcohol in a Quebec study, male rats attempted sex with female rats who had just rejected them. Sound familiar?

> Drinking carbonated beverages can give you gas, as can drinking through a straw or chewing gum, because you take in air.

The term *cocktails* came about after a barmaid decorated her tavern with the tail feathers of cocks, and someone asked for a cocktail. She served him a drink with feathers in it.

Drinking to forget? Well, forget it. Alcohol not only doesn't help you forget, but it can help you *remember* something. Alcohol has been shown to help you recall events that happened just before you started drinking.

Alcohol affects you differently depending on what time of the day you drink it. For example, wine with lunch can put you to sleep, but the same glass can make you feel better at dinner.

Whenever you drink, you make some of the cells in your brain inactive, thereby putting them out of commission. If that didn't happen, you wouldn't drink.

Other Facts to Drink To

- If you place a tiny amount of liquor on a scorpion, it will go crazy and **sting itself to death.**
- A raisin dropped in a glass of fresh champagne bounces up and down from the bottom to the top of the glass.
- Whether or not you drink, your body produces slightly under an ounce of alcohol each day.
- **Driving while talking on the phone** is as dangerous as drunk driving.
- Coffee not only won't sober you up, but it may make you *more* drunk.

> The good news: A substance (resveratrol) in red wine seems to stop even drug-resistant strains of herpes.
>
> The bad news: You have to rub it on, not drink it.

Funny Quotes about Alcohol

- "When I read about the evils of drinking, I gave up reading." —Henny Youngman
- "I swore off drinking . . . and in fourteen days I lost two weeks." —Joe E. Lewis
- Lady Astor: "Sir, you are a drunk." Winston Churchill: "Yes, Madame, I am. But in the morning I will be sober and you will still be ugly."
- Greta Garbo, when asked if she wanted scotch or water, said "Scotch. Water makes you rust."
- "I feel sorry for people who don't drink. When they wake up in the morning, that's as good as they're going to feel all day."—Frank Sinatra
- "A woman drove me to drink and I didn't even thank her." —W. C. Fields
- "I only drink to steady my nerves. Sometimes I'm so steady I don't move for months."—W. C. Fields
- "Always remember that I have taken more out of alcohol than alcohol has taken out of me."—Winston Churchill
- "Work is the curse of the drinking classes."—Oscar Wilde
- "I drink to make other people interesting."—George Jean Nathan

Other Alcoholic Musings

- A heavy drinker is someone who drinks twice what you do.
- I'm not an alcoholic. I'm a drunk. Alcoholics go to meetings.
- A bartender is a pharmacist with a limited inventory.
- I have a problem with drinking: two hands and only one mouth.
- Here's champagne to your real friends . . . and real pain to your sham friends.
- Drunk is feeling sophisticated when you can't say it.
- I never drink anything stronger than gin before breakfast.

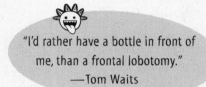

"I'd rather have a bottle in front of
me, than a frontal lobotomy."
—Tom Waits

How to Get Drunk Without Drinking
(and Beat a Breathalyzer)

Women who don't want the smell of alcohol on their breath have dunked unused **tampons** into alcohol and inserted them vaginally. The alcohol traveled through their bodies and they became intoxicated.

If you cut a deep hole in a **watermelon,** put vodka in it, and then eat the watermelon, you can get drunk.

Kava tea, a light stimulant, is also a natural treatment for anxiety and insomnia. But it may be almost too relaxing, if people drive after drinking too much. After drinking twenty-three cups of kava tea, one dummy was picked up for driving on a highway shoulder. (Maybe he was just looking for a place to pee.)

Mistletoe in tea can make people feel inebriated.

Nutmeg in larger quantities (a few tablespoons) can make people drunk—but also nauseous. **SEE "HE'LL PEE FOR YOU," PAGE 110.**

Absinthe Made His Head Grow Nuttier

Ear ye! Ear ye! Remember that crazy painter Vincent van Gogh who cut off his ear? One theory is that it was toxic liquor that left him "a few bristles short of a brush." A book on the yellow-obsessed painter titled *Vincent van Gogh: Chemicals, Crises and Creativity* says that van Gogh may have been whacked out on absinthe. Once favored by the Parisian Eurotrash, this green drink contains a potent neurotoxin and is very dangerous—so bad that "the green fairy" can't even be purchased in the United States.

DRUNK DRIVING
Don't Drink to These Facts

In thirty-four states, the legal blood alcohol level is .10—and that's five times more than Sweden at .02, and twice as lax as France, where 0.5 means you're too drunk to drive. Our punishments—if someone is punished at all—are also much more lenient than in many other countries. According to *How Much is Too Much?*, an interesting book published several years ago:

- In El Salvador, **drunk drivers can be shot.** (Fortunately, they have few automobiles.)
- In South Africa, the penalty is twenty years in jail and a $3,800 fine.
- In Australia, the drunk driver's name is listed in the local newspaper in a column titled **"He's Drunk and in Jail."**

In Turkey, a drunk driver may be taken twenty miles from home and forced to walk back.

Watch Out for Flashlights If You've Been Drinking

If a policeman stops you while driving and he comes over to you with a flashlight, he may be preparing to give you a sobriety test. The newest **alcohol detection device** is hidden in a flashlight, and it takes only four seconds to work.

The light in the flash samples the air around you, and if you're drunk, the bar on it turns red. If you're sober, green. It works even if the drinker is chewing gum or has incense in the car.

According to the *Washington Post*, the "Sniffer" catches 20 to 30 percent more drunk drivers than standard methods. It's also easier for the police, because they don't have to stick their heads in a car to see if there's a scent of alcohol. They also don't have to smell air or breath, nor do they waste a lot of time watching people fall on their asses as they try to walk a straight line.

Drunk Walking Can Be as Dangerous as Drunk Driving

A bartender who suggests that a person who is too drunk to drive home should walk home instead may be putting himself in danger. Several studies have found that as many people are **fatally injured** *walking* **while drunk** as driving while drunk—about 50 percent.

It may be an even bigger problem than that. Besides the injury to the drunk walker, there may also be accidents to *other* drivers as well as pedestrians, because many accidents are caused when a driver swerves to avoid hitting a pedestrian—who may be drunk.

The reason it's dangerous to walk while drunk is the same reason it's dangerous to drive that way: Alcohol affects eyesight, judgment, physical reaction, psychomotor skills, and the ability to negotiate or take evasive action if there's a horn honk or whatever.

Despite the danger, though, very few places have any laws against walking while intoxicated, which would be almost impossible to enforce anyway.

How to Cut Down Drinking

- **Measure your drinks.** Remember that all drinks aren't created equal. Use shot glasses when making mixed drinks, and four-ounce wine glasses for wine.
- **Drink wine or beer** as opposed to hard liquor. Beer, especially, will get you fuller quicker, so ultimately you'll drink less.
- Drink slowly to stretch drinks out over a longer period of time.
- Don't "binge" drink. People who have all their drinks on the weekend have much higher mortality rates.
- **Eat while you're drinking,** but stay away from salty snacks because they'll just make you want more to drink. (Why do you think bars serve free peanuts and pretzels?)
- Women should not try to match their drinks to men. Women's bodies metabolize alcohol less efficiently; along with a woman's smaller size, this makes drinks hit them harder.

SOURCE: *How Much is Too Much?*

Watch Out for Soda Pop Too

- Think soda pop doesn't qualify as alcohol? You're right, but some prohibitionists wanted to ban soft drinks, along with alcohol, believing that carbonated water was **a mild intoxicant.**
- Because it was illegal to sell carbonated drinks on Sunday, store owners developed "sundaes"—those delicious ice cream, fruit, and chocolate goodies, which contain no fizz.
- Most of the caffeine in soft drinks comes from the leftovers of processing decaffeinated coffees.
- Almost one million Americans drink **carbonated sodas for breakfast.**

SOURCE: *The Whole Pop Catalog*

BEER
Mostly Good News

- Beer may help reduce your risk of getting kidney stones by 40 percent, researchers in Finland learned.
- A study at the University of Wisconsin Medical School found that an occasional beer may help **prevent heart attacks and strokes,** especially dark beer, which contains flavonoids that may unclog arteries.
- Three tests confirm that beer—especially the darker brews—contains **antioxidants** that shield cells from the effects of free radicals. These may play a role in preventing aging and age-related diseases.

Why Beer Is Better Than Milk

PETA, those fun folks who like to throw ink at $20,000 mink coats and scream at people who squash mosquitoes, in another highly controversial campaign, took ads out for college students, urging them to drink beer instead of milk. Of course they didn't mention that it's a lot safer to drive on milk than beer. Instead, they pointed out these alleged health benefits of milk over beer:

- Beer has no cholesterol, unlike milk.
- Beer has no hormones or antibiotics, and milk contains them.
- Beer has a small amount of fiber in it, while milk has none.
- Beer has complex carbohydrates, and milk doesn't

Why Beer Is Better Than Jesus

- Beer has never caused a major war.
- No one will kill you for not drinking beer.
- You don't have to wait more than 2,000 years for a second beer.
- Nobody's ever been burned at the stake, hanged, or tortured over a brand of beer.
- When you have a beer, you don't knock on people's doors trying to give them away.

But, in Jesus's favor . . .
- He doesn't go flat after an hour.
- Nobody ever woke up naked with a goat after a night with Him.
- He doesn't make you run to the bathroom every twenty minutes.

Beer Isn't Just for Breakfast Anymore

How fast and how much do people drink? It's said that you can tell someone's nationality by how many wet rings are on the glass when he's finishing a pint.

- An American leaves seventeen to twenty rings.
- An Irishman leaves five to six rings.
- An Australian leaves only one ring, drinking it in a single gulp.

Men with mustaches lose a total of 162,000 pints of beer in the hair, costing them more than half a million dollars each year. People with full beards lose even more, according to a study by Guinness Beer, which would like you to lose as much beer as possible so you'll have to buy more.

If the person next to you pours a little salt in his beer, he's doing this to try to enhance its flavor, get the carbonation going again, and restore the foamy head.

Even weirder, if the man next to you rubs his finger in the crease between his nose and cheek, and then drags his finger through the foam in his beer, he's trying to dissolve the foam, which **the oil from his face** may do.

A recent study showed that raising the tax on a six-pack of beer by twenty cents **reduced the rate of gonorrhea** by up to 9 percent, because alcohol is linked to risky sexual behavior in young people.

"Beer is proof that God loves us and wants us to be happy."
—Benjamin Franklin

More Facts for What Ales You

- The average American drinks **235 bottles of beer a year.**
- Although most people think that Germans are big beer drinkers, Americans drink twice as much as they do.
- In Natchez, Mississippi, there's a law that **elephants can't drink beer.**
- If you can't get the real thing, there's a company that makes beer-flavored ice cream.
- If you want to tenderize a piece of beef (and make it taste better), marinate it in beer an hour before cooking.

How to Avoid Hangovers

It's been said that you've got a drinking problem if every woman you see when you're drinking has an exact twin. And if you've got a drinking problem, you probably have a hangover problem. Here are a couple of ways to lessen it:

Light-colored beer is more likely to cause a hangover than dark-colored beer, according to a study at the University of Connecticut Alcohol Research Center. That's because light-colored beer contains more carbonation, which increases the speed at which the alcohol goes through your system.

Do you get a headache from red wine? One study showed that, in most cases, two aspirin tablets taken thirty minutes before drinking prevented headaches.

The good news: A study found that the hops that flavor beer contain ingredients that help you fight disease.

The bad news: You'd have to quaff 450 one-liter glasses of beer each day to receive the benefits. (Who are these lucky people sitting around and getting paid to drink beer for studies?)

There's a British beer called Old Fart.

"Without question, the greatest invention in the history of mankind is beer. Oh, I grant you that the wheel was also a fine invention, but the wheel does not go nearly as well with pizza."
—Dave Barry

SMOKING
Sure, Go Ahead and Keep Smoking

A study indicated that almost half of smokers are **mentally ill.** So if you smoke and you're not nuts, then watch out for the person smoking next to you because he may be.

"I started smoking to lose weight. After I dropped that lung, I felt pretty good."
—Michael Meehan

Believe or not, you may upset more people if you smoke than if you fornicate. A young couple on a British train had intercourse in front of the other passengers. As incredible as that was, it was only *after*, when each lit up a cigarette, that the people in the no-smoking car complained—about the smoking—and called the conductor.

Tobacco is the only product that kills one-third of the people who use it. Cigarettes kill more people each year than AIDS, alcohol, auto accidents, homicide, illegal drugs, fires, and suicides combined, according to Smokefree Education Services.

Secondary smoke causes more deaths than suicide, AIDS, homicides, or fires.

Even an unlit cigarette can harm people with weakened immune systems because it **contains a mold** that can endanger lives. (So can smoking marijuana, but for that matter, plants, flowers, and pepper may also contain this mold.)

And a bit of good news for those slinking off to have a cigarette anyway: One study showed that nicotine **stimulates you to remember better,** boosting the strength of signals between brain cells.

A New Way to Quit Smoking

As everyone knows, smoking is the way to an early grave. This might not be so bad, for soon it will be the only place you can smoke in peace without being hassled by fanatical anti-smoking zealots. But here's something to smile about. **Nitrous oxide, or laughing gas,** might help you quit smoking. When seven smokers were given nitrous oxide, five quit—for at least three days. Better still, four still weren't smoking a month later (although they may have still been laughing).

Holy Smoke! A Few Famous Smokers

- The most famous contemporary cigar smoker in the world, **Fidel Castro**, hasn't smoked in over ten years.
- According to Michael Caine's *Almanac of Amazing Facts,* **Sir Winston Churchill** rationed himself to fifteen cigars a day.
- **Russell Crowe,** who played the anti-cigarette activist in the *Insider,* is a smoker—and started at the age of ten.
- A famous movie blooper is related to pipe smoking. In *Swing Time,* **Fred Astaire** takes a few puffs on his pipe and then puts the pipe in his jacket pocket—while it's still lit!

Smoking in History

Put this in your pipe and puff on it. When the Indians smoked tobacco, not only was their tobacco a stronger strain than what we inhale today, but they smoked **through their noses,** sticking the pipes up their nostrils. This gave them an immediate and stronger hit than the Western way of lighting up.

Oscar Wilde: "Do you mind if I smoke."
Sarah Bernhardt: "I don't care if you burn."

Historically, execution has been one (failed) method of trying to stop people from smoking. (Although, at least it did get the executed person to quit.)

Benjamin Franklin paid for the Continental Congress by getting a loan on tobacco futures. The money also helped finance the American Revolution.

The North may have **won the Civil War** because of three cigars. Two union soldiers found the cigars with some papers wrapped around them. They were Robert E. Lee's battle plans.

"In the second grade, a teacher came in and gave us all a lecture about not smoking, and then they sent us over to art and crafts to make ashtrays for Mother's Day."
—Paul Clay

DRUGS
Pot Luck (Or, Where You Shouldn't Smoke Marijuana)

Alternet.org conducted a study of marijuana arrests in the United States and found that:

- ℮ Every 45 seconds someone in America is arrested for marijuana.
- ℮ About 85 percent of these arrests are for possession only, not for selling.
- ℮ Almost half of all marijuana arrests in the United States—almost 700,000 each year—occur in only ten counties.
- ℮ Counties in Alaska and Texas have the highest arrest rate for marijuana; Pennsylvania, North Dakota, and Hawaii have the lowest.

Within those counties, the places where most marijuana arrests occurred were:

- ℮ International airports
- ℮ Ski resorts
- ℮ State and national parks and wilderness areas
- ℮ Amusement and theme parks
- ℮ Sports complexes
- ℮ Music venues
- ℮ Border regions with Mexico and Canada

When asked to take a drug test, former NBA player Kurt Rambis said, "I'm in favor of it, as long as it's multiple choice."

Drugs Have Always Been with Us

People have been smoking marijuana for at least 1,500 years. Not only for pleasure, but it may also have been used as **a painkiller for women in labor.**

Even the stronger stuff was used by the powerful. According to *Maxim* magazine, there are "Rumors that James Madison took opium, George Washington smoked opium to numb the pain of his miserable dentures, **Benjamin Franklin** got hooked on laudanum because of kidney stones, and **George Washington** and **Thomas Jefferson** grew hemp, marijuana's leafy green cousin."

George H. W. Bush was born with a silver spoon in his mouth—and George W. Bush was born with a silver spoon in his nose.

Hemp is just marijuana grown differently, but there's some reason to think **George Washington** may have been growing the more interesting stuff. In his logs, he wrote that he "began to separate the Male from the Female hemp." That's generally done if you're growing it for its intoxicating properties, not for rope.

He'll Pee for You

An entrepreneur who doesn't smoke, drink, or use drugs sells his urine, which he calls "liquid gold," to people who have to take a drug test. For less than $10, he sells a kit that contains a tube to attach to one's body to activate a heating packet so that the urine will be warm—as if it came right out of the person naturally. Because this tube runs down to the person's genitals, even if someone is monitoring the test, it looks like they're really urinating—so long as they don't have to take off their pants. SEE "THE PENIS," PAGE 76.

The paper on which the **Declaration of Independence** was written was made of hemp. And the first American flags were made of hemp cloth too.

At the turn of the twentieth century, Bayer advertised heroin as being effective against coughs.

According to *Playboy's* "After Hours," a popular way to quiet crying babies long ago was to give them "Mrs. Winslow's Soothing Syrup" for babies—which contained **morphine**.

Drug Dealers Makes Less Than the Minimum Wage

Forget the image of street drug dealers raking in the dough. The big pushers make it, true, but one-third of them are in prison at any one time so the price they pay for the price they receive is pretty high.

But according to a study by a professor of economics at the University of Chicago, those on the lowest rung, the street drug pushers, the ones who risk arrest on the street to get people to buy their drugs, averaged only about three dollars an hour.

Unemployment pays better, the hours are much better, and those collecting it are far less likely to get arrested.

"Drugs are a very serious problem.
I knew a fellow whose habit got so
bad, I stopped selling to him."
—Flip Wilson

Sports

SPORTS TRIVIA
That's Not So Fine!

When he accidentally spit on an eight-year-old girl, **Charles Barkley** was fined $10,000 by the NBA. But John McEnroe, who deliberately swore when he lost in the French Open's first round, only received a $7,500 fine.

When he had to pay a fine for throwing a tantrum after being called out on strikes, **Andre Dawson** made the check out with the memo saying, "Donation for the Blind."

"Luge strategy? Lie flat and try not to die."
—Tim Steeves

Writer **John Viscardi** wrote that the IRS wanted to tax the baseball fan $500,000 who caught Mark McGwire's record-breaking ball even though he returned it. But because the fan held (and therefore legally "owned") an object supposedly worth $1 million, even just for an inning, the government wanted half of that million.

In **Japan,** if someone gets a hole in one, in a sense they're fined—by their friends for whom they have to buy expensive gifts. Plus, a hole in one means they have to give a huge tip to the caddy *and* host a reception *and* invite hundreds of guests *and* plant a commemorative tree at the country club. Perhaps insurance companies there should offer hole-in-one insurance to ensure that the lucky golfer doesn't go broke because of his good fortune.

"Last week when Dennis Rodman said unpleasant things about the Mormons, the NBA slapped him with a $50,000 fine. But think about it. What's $50,000 to him? He's usually got that kind of cash stuffed in his bra."
—Jay Leno

When **Roger Clemens** threw a splintered bat toward Mike Piazza, he was fined $50,000—which was than one-third of 1 percent of his $15 million salary.

A twenty-seven-year-old millionaire was fined $71,400 for going fifteen miles over the speed limit in Finland, where traffic fines are based on how much money one makes. (The millionaire had been fined close to $50,000 before this for "zigzagging dangerously.")

Hip Hip Hooray! Cheerleading Today

According to *Time* magazine, fourteen states now call cheerleading a sport. Here are some other facts about it:

- Almost 200 colleges offer cheerleading scholarships.
- **Cheerleading injuries are five times higher** than those of football injuries among high school kids, partly because of the elaborate stunts they perform.
- Cheerleading injuries also tend to be more severe than in other sports.
- According to an orthopedic specialist, the average cheerleader loses twenty-eight to thirty-five days per injury, more than any other sport.

Famous People Who Were Cheerleaders

According to *Celebrities: Jokes, Quotes, and Anecdotes 2001 Calendar*, the following were all cheerleaders at one time:

Kathie Lee Gifford	Susan Lucci
Madonna	Alicia Silverstone
Meryl Streep	Steve Martin
Kim Basinger	Sandra Bullock
Katie Couric	Cameron Diaz
Sally Field	Calista Flockhart
George W. Bush	Ronald Reagan
Dwight David Eisenhower	

U.S. Presidents Who Were Good Wrestlers

George Washington	Ulysses S. Grant
Andrew Jackson	Chester A. Arthur
Zachary Taylor	Calvin Coolidge
William Howard Taft	Theodore Roosevelt
Abraham Lincoln (Wrestling Champion at 21)	

Karate Kids

Karate has a reputation not only for bad movies but also for extreme danger, yet a report on children who studied karate did not bear this out. In fact, the report concluded that karate may actually be a much safer sport than people assume. Here's how it breaks down.

"Karate is a form of martial arts in which people who have had years and years of training can, using only their hands and feet, make some of the worst movies in the history of the world."
—Dave Barry

- The injury risk in children and adolescents for karate was about 5 percent.
- For soccer, the injury rate was almost 8 percent
- For baseball, it ranged from 2 to 8 percent.
- For hockey, it was an astounding 33 percent injury rate.

Other Interesting Sports Trivia

Tiger Woods receives ten cents for every box of Wheaties that is sold (for a little less than $3 a pop) with his picture on the box. *The Oregonian* wrote that the farmer who grows the wheat in it gets only a nickel from the same box.

The New York Giants once offered Cuban leader **Fidel Castro** a chance to pitch for them, after being impressed by his sports skills while he was on tour in 1948. Castro would have received a standard contract with a $5,000 signing bonus (had he not chosen instead to stay in Cuba and become a dictator) according to *Nash & Zullo's Believe It or Else: Baseball Edition*. A former president of the Giants said that "There's no question he would have made it to the major leagues."

In 1951, the Cleveland Indians had a midget playing on the team who was 3'7" tall.

A Dutch study found that almost three-quarters of long-distance runners (and cyclists) had intestinal problems, including flatulence and an occasional urgent need to move their bowels. Bicyclists' problems may stem from their putting pressure on the esophagus, which traps gas.

According to the *Guinness Book of Sports Records,* **the longest boxing match in history** went 110 rounds and lasted seven hours and nineteen minutes—before it was declared a draw.

According to a poll by the Field of Dreams, a memorabilia store in Minneapolis, **Ken Griffey Jr., Dan Marino,** and **Muhammad Ali** are the best athletes of whom to collect memorabilia.

According to a five-city survey, three out of four American men would rather go to the Super Bowl than spend a romantic evening in a cozy hotel with a sexy woman.

Sports Factoids

- A billiard player walks an average of three miles per game.
- The reason it's called a boxing ring is that boxing once took place in a round area.
- Babe Ruth held the record for home runs—as well as the record for striking out.
- The only two days of the year in which there are no professional sports games (MSP, NBA, NHL, or NFL) are the day before and after the Major League All-Star Game.
- A baseball has 108 stitches.
- The longest baseball game ever played was in 1981, between the Rochester Red Wings and the Pawtucket Red Sox. They tied 2–2 after thirty-two innings.

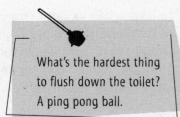

What's the hardest thing to flush down the toilet? A ping pong ball.

- It takes 3,000 cows to supply the NFL with enough leather for a year's supply of footballs.
- Golf was invented in Scotland and was a Gentlemen Only, Ladies Forbidden game—ergo GOLF.
- There are 336 dimples on a regulation golf ball, which enables a golf ball to travel faster and further than a smooth ball of the same size.
- More people are struck by lightening on golf courses than anyplace else.

Stories about Celebrities and Sports

According to *New York Post* reporter Neal Travis, former star of the Chicago Bulls **Michael Jordan** will never be able to play a good game of golf because he can't grip a driver. It seems that he accidentally slashed the tendons of his right index finger. This accident, which rightly teed him off, occurred when he was playing around with a cigar cutter at a casino in the Bahamas.

Michael Douglas had a multimillion-dollar lawsuit filed against him by a golf caddy who claimed he **lost his testicles** as a result of a bad shot by Douglas. Talk about a slice into the wood(y)! Douglas tried to deny it, claiming it was *another* golfer who hit the man. But one day before the case was scheduled to go to trial, Douglas settled—probably for more than $1 million.

Professional boxers say that **Sylvester Stallone**'s boxing in his movies is a joke—and those who know him say he's terrified of being punched in the face. (Who isn't?)

Here's a statement that's par for the course for "The Greatest," **Muhammad Ali.** When asked if he played golf, he said, "I am the best. I just haven't played yet."

Former boxer **Mike Tyson,** who spent time in jail for sexual assault and was once called a serial buttocks fondler, now keeps **a camera in his bedroom.** That way, he can prove (or disprove) what really happened if he's ever accused of assault again. Of course, he doesn't have to do it in his bedroom. . . .

Unlike most entrants, **Princess Anne** was never asked to undergo a sex test when she was an Olympic competitor.

"My brother-in-law died. He was a karate expert, then he joined the army. The first time he saluted, he killed himself."
—Henny Youngman

SPORTS QUOTES
Shocking Quotes

- "One of the reasons Arnie (Arnold Palmer) is playing so well is that before each tee-shot, his wife takes out his balls and kisses them. Oh my God, what have I just said?"—USTV commentator
- "I like to hurt women when I make love to them . . . to see them bleed."—Mike Tyson
- "This is really a lovely horse. I once rode her mother."—Ted Walsh, horse racing commentator
- When asked whether Magic Johnson's return to the NBA would put other players at risk for HIV, Western Kentucky University student Joe Schmidt said, "It would be an honor to get HIV from playing Magic Johnson on an NBA court."
- When Oiler coach Bum Phillips was asked by Bob Costas why he takes his wife along with him whenever he goes on a road trip, Phillips told him, "Because she's too ugly to kiss goodbye."
- Branch Rickey, a baseball player, said of getting old: "First you forget to zip your fly. Then you forget to unzip your fly."

Funny Quotes

- When Michael Jordon was asked if he had room to store all his trophies he said, "I've always got room, even if it means my wife has to move or the kids have to go."
- "I happen to love women's sports—sometimes even for the right reasons."—Dennis Miller
- "If swimming is so good for your shape, then why do whales look like they do?"—George Carlin
- "Men hate to lose. I once beat my husband at tennis. I asked him, 'Are we going to have sex again?' He said, 'Yes, but not with each other.'"—Rita Rudner
- Here's something someone *didn't* say, which lead to the firing of the editor of the newspaper at Penn State University, who made it up: "That's the fun part of coaching—you have eighteen- to twenty-two-year-olds paying your mortgage and munching your box."

Stupid Sports Quotes

- "The first time I slept with a girl I didn't know where to put my peter."—Billy Martin, baseball manager
- "I've never had major knee surgery on any other part of my body."—University of Kentucky basketball forward

- When he was on Japanese television, boxer Bruce Seldon was asked if he had anything special to say to the people of Japan. His response: "I love Chinese food."
- "This is unparalyzed in the state's history."—Gib Lewis, Texas Speaker of the House
- "It was pretty good. Even the music was nice."—Yogi Berra, after attending an opera

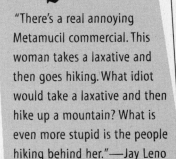

"There's a real annoying Metamucil commercial. This woman takes a laxative and then goes hiking. What idiot would take a laxative and then hike up a mountain? What is even more stupid is the people hiking behind her."—Jay Leno

- When a Chicago Blackhawk left wing was asked why he kept a color photo of himself above his locker he said, "That's so when I forget how to spell my name, I can still find my clothes."
- "We now have exactly the same situation as we had at the start of the race, only exactly the opposite."—Murray Walker
- "What will you do when you leave football, Jack. Stay in football?"—Stuart Hall, Radio 5 Live
- On the difficulties of adjusting to playing football and living in Italy, Ian Rush said, "It was like being in a foreign country."
- "Strangely, in slow motion, the ball seemed to hang in the air for even longer."—David Acfield
- "I'm going to graduate on time, no matter how long it takes." —Senior basketball player at the University of Pittsburgh

Boxing Quotes

- A veteran trainer said of his boxer: "He's a guy who gets up at six o'clock in the morning regardless of what time it is."
- "It's just a job. Grass grows, birds fly, and waves pound the sand. I just beat people up." —Muhammad Ali
- "Sure there have been injuries and deaths in boxing—but none of them serious."—Alan Minter

Men's Health, whose motto is "Never Miss an Opportunity to Exercise," suggests that their readers can build the tibialis interior muscles while on the toilet. "Start with both feet flat on the floor (and, well, your butt in its usual position). Next, lift your toes as high as you can while pressing your heels into the floor."

Comments on Sports Stupidities

- On Mike Tyson after he got out of jail: "Why would anyone expect him to come out smarter? He went to *prison* for three years, not Princeton."
- Steve Spurrier, a football coach in Florida, after saying that a fire at Auburn's football dorm had destroyed twenty books: "But the real tragedy was that fifteen hadn't been colored in yet."
- A Dallas Cowboy linebacker said about Pittsburgh Steeler Terry Bradshaw, "He couldn't spell *cat* if you spotted him the *c* and the *t*."

Exercise

It has been said that for every mile you jog, you add one minute to your life, and this enables you, at eighty-five, to spend **an additional five months in a nursing home** at $5,000 a month. Here are some more reasons (not) to exercise:

- I don't jog. It makes the ice jump right out of my vodka tonic.
- If you are going to try cross-country skiing, start with a small country.
- I'm in shape. Round is a shape.
- If God had wanted us to bend over, he would have put diamonds on the floor.
- If you're healthy, you don't need exercise. If you're sick, it's dangerous to do it.
- One reason to smile is that every seven minutes of every day, someone in an aerobics class pulls a hamstring.
- Olympic events in hell: synchronized sinning and disfigure skating.
- "My mother started walking five miles a day when she was sixty. She's ninety-seven now and we have no idea where she is."—Rita Rudner
- "I get my exercise running to the funerals of my friends who have exercised."—Barry Gray
- "He does forty-five minutes on the treadmill a day. He's on his stomach. It's like a loofah."—Bob Saget, *That's Funny*
- I'm not into working out. My philosophy is no pain, no pain."—Carol Leifer
- "The only reason I would take up jogging is so that I could take up heavy breathing again."—Erma Bombeck

BASEBALL
Watch out for Those Balls

The next time you hear about baseball players **playing with their balls** at the pitcher's mound, it might not be what you think. The pitching coach for the Cleveland Indians, Dave Duncan, estimates that roughly half of all major league pitchers play with their balls in various illegal ways.

The most famous is the "spit" ball (obviously, spitting on the ball), sometimes with tobacco mixed in. But the book *Bigger Secrets* revealed some more sophisticated methods. Such as doctoring the ball with Vaseline, **K-Y jelly,** flour, soap, licorice, Slippery Elm lozenges, flour, rosin, Metamucil, and almost anything else slick you can think of.

Another method is either freezing or microwaving the balls. Cold balls don't bounce as well, and **hot balls bounce better.** So you would want your opponent's balls froze, and your own balls toasty warm. (Everyone knows that cold balls are no good, right?)

"I was captain of the latent-paranoid softball team. I used to steal second base and feel guilty and go back."
—Woody Allen

The good part (for the cheater) is that it's difficult to prove anything's been done to yours, or theirs, without actually cutting their balls open and measuring the internal temperature. By the time anyone might manage to do that, the balls would already be back at room temperature.

Many say that cheating is done all the time, but no one is caught. The rare cases in which players are caught have generally been blatant. In one infamous case, as Yankee **Graig Nettles** hit a ball in a Detroit game in 1974, his bat splintered and the top came off. He stood there, with the (illegal) cork exposed, looking "Like a bald man whose wig had blown away."

Better Nettles had stuck to just fooling around with his balls.

"It's terrible what they do to umpires. When they first go out on the field the band starts playing *Oh Say Can You See?*"
—Goodman Ace

☺ Sexual Baseball Terms

- First base = Kissing
- Second base = Touching, tongue kissing, and so on
- Home run = Intercourse
- Strike out = No intercourse
- Relief pitcher = Vibrator
- Minor league = Underage woman
- Switch hitter = Bisexual
- Plays for the other team = Homosexual

GOLF
☺ Bedroom Golf for Men

- Each player furnishes his own equipment, one club and two balls.
- Play on a course must be approved by the owner of the hole.
- You shouldn't play the hole immediately upon arrival at the course, but you should admire it for a respectable amount of time.
- You must act like playing golf wasn't the reason you came.
- You shouldn't mention other courses you've played to the owner of the course being played.
- You must be certain that it's not a private course before you play on it or the owner may become very upset.
- You must obtain the course owner's permission before attempting to play the back nine.
- An outstanding performance is to play the same hole several times in one match.

Golf Quotes

- "It's good sportsmanship to not pick up lost golf balls while they are still rolling."—Mark Twain
- "I'd give up golf if I didn't have so many sweaters."—Bob Hope
- "I hate golf, I hate golf, I hate golf, NICE SHOT, I love golf . . ." —Stephanie Nilan
- Best excuse for a bad shot: "The car dealer overcharged me so I couldn't afford good golf balls."
- Second best excuse for a bad shot: "I didn't put deodorant on this morning and the smell is making my eyes water."
- "The reason most people play golf is to wear clothes they would not be caught dead in otherwise."—Roger Simon
- "I play in the low '80s. If it's any hotter than that, I won't play." —Joe E. Lewis

When Kennedy became president, one aide said, "This administration is going to do for sex what the last one did for golf."

SEE "STORIES ABOUT CELEBRITIES AND SPORTS," PAGE 115.

Presidential Golfers

Some presidents have been above par as golfers, and presidential golf expert, author of *Presidential Lies: The Illustrated History of White House Golf*, wrote about a few of them:

JFK was the best of all presidential golfers. Although he rarely played a full eighteen holes because of his bad back, he often shot forty or less for nine holes and would have had a handicap in the seven to ten range.

Gerald Ford, even as he approached the age of eighty, had a handicap in the fifteen ti seventeen range. He also once accidentally hit someone with his ball, leading him to say later about his game, "I know I'm getting better because I'm hitting fewer spectators."

Bill Clinton was in a league by himself, playing slowly and with liberal use of mulligans. *New York Daily News* columnist Mitchell Fink quoted someone who had played golf with him as saying, "He shot a ninety, but at the end of the game, his scorecard said eighty-four."

Other good golfers:
- Dwight D. Eisenhower, although he didn't take up golf until he was thirty-seven
- Richard Nixon, who didn't start playing seriously until he was in his forties
- FDR
- George H. W. Bush
- Ronald Reagan

Golf Terms That Sound Dirty . . . but Aren't

- Nuts, my shaft is bent.
- After eighteen holes I can barely walk.
- Look at the size of his putter.
- Keep your head down and spread your legs a bit more.
- Mind if I join your threesome?

FISHING
True Fishing Stories

Fishing is not only the most dangerous job, it's also the most dangerous *sport*. Some of the following are causes of noncommercial accidents, and others just weird fishing stories:

A Brazilian angler **choked to death** when a six-inch-long fish jumped out of a river into his mouth and choked him when he was yawning.

When an Ohio fisherman held up an eight-inch fish he had just caught, the squirming fish fell into his mouth. He was unable to grab hold of the wiggling tail and choked to death.

A Mexican angler was seriously injured when he caught a ten-foot marlin that **jabbed its spear right through him.**

Fish occasionally pull fishermen into the water, and death results immediately if the person gets entangled in the line. In one case, **a nine-foot-long catfish** pulled an Austrian fisherman right out of his boat, and towed him until he died.

Another man who lived was dragged through the water at twenty miles per hour by a marlin he had hooked, when the hook went through his right hand and the fish almost reeled *him* in.

Dumb Fishermen

Old fishermen never die— they just smell that way.

A forty-three-year-old Russian fisherman got a brilliant idea for catching fish: He connected a power cable to his home and dropped the other end of the cable into the water. Sure enough, the shock killed a lot of fish, who lay **floating belly-up in the water,** just waiting for him to take them home. But the fisherman was so excited over his "catch" that he waded into the water to collect the fish, forgetting to remove the live wire from the water first.

A New Zealand fisherman once fought to hold onto a 1,500-pound black marlin for thirty-two hours and five minutes, during which time the fish **towed his boat for fifty miles.** He lost the fish when the line broke. (The largest fish ever actually caught, by the way, was a 2,664-pound great white shark caught in Australia.)

Smart Fisherman

One man who wanted to go fishing but didn't have any bait used some **silly putty** belonging to his son. He caught a three-pound bass with it.

Russian fishermen discovered that the shiny blonde hair on a **Barbie doll** was a good lure for fish. And they're using it!

Smart Fish

Think twice before throwing that fish back. It has been found that fish can learn from experience to avoid your bait the next time. (Of course, if you don't throw it back, it's never going to learn at all.)

Farting Fish?

A full-scale nuclear alert was set off by a snafu so ridiculous it could make it hard to sleep at night, thinking about the good hands and sound minds that control the world's nuclear arsenals. It seems that a fleet of NATO ships was actually dispatched to the Baltic Sea after defenses detected "propeller-like" noises off the coast of Sweden. Fortunately, it was not the start of World War III, but, according to the official explanation, probably "a shoal of herring passing wind."

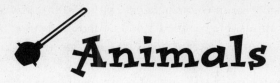

Animals

SHOWBIZ PETS (OR, PAWS CÉLÈBRE)

If you think dogs can't count, you should try putting three dog biscuits in your pocket and then giving Fido only two of them. Here are some ways show business people make animals look almost as smart as they are.

- To make a dog look like it's looking at a picture in a book, they **smear some cheese** on the page.
- To get a dog to look like it's counting something—say apples—in front of it, they throw pebbles at each apple so that the dog will look at each one.
- **To make a spider move** in a movie, they blow air on it through a straw.
- It isn't politically correct to kill animals for entertainment anymore. So if you see someone squashing a bug—for example, the killing of a cockroach in *Erin Brockovich*—assume the bug was already dead. Sometimes, dead bugs are stuffed with something like suntan cream to fluff it out so it will squish more when someone steps on it.

Funny Names for Show Animals

- CATS: Bing Clawsby, Joan Pawford
- SNAKES: Boa Derrick, Julius Squeezer, Ponty Python
- FERRET: Ferret Fawcett Major
- BUFFALO: Cicely Bison

Famous Pets

- **Eddie, the dog on** *Frasier,* was rumored to have attacked and seriously hurt a stray cat on the set, but it was hushed up so as not to turn off cat-lovers. Eddie, by the way, is really named "Moose," and his "wife," with whom he has three pups, is the stand-in for him on the show.

- The grizzly bear in *Grizzly Adams* made $9,000 a day and $15,000 extra for stunts. He weighed 1,500 pounds and stood 9'3" tall.
- There were nine different dogs used for *Lassie,* and the main one was female (females shed less than males).
- **Toto, the dog in** *The Wizard of Oz,* was paid more money to do the movie than Judy Garland.
- **Morris the Cat** was discovered in a New England animal shelter.

Literary Dogs

"Millie," the alleged author of an auto-bark-ography of her life in the White House, supposedly barked her autobiography to **Barbara Bush,** mother of current president George W. Bush. The book earned more than three times what Millie's master earned as president of the United States.

ANIMAL TRIVIA
Like, Who Cares?

- One type of bloodsucking louse lives its entire life **inside the nostril of a seal.**
- Ants not only make war with other ants, but they turn the captive ants that they don't kill into slaves.
- Iguanas can—and have been—revived by mouth-to-mouth resuscitation. One woman successfully used **CPR on her pet lizard** after it fell into a swimming pool.
- Orangutans warn outsiders to keep out of their territory by **burping.**
- Not only is a tiger's fur striped, but its skin underneath is striped as well.
- A goldfish can remember something for three seconds.
- Bats always turn left when exiting a cave.
- You can lead a cow upstairs, but not downstairs.
- **Leeches have thirty-two brains.**
- Sea slugs have 25,000 teeth.
- President **John Quincy Adams** kept a pet alligator.
- The average kangaroo has an IQ that's 40 percent higher than the brightest dog or cat.
- A locust was tried for its crimes, found guilty, and executed in 1866.
- An elephant's tusk—sometimes weighing over two hundred pounds—is really its teeth.
- Most lipstick contains scales from fish.

Maybe These Facts Are Worth Caring About

- More than 100,000 Saint Bernards are killed in China every year, to be served in restaurants.

- The groundhog has only predicted the weather correctly one-quarter of the time in the past sixty years. When it rushes back and forth from its home, it's probably looking for sex, not shadows. So you might as well ignore those groundhog reports.

- Australia's cattle and sheep emit **prodigious amounts of gas,** probably contributing to the Greenhouse Effect. (The situation there is so bad that the Australian government has proposed a tax on the animals' farting to get their owners to do something to reduce it!)

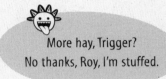

More hay, Trigger?
No thanks, Roy, I'm stuffed.

- When a lobster makes a "screaming" sound as you put it in boiling water, it's not really crying out in pain. It's probably just the noise of heated air escaping from its shell.

- A koala's fingerprints can't be distinguished from people's fingerprints, which could be used as **a unique murder defense.**

- Go ahead and swat that fly. A common housefly can give you **thirty different diseases.**

- Got ants? You can kill the queen of an ant colony by leaving out a small piece of apple. Her underlings will bring it to her, the fool will eat it, and the acid in the apple will destroy her digestive system.

- Know why that mosquito hurts? The little bugger's got **almost fifty teeth** and stabs you with its long proboscis.

- A bat is more likely to bite someone with bad breath.

Donkeys are the loudest wind breakers in the animal kingdom.

WHAT YOU DON'T KNOW ABOUT YOUR PET

Got a pet bird? Better get regular checkups. As a bird owner, you've got twice the chance of getting **lung cancer** if you've had that bird for up to ten years. And three times the likelihood of contracting the disease if you've been exposed to him or her for more than ten years.

"Animals are great, but they won't pick you up at the airport."
—Bob Goldthwait

If you're allergic to cats but really want one, get a light-colored cat. Black cats are six times more likely to cause allergy problems because their coats contain more allergy-triggering proteins than cats with light hair.

Weimaraner dogs (best known from William Wegman's photos) were originally bred in Germany for hunting deer. Their unique method: They would **grab the deer's genitals and rip them off.** Beware, some have been known to try the same thing with humans.

Politically Correct "Pets"

Political correctness now applies to pets, whoops, **"companion animals,"** as they're now supposed to be called.

- People who live with "companion animals," such as dogs, cats, and ferrets, should now be called "pet guardians."
- Mutts should be respectfully referred to as "random breeds."
- Declawing a cat is **"mutilative elective surgery."**
- Hunters are "animal assassins."
- And never say you "own" a dog or cat. As anyone who "owns" one can tell you, they own you!

SEE "POLITICALLY CORRECT SEX," PAGE 93.

"My goldfish got a bladder infection. I didn't know it was uninating thirty-seven times a day until it's bowl tipped over, full."
—Howie Mandel, *Joke Soup*

ANIMAL SEX
Animal Penises (Monkey Do, Monkey Dong)

When bulls are used for bullfights, the public thinks that what makes them angry are the red capes. Because bulls can't distinguish color at all, they're responding not only to the waving of the (colorless) cape, but to something that really pisses them off. Special **"bucking" straps that pinch their penises** are often put on to make them really see red.

An elephant has the world's largest penis, sometimes growing as long as six feet and weighing an average of **sixty pounds.**

Here are some more factoids about animal penises
- Snakes (and some lizards) have two penises.
- A whale's penis is called a **dork.**
- The gigantic gorilla has a penis two-thirds the size of a human's, and it's as thin as a cigarette.
- The **sperm whale** got its name because sailors used to think that the white oil on top of its head looked like sperm.
- Swans are the only birds with penises.

Some Animal Sex Is Like Some People Sex

Horny Dogs
A Bichon Frise in England kept humping a woman's leg—not while she was home alone but while she was on a stage in front of hundreds of people. The actress was playing the role of Dorothy in *The Wizard of Oz*, and whenever the dog would see her, he would "Latch on to her leg and start thrusting furiously," to the amusement of the audience (except for moms with children). Guess they weren't in Kansas anymore.

Nympho Cats
Cats can mate thirty times a day, and a male cat will do anything to get to a female cat in heat, even pursuing her for days. But once he finds her, it's hardly the cat's meow for her. Mating lasts for a few seconds, and it's a **slam-bam-without-even-a-thank-you-ma'am affair.** There's no foreplay, afterplay, smooching, cuddling, cocktails before, or cigarette afterward.

"All birds masturbate. And you thought that was shit on your car?"
—Bill Maher

Limp Chimps

Chimpanzees often make love **twenty times a day.** Female chimpanzees masturbate with their fingers, twigs, and when available, water faucets. Capuchin monkeys sometimes greet each other by showing off their erections. Female baboons conduct **a form of prostitution** by stealing food during sex.

According to *That's Disgusting: An Adult Guide to What's Gross, Tasteless, Rude, Crude, and Lewd,* a Dutch company found they could keep their urinals cleaner if they etched a fly in to them. Men trying to drown the fly reduced spillage by 80 percent.

Other Animal Sex

Some hippopotamuses just don't know how to do it. According to FunTrivia.com, the pygmy hippopotamus at the San Francisco Zoo has lived with his mate for thirty-five years and still can't get it right. Zoo officials said, **"He'd put it in her ear. He'd put it under her arm.** In twenty-six years he never put it in the right spot."

Dolphins have been guilty of **sexual harassment** because they sometimes corner women and rub their penises on them.

Flamingos become more sexually aroused if they're in a group. (In fact, mirrors are sometimes placed near them to encourage them to mate.)

Ostriches in captivity are often unable to become sexually aroused unless they're being watched by human beings. They're also often more attracted to their handlers than to the ostriches with whom they're supposed to mate.

Snakes may make love for a day at a time.

Some bull elephants go to the front of the females and stroke their faces before they mate.

Ferrets have orgasms.

Sexy Insects

- Mosquito sex lasts two seconds.
- Many male insects **lose their genitals** when mating.
- Not only does a female black widow spider eat her sexual partner after mating, but she may devour as many as twenty-five partners in one day.

SOURCE: USELESS-SEX.COM

Are Cats Kinky?

- **Cats masturbate,** and that little shudder afterward doesn't mean they're cold. They can have tiny orgasms as well.
- A sexually aroused cat may come on to a dog.
- A male cat may impregnate his own sister and attempt sex with his own kittens.

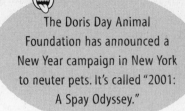

The Doris Day Animal Foundation has announced a New Year campaign in New York to neuter pets. It's called "2001: A Spay Odyssey."

- Cats may be aroused by their owner's arms, armpits, head, and breasts, also by **soft pillows, fuzzy slippers, smelly clothes,** and so forth.
- Cats may act seductively toward their owners during their fertile period, even displaying themselves. **SEE "ANIMAL SEX," PAGE 129.**

SOURCE: *277 Secrets Your Cat Wants You to Know*

PROTECTING YOURSELF FROM ANIMAL ATTACKS
Deer Me! What Is Predator Urine?

Some people try to keep deer from entering their gardens by sprinkling "predator urine" around. This supposedly fools deer into thinking your house is surrounded by foxes, bobcats, and coyotes, all of whom are just peeing up a storm on your perimeter. Predator urine is sold on the Internet, and the owners claim it's real, but they get pretty foxy when you ask them exactly how they obtained it. In fact, the whole subject creates a lot of nonsensical, unanswered questions:

- Does someone have **a pee pen** where captive animals have been trained to give up their most precious bodily fluid (well, second most precious)?
- Are animals forced to drink vast amounts of water while **piss-wranglers** follow them around with gallon jugs?
- Does someone run some water to make them want to go more?
- If they eat asparagus, does their urine smell so funny it's usable?
- Is the urine really from animals or is it just chemically similar?
- **And, of course, does it work?** An animal control Web site says they don't think so, and if it did, you would have to use so much of it that it would be just as effective at repelling people as deer.

How to Save Yourself from Killer Bees

You can't bee too cautious—they've killed more than a thousand people so far. Furthermore, they're increasing both in number and in the number of states they're in. Here's the lowdown:

- Don't think you can outrun them. They've chased people **for more than a mile.**
- You can't save yourself by jumping into water—they'll just wait until you come up for air from the lake, stream, pool, or whatever.
- If you're bee-ing attacked, cover your face and as much of the rest of your body as you can.
- Look for an enclosure (house? car?) even if it means bringing a few of them in with you. It's better than staying outside with the swarm.

SOURCE: PORTIONS FROM *The Worst-Case Scenario Survival Handbook,* USED WITH PERMISSION OF QUIRK PRODUCTIONS

Protecting Yourself from Snakes

- A snake can bite you—and kill you—*after* it's dead.
- Don't think a snake is safe because it's small. Just-born snakes can be as dangerous as their parents.
- Walk in snake territory as heavily as you can so they feel the vibration and will slither away.
- If you see one snake there may be others, so watch out.
- Many people never feel a venomous snake biting them.

Most snakes will release you if you wave an open alcohol bottle at them—or as a last resort, pour it on their nose. In some instances, killing them while they're trying to do the same to you works. One man saved himself by bitiing a snake as hard as he could while the snake was doing the same to him and the snake released him.

- The majority of people who are bitten play with their own snakes while **drunk or on drugs.**
- If you see a rattlesnake nearby, don't move. They'll usually slither away, because they'd rather be heard than seen, and they don't like moving targets. If you are bitten, don't panic; you'll probably survive. About 8,000 people in Canada and the United States are bitten each year—but only about ten to fifteen people die from it.
- You only have to worry about being **swallowed by a snake** if it's over twenty-five feet long; otherwise, it can't open its mouth wide enough to get past your shoulders.

- Certain species of cobras will spit in your eye, which can lead to **blindness.**
- If a python decides to **squeeze you to death,** nothing will stop him. A few years ago a python continued to squeeze a woman—even after authorities decapitated it.
- If you are bitten, make a mental note of the coloring of the snake to make it easier for a doctor to determine what type of venom antidote you need.
- Don't do the "movie maneuver" of sucking venom out of the bite. It could make the bite—and you—worse. Just get to a hospital as fast as you can.

SOURCE: *277 Secrets Your Snake Wants You to Know*

How to Protect Yourself from Sharks and Killer Whales

Only 10 percent of all sharks attack humans, and you have about a 30 percent chance of surviving an attack if it occurs. So it's not instant death if one circles around you. Obviously it's best to avoid it, and you can use these tips.

- Don't swim where there are a lot of fish because that's natural bait for shark.
- Avoid staying near dead fish.
- Stay out of potentially dangerous water if you're bleeding from an open wound or if you're **a menstruating woman.**
- Don't wear bright or high-contrast clothing, because sharks can see **contrast more easily than complementary colors.**
- For the same reason, be cautious if your tan is very uneven.
- Avoid wearing (or carrying) anything shiny, such as jewelry.
- If you see a shark, don't splash. Try to get back to shore or a safe place without churning the water up too much. They may think another fish is competing with them for food—and try to get rid of the competition.

"Sharks don't eat you—they bite you and spit you out. Scientists don't know why. I know. When a shark bites you you shit in your pants."
—David Brenner

- If you're on a surfboard, keep your limbs on it. Don't get on your stomach and paddle or you'll look like a fish to them. Try to move as little as possible.

- **If the shark's right next to you,** hit it with anything you've got, such as a camera.
- **If its teeth are in you** and you can't get free, poke it in the eye or grab its gill openings. Both will cause it pain, and may make it uncomfortable enough to let go.

SOURCE: PORTIONS FROM *The Worst-Case Scenario Survival Handbook,*
USED WITH PERMISSION OF QUIRK PRODUCTIONS

> Suppositories for elephants are almost one foot long, weigh two pounds, and require four people to insert them.

As for killer whales, they're no fun either: They kill sharks by torpedoing them, ramming into their stomachs from underneath so **the shark explodes.** Fortunately, it's not likely they'll do that to you. A big danger is that if you're in a small boat, and a whale decides to breach under it, you can be thrown in the water. And if the water is cold, you aren't going to have a whale of a good time.

The Bear Facts: How to Protect Yourself

Although many people are afraid of them, bear attacks are rare. Bears, like most animals, go about their daily routine, looking for food, sleeping, and of course, shitting in the woods. Here are some ways to protect yourself, some of which appeared on eHow.com:

Do bear sprays work?
Maybe, if they are used properly. They are supposed to be sprayed in the bear's face when it's really close, but many people foolishly think they're supposed to spritz their sleeping or eating areas to keep bears away. These people are called dinner. Spritzing your tent or your clothes can actually *attract* bears who may become curious about the strange smell.

What should you do if a bear runs after you?
If there's a group of you, it's better to stick together than to scatter. If you all wave your arms, scream, throw rocks, or bang pots together, the bear may think you're a large and dangerous, albeit very odd, animal.

None of you are going to outrun a bear because **bears can go faster than an Olympic sprinter.** You are, however, better off running downhill, since their center of gravity makes it harder for them to run that way. If you decide to run like hell, throw something down as you go, say your camera or a jacket, which may distract them and lighten your load. But don't throw your backpack down because that may give you needed protection in case of an attack.

Should you climb a tree?
Black bears can climb trees also, and probably better than you can. Furthermore, the branches you would hang onto may break and put you in a worse spot than you were in before.

Should I tiptoe around so bears don't hear me?
No, bears don't like to be surprised, so when you leave your tent, wear a bell if you're going out walking. Or be sure to make a lot of noise so the bear is likely to avoid you.

What about cars?
What about cars? Bears in Yosemite prefer **Hondas.** God knows how much of your tax money was spent to learn that.

DOGS
A Few Doggone Interesting Facts

According to *277 Secrets Your Dog Wants You to Know*, **dogs can get two different types of VD,** one of them from fooling around, just like people. As many as one in ten dogs carry this type, which can be transmitted to humans by handling aborted fetuses from female dogs with the disease.

FunFacts.com says that two dogs survived the *Titanic* sinking. Two Pomeranians went with their owners in early lifeboats that carried few passengers, so no one objected to space being taken up by dogs.

If your lawn has been ruined in one spot from a dog's pee, the culprit was probably a female dog. Females urinate straight into the ground, all at once, which can discolor and ruin the grass. **Male dogs release small quantities of urine** and spread it out. Because they lift their legs to urinate, some of the urine is dissipated and does not hit the ground below at all.

In Germany in the 1880s, there was a very unpopular tax collector who bred a particularly fierce breed of dog to help him collect taxes. The tax collector's name was **Ludwig Doberman.**

In the 1880s, **Thomas Jefferson** instituted the first dog license, so if you have to buy one, blame him, not the place you're paying the money to.

"The difference between dogs and men is that you know where dogs sleep at night."
—Greg Louganis

Americans spend more on dog food than on baby food, which means something, but no one's sure what.

A full-grown dog can understand about forty expressions. These are mostly "signaling actions," for example, if you get up, your dog understands that you may take him or her out.

Kathie Lee Gifford's dog is named Regis. She claims she wasn't trying to "dog" her former co-host.

A legal argument over a dog has made it to the state Supreme Court and so far has cost American taxpayers $200,000. A ten-year-old Lhasa Apso bit two women seven years ago, and the debate continues to rage over whether the dog should be put to sleep or not. Meanwhile, the dog is in a shelter and its owner in the doghouse.

My Dog Can Lick Your Dog

Part of the reason dogs lick us is because they like salt. A Japanese study found that salt enhanced their taste responses. But dogs also lick other dogs and that's not because of salt. They do it as a form of greeting or perhaps to help them recognize the scent on the other dog. Puppies also lick their mother's faces, soliciting food from them in this manner. (That's why cats don't lick your face; they don't lick their mother's faces to get food.) So maybe dogs lick us for *all* these reasons. We're their parents, their friends, their pack mates—and they love us not just because we're so sweet, but because we're so salty.

SOURCE: *277 Secrets Your Dog Wants You to Know*

Dog Quotes

- We wonder why dogs always drink out of toilets, but from a dog's point of view, they wonder why we keep peeing in their water.
- "Dogs need to sniff the ground. It's how they keep abreast of current events. The ground is a giant dog newspaper, containing . . . late-breaking dog news items . . . [often] continued in the next yard."—Dave Barry
- "It is said that a family can be torn apart by something as simple as a pack of wild dogs."—Jack Hardy

Puppy Love

- "There is no psychiatrist in the world like a puppy licking your face."—Ben Williams
- "Don't accept your dog's admiration as conclusive evidence that you are wonderful."—Ann Landers
- "If heaven went by merit, you would stay out and your dog would go in."—Mark Twain

On the Steve Allen show in 1956, when Elvis was singing "Hound Dog" to a basset hound on a stool, the dog was peeing.

Signs Your Dog Is Reading Martha Stewart

- The dog droppings in your backyard have been sculpted into swans.
- Dog hair has been collected and put into baskets with nesting material for the birds.
- There's potpourri hanging from his or her collar.
- The pooper scooper is decorated with rafia.

Dog Property Laws

- If I like it, it's mine.
- If it's in my mouth, it's mine.
- If I had it a while ago, it's mine.
- If I'm chewing it, it's mine.
- If you put it down, it's mine.
- If it's broken, it's yours.

"Acquiring a dog may be the only opportunity a human ever has to choose a relative."
—Mordecai Siegal

How to Be as Happy as Your Dog

Be in the present. Dogs have no sense of the past or future. "You won't find Munchie at the local dog bar nursing a beer over a lost love. . . . He loves whatever is in front of him."

Take care of yourself. Ever notice how much your dog sleeps?

Entertain yourself. Dogs play with toys and make their own entertainment, from chasing cats to "sniffing dead critters." (Not recommended for you, but you get the idea.)

Let yourself be loved. Has your dog ever stopped you from rubbing its tummy or scratching its ears?

Relax.

SOURCE: ALAN COHEN, *New Frontier Magazine*

WHY DOGS ARE LIKE MEN
- Both are fascinated with women's crotches.
- Both fart frequently and shamelessly.
- Both are suspicious of the postman.

CATS
Feline Facts

- The owner of a stud cat in Bucharest was able to raise its fees to $1,000 a night when she changed his name to **Bill Clinton.**
- If you cut off a cat's whiskers, it can't stand up.
- **Cats don't have collarbones,** so they can squeeze through any space large enough for them to get their head through.
- Cats have 230 bones in their body (mostly in their tail) and people have 206.
- A twelve-year-old cat may have spent three years of its life grooming itself.
- A fifteen-year-old cat may have only been awake for five to seven years of its life, spending the rest of its time sleeping.
- Some people are so phobic about cats—**Julius Caesar, Napoleon, and Henry II**—that they practically faint when they see one.
- A fifteen-year-old girl in Utah recently got the (pneumonic) plague from her cat. The cat became infected from a flea-infested colony of rodents.
- There are almost no entirely **black cats,** although they were once very common. Usually black cats have *some* white coloration, because totally black cats were considered evil and bad luck, and they were not kept or bred.

Cat urine glows if you place a black light over it.

- Be careful of canned cat food that is red, because it may contain a carcinogen.
- **Most adult cats get diarrhea from milk.**

 ## Signs That Your Cat Is Planning to Kill You

- He actually does have your tongue.
- You find "feline of fortune" magazines behind the couch.
- You wake up to find a bird's head in your bed.

All I Need to Know about Life I Learned from My Cat

- Climb your way to the top—that's why the drapes are there.
- A small bird or rodent left on their bed tells them you care.
- Life is hard, then you nap.

SOURCE: *Art Tops* BY PORTAL PUBLICATIONS, LTD.

WHY CATS ARE BETTER THAN MEN
℮ A cat hits the litterbox.
℮ You have a better chance of training a cat.
℮ You never have to spend time with your cat's mother.

CATS VERSUS DOGS
Interesting Facts

Do cats beat dogs paws down—or is it vice versa in the battle of the two most popular pets?

℮ A Harvard University study concluded that cats were smarter than dogs because the only way to determine how smart an animal really is would be to watch how it performs in the wild. Cats turned out to have much stronger **survival skills,** rating 7.2 on a scale of how well they fared on their own, as compared to the dogs' 5.3 rating.

> Cats recognize dog breeds. If they're raised with certain kinds of dogs, they may not be frightened of other dogs of that breed, but scared by other breeds.

℮ Another study showed that a dog's memory lasts about five minutes, while a cat's can last about sixteen hours.
℮ Cats have about one hundred vocal sounds. Dogs have about ten.

Other Differences Between Cats and Dogs

℮ Buy a dog a toy and it will play with it forever. Buy a cat a present and it will play with the wrapper for ten minutes.

℮ Dogs shed. Cats shred.

℮ Dogs believe they are human. Cats believe they are God.

℮ Dogs have owners. Cats have staff.

℮ Dogs mark their territory. Cats simply assume that all territory is theirs.

Is Marijuana Worse for Dogs or Cats?

Small quantities will probably physically harm a cat more than a dog, but psychologically, it will harm a dog more. That's because the marijuana plant is related to catnip and they're used to tripping out on the faux stuff. But marijuana still **can make them hallucinate,** possibly have seizures, and even die.

When dogs are given marijuana—sometimes blown in their faces by their stoned owners—they have no idea what's going on. They may become extremely confused and agitated because they don't have experience with something like catnip to help them put it in perspective (as if dogs had perspective).

So, to play it safe, keep both from your stash. If Fido or Fluffy want to share your joint with you, **just say no.** You might be arrested for it. A man was recently arrested, jailed, and fined for attempted poisoning after a photo of him holding his cat by its head and forcing its nose and mouth into the opening of a bong somehow ended up at a police station.

SOURCE: *277 Secrets Your Cat Wants You to Know*

When the Parisians decided to run a campaign to clean up all the dog *merde* in the streets, a South African newspaper ran a story titled "Super Pooper-Scoopers to Fight Turd Reich."

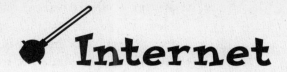

Internet

PORNOGRAPHY
G-Rated Stories about Computer Porn

Someone once wrote, "No matter what kind of twisted sexual mutant you happen to be, on the Internet, if you type in **'Find people who have sex with goats that are on fire,'** the computer will say, 'Specify type of goat.'" Here are a few other things on or about the Internet:

Porn again or born-again? Do you think born-again Christians behave better than the rest of us? One in five born-agains admitted in a survey by Focus on the Family that they had viewed what is euphemistically called "adult Web sites." And that number of righteous hypocrites viewing porn sites is no higher or lower than the rest of the population.

Porn free! A man invented a **"Beaverbox,"** which is enables people to visit porn sites without their computers crashing. Porn sites crash more frequently than regular ones because some engage in "mouse trapping" (refusing to let you shut them off) or send you to additional sites.

Parents with children can easily remove the Beaverbox from the hard drive so the children don't discover it and use it to find their parents' favorite pictures.

If you think the Internet is filled with perverts, you're wrong! It's actually filled with sports fans. One survey found that almost twice as many people have logged onto **sports Web sites** than porno sites, 32 percent to 17 percent.

Few, if any, people ever read the long disclaimers in tiny print that appear on the front page of porn Web sites. But **buried in the fine print,** a few of them have said that the site can terminate someone's modem connection and substitute an international long-distance connection *to another country.* One person was unwittingly connected to another site via a country in Africa—at $7.31 per minute.

Beaver College had to change its name (to Acadia) partially because it was the source of much winking and leering. They claimed the major reason, though, was that people searching the Internet for information on the college couldn't find anything if their computer had a filter installed to block sexually explicit material—such as words like "beaver."

SOURCE: WIRELESS FLASH

 ## Movies That Should Have Been Porn Flicks

Big Daddy
My Dog Skip
Toy Story
Moby Dick
Reindeer Games
In Too Deep

Grease
Sister Act
Free Willy
Octopussy
My Giant

WEB SITES

If someone was sick enough to think of it, it's probably on the Internet. Here are some goodies I've stumbled across. In most cases the exact Web sites aren't given because Web addresses tend to disappear or change. Use a search engine (such as Google.com) to look for them if you want to. For those of you who find these sites fairly tame, check out *That's Disgusting Too: The 200 Most Disgusting Sites on the Internet.*

 ## Hilarious Porn Movie Titles

- Snow White and the Seven Sailors
- Pulp Friction
- Romancing the Bone
- Saving Ryan's Privates
- Rambone
- Forrest Hump
- Sorest Rump
- Glad He Ate Her (Gladiator)

SOURCE: BBSPOT.COM "TOP TEN"

Weirdo Web Sites We Could Live Without

Naked News is what Fark.com calls "the program with nothing to hide—and they're not kidding." You choose a totally naked woman who will give you your choice of the day's news: that the world is about to end, that Bush is still president, or whatever you consider to be bad news.

Moon of the Month Contest asks people to send a photo of their posterior. "No professional photos please," it says.

The Seven Words You Aren't Supposed to Say on Television is translated here into dozens of languages, including Azerbaidjhan, Sanskrit, and Yiddish.

Frequently asked questions about **Elvis in Latin,** along with available CDs such as *Tenere me ama* ("Love Me Tender"). They're serious.

Clone Your Bone is a penis-casting kit where you can replicate your organ in wax. Also available at the site is "Match Your Snatch" where you can make "an exact copy of your lovely labia." Comes with optional magnets.

Dull Men's Club Chat Room: Join in on discussions about whether airport luggage should go clockwise or counterclockwise, the best type of coat hangers to collect, and so on.

Skinema, or the skin of celebrities, is a site put up by a dermatologist. It includes a section on "Stars with Scars" like Harrison Ford's chin scar, Demi Moore and Leonardo DiCaprio's chicken pox scars, and so on.

Errrggg

A Web Site That Sells People Back What Thieves Stole from Them: Alas, TheBurglar.com, an English Web site designed to help crooks fence their stuff was closed down and accused of breaking the Theft Act. (Shouldn't the Web masters have thought of this problem before they put money into it?)

Museum of Dirt includes celebrity dirt from Jim Morrison's grave, O. J. Simpson's front yard, and even super-fortified dirt from Martha Stewart's yard.

Alien Implant Probes: According to CuriousTimes.com, if you're jealous when you read about all those people who have been abducted by aliens, you can go right over to Alien Abductions, which will implant into your brain memories of your very own out-of-town visitors.

Borrring

Encounters with Stars: Chat Soup has a section in which people like Pat Boone's podiatrist's assistant talk about their four-second encounters with such superstars, thereby spicing up their pathetically dull lives.

Pig Ear Notches: Pig's ears are notched in a certain way by their owners to help them keep track of litters and genetic lines. Pig-out here by learning how to tell one pig from another.

Watching Corn Grow: Here's a Web cam where you can watch corn grow twenty-four hours a day. At least it beats watching paint dry—wait, there's a Web site for that too.

Stinky Meat: This meaty site shows the composition of a piece of raw meat. A sure-fire crowd pleaser—developed by Harvard students no less—it has gotten more than three million hits.

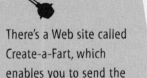

There's a Web site called Create-a-Fart, which enables you to send the sound of farting to another Web user.

Sicko Web Sites

Jumper Pools: Visitors to the site can guess where and when the next leap will be, and whether the person will hit water, rocks, or a boat.

PsychoExgirlfriend.com: Fifty messages were supposedly left on an answering service of a man who jilted a woman. He put them up so everyone could listen to what she said and either laugh or commiserate.

Ghoul Pools: These are Web sites where people choose the names of people who they think will kick the bucket that year. Nice, eh?

Public Urinators: The Barking Dogs Crime Watch Group in Dallas got tired of drunks relieving themselves in public. They started taking pictures of people caught in the act, and then posted them on the Internet.

Penile Pump Implant Surgery: Haven't you always wanted to watch someone getting a penile implant? Happily you haven't, nor did most people, who stayed away in droves from a live-action, forty-minute surgical implant procedure, proving that apparently there is hope for civilization after all.

Disgusting Sites

- **GretaGarbage.com** contains excerpts from a really disgusting (but funny) book titled *That's Disgusting: An Adult Guide to What's Gross, Tasteless, Rude, Crude, and Lewd* plus samples from a second book titled *That's Disgusting Too: The 200 Most Disgusting Sites on the Internet.*

- **Crap-O-Gram** offers, yep, crap from various animals (including elephants). If that isn't artistic enough for your tastes, you can always buy buffalo dung in the shape of Texas.

- **Used Panties:** Not only do you get to choose the type of panties you want (say, thongs) but you can pick which model you'd want to have worn them before they send them to you. The panties were probably really worn by some toothless hag in Lightyourfart, Arkansas—but hey, you never know.

Are These for Real?

Salon.com's article "AllThePornYouCanEat.com" listed a few more fun sites :

- IJustHadaRectalExamineOnline.com
- Looking-Up-the-Butt-of-a-Dead-Bear.com
- ButIDontNeedMyToothPasteDelivered.com
- BlowtheDotOutYourAss.com

Never Made It to the Internet

- FuckYouandtheStartUpYouRodeInOn.com
- PenisEnlargementGiftCertificates.com
- SoiledCelebrityProphylactics.com
- ShredsofSomeoneSoulforAuction.com

SOURCE: SALON.COM

Greta Garbage's Favorite Sites

- **Best miscellaneous sites:** GretaGarbage.com, Beer.com, CertifiedBitches.com, HeartlessBastards.com
- **Best link sites:** Cruel.com, Fark.com
- **Best offbeat news sites:** Chuck Shepherd's NewsoftheWeird.com, http://abcnews.go.com/section/us/WolfFiles (Buck Wolf's The Wolf Files), ThisIsTrue.com, Lewis Lapham's BizarreNews.com (and mailing list), ObscureStore.com, FlashNews.com (Wireless Flash), CuriousTimes.com, BizarreMag.com, World-Sex-News.com
- **Best trivia sites:** UselessKnowledge.com, UselessFacts.net, Corsinet.com (Brain Candy), AbsoluteTrivia.com, FunTrivia.com, DumbFacts.com
- **Best health sites:** HealthScout.com, HealthCentral.com
- **Best newsgroups:** alt.showbiz. gossip, alt.gossip.celebrities, alt.fan.cecil-adams

"What do people mean when they say their computer went down on them?"
—Marilyn Pittman

GEEK SHEIK
Computer Buzzwords

- **Mouse potato:** Like a couch potato is always watching television, a mouse potato is always on his or her computer.
- **Mouse trapping:** When a Web site grabs control of your mouse and won't let you get off the site.
- **Dirt road:** Slow connection to the Internet.
- **Sundowner:** Someone who stays up all night on the Internet.
- **Mouse arrest:** Spending too much time tied to a computer could you give you the feeling of being handcuffed to it.
- **Vulture capitalist:** People who pick over the bones of dead dot-com companies.
- **Screenager:** Internet or computer-addicted teenager.
- **Geek god:** A handsome computer nerd.
- **Face mail:** Talking to someone offline, in person.
- **Treeware:** Printed material.
- **404:** A clueless person (based on a computer term).
- **Angry fruit salad:** A computer interface with too many colors.
- **Lasagna software:** Software composed of too many overlapping dialog boxes.

A "bio break" is computereze for going to the bathroom.

What You Can Learn from Video Games

- That you can vanquish most bad guys if you have enough quarters.
- That death is reversible (but only for you).
- That you'll frequently encounter ninjas as you walk along the street.
- That whenever fat, evil men are about to die, they begin flashing red or yellow.
- That 200 to 1 odds against you is not a problem.
- And that you only live three times.

How to Keep Your Cat Off Your Computer

"Do not meddle in the affairs of cats, for they are subtle and will piss on your computer," someone once wrote about cats. They should know, because kitty littering of computers is enough of an issue that the *Wall Street Journal's* main tech writer, Walter Mossberg, devoted space to this nontechie problem. The letters he received about it afterward offered suggestions such as:

- Build a low, comfortable shelf with a heating pad above the monitor for your cat to sit on.
- Get your cat to avoid the top of the monitor by pasting, spraying, or gluing something like sandpaper or double sticky tape on it, which cats don't like.
- Keep a spray bottle of water next to your computer and blast cats when they come near.
- Finally, you can buy Paw Sense software "which can detect 'catlike typing' on four keys at once, or nonsensical patterns." It then realizes there's a cat on the keyboard, and emits a screeching sound while the keyboard locks until you type the word *human*.

Now that they've gotten rid of the cat problem, if they could just figure out a way to keep all those snakes out of the chat rooms.

Really Weird Things They've Auctioned at Ebay

Here's what they were selling, and what they received (besides publicity). In some cases good taste was the winner and the item was removed.

- **A sexual slave:** "One night with my wife" had a starting bid of $15,000 and was auctioned by a man who wanted money for a down payment on a house. For this, he was more than willing to give up his twenty-three-year-old 36C-cup wife to be a "sex slave" for one night.

> One man sold his soul in a jar on Ebay, supposedly for $1,000. (Jay Leno said that the man was a law student, so he didn't need his soul.)

- **A man's past:** This included "Multiple bad hair days. A few bad relationships. Boredom in Iowa. Time roaming in Saudi Arabia. A fractured left elbow. Pinched nerves in right elbow. Two stiches above left eye. Three stitches over right eye. Five stitches on back of head. Many ingrown toe nails. Lots of mistakes. Many regrets. Lots of moving. Stepping in poop bare foot. Getting pooped on by a bird. An annoying brother. And much, much more!"

- **A testicle:** A testicle for trade (huh?) with a starting bid of $500,000.
- *Survivor* **underpants:** Underpants owned but never worn by Kelly Wigglesworth, one of the last four survivors from the original show, were put up for auction for $149.95. No one bid.
- **Virginity:** The offer of the virginity of a woman turned out to be a dark prank, for those all over the world who bid on it learned afterward that their names, addresses, and messages were posted on the Internet by the sneaky "virginity" seller. The high bidder, by the way, was an American who bid $2,000.
- **A brother:** Someone tried to sell his "annoying little brother" for $1.50.
- **A cat:** "Irksome cat (throws up constantly)" for 1 cent.
- **Toenails:** "Freshly bitten off" clippings for $50.
- **Killer nails:** Fingernails from a serial killer for $9.99.
- **Elian Gonazales:** Yep, the over-hyped child himself was actually auctioned by someone as a joke, because obviously they didn't have him. And someone else also poked fun at the media hype by offering "air from Miami" that "might have been breathed by Elian Gonzales."

Microsoft Graffiti

Mad magazine listed some of the writings that might be found on the walls of the bathrooms at Microsoft:

- Bill Gates downloads here.
- Do not flush mouse pads down the toilet.
- To flush, press handle. You don't need to hold control, alt, and delete at the same time.
- Your mother's so fat that it took me twenty-five minutes to download her picture from the Web.

- **Sperm:** High IQ sperm with a starting bid of $250.
- **Execution:** Seats to the execution of a death row inmate—who wanted to establish a trust fund for his estranged daughter—for $100. The man was executed for a briefcase bomb that killed three innocent people.
- **An electric chair:** This slightly used chair received a bid for $25,000, but the owner withdrew it—and sold it for more to Ripley's Believe It Or Not.

SOURCES: *Knight-Ridder*, OUTRAGEOUSAUCTIONS.COM, *Maxim*

Slogans for Microsoft

- I still miss Windows, but my aim is getting better.
- I'll never forget the first time I ran Windows, but I'm trying.
- Double your drive space. Delete Windows.
- How do you want to crash today?

Is reading this book while you're on the toilet a type of multitasking?

Unofficial Smilies

:-)~	User drools.
:-)	User is taking a leak.
:- ~)	User has a cold.
:-#	User wears braces.
:^)	User has a broken nose.
:-&	User is tongue tied.
+- :)	User is the Pope.
0 :-)	User is an angel.
:-X	User's lips are sealed.
C=:)	User is a chef.
{: -)	User is wearing headphones.
(: -)	User is bald.
(-:	User is left handed.
< ;)	User is a dunce.
.-)	User has only one eye.
: -)————	User is smiling with an erection.

Creative Chat Room Acronyms

IITYWYBMAB	If I Tell You, Will You Buy Me a Beer?
AWGTGTTA	Are We Going to Go Through This Again?
BIOYIOP	Blow It Out Your Input-Output Port.
DNPM	Damned Near Pissed Myself.
ESOSL	Endless Snorts of Stupid Laughter.
GD&R	Grin, Duck, & Run.
INMDO	In My Conceited Dogmatic Opinion.
LMAO	Laughing My Ass Off.
YABWFTNOTNG	Yet Another Bozo Who Forgot the Name Of the News Group (meaning that the person is off topic on a newsgroup).

SOURCE: *A Man's Life*

☼ Computer Commandments

℮ Thou shalt remember thy name and thy password.
℮ Thou shalt not covet they neighbor's password, nor thy neighbor's real name, computer, software, nor any other thing of thy neighbor's.
℮ Thou shalt only call technical assistance two times a day.
℮ Thou shalt delete thine ancient e-mail.
℮ Thou shalt not post messages after imbibing excessively of ale.
℮ If thou doth promise to reply to a message and thou doth not, then surely thou shalt spill liquid into thy keyboard and shorteth out thy central processing unit after your warranty, including parts, has ceaseth.

Before Computers

℮ A keyboard was a piano.
℮ A mouse was a rodent.
℮ A CD was a bank account.
℮ LOL was a little old lady.
℮ Compress had something to do with garbage.
℮ Memory loss happened to you when you got older.
℮ If you unzipped anything in public, they'd send you to jail.
℮ If you had a 3 1/2-inch floppy you kept it a secret.

The following conversation supposedly occurred between a "newbie" and a technical support person.

TECH: Now press Control and Escape at the same time and then type the letter "P" to bring up the Program Manager.
CUSTOMER: I don't have a "P."
TECH: "P" on your keyboard.
CUSTOMER: I'm not going to do that.

Artsy-Fartsy Stuff

MUSIC
Original Names of Famous Bands

- The Beatles were Johnny and the Moondogs.
- Grateful Dead were Warlocks.
- Led Zeppelin was New Yardbirds.
- The Beach Boys were Carl and the Passions.
- The Bee Gees were Rattlesnakes.
- Earth, Wind & Fire were Salty Peppers.
- Simon and Garfunkel were Tom and Jerry.

> Sonny and Cher were Caesar and Cleo.

The Worst Real Band Names

- Bassholes
- Alcoholics Unanimous
- Boner Donors
- The Armadildoes
- Attila the Stockbroker
- The Bourbon Tabernacle Choir
- Cap'n Crunch and the Cereal Killers
- Clitaurus Rex
- A Life-Threatening Buttocks Condition
- Dead Kennedys
- We'll Suck for Food
- The Poo Poo Platters
- Assrash
- Union of Uranus
- Pull My Finger Chili Cookoff
- I Rule over Martha Stewart

SOURCE: "THE CANONICAL LIST OF WEIRD BAND NAMES" AT WWW.MCS.NET /~SHOCHBER /BANDNAME.HTML

Funny Rap Band Names

New York magazine had a competition for most original name for a rap group. The winners were:

- Phi Beta Rappa
- Noyz 'R Us
- Death 'N Taxis
- Gunga Din
- Raparazzi
- The Dread Lo

Hilarious (Real) Song Titles

- "If My Nose Were Full of Nickels, I'd Blow It All on You"
- "My Head Hurts, My Feet Stink, and I Don't Love Jesus"
- "We Used to Kiss Each Other on the Lips, Now It's All Over"
- "Wake Up and Smell the Whiskey"
- "You're as Young as the Women You Feel"
- "You're the Reason Our Kids Are So Ugly"
- "The Pint of No Return"
- "Get Your Biscuits in the Oven and Your Buns in the Bed"
- "If the Man in the Moon Were a Coon"
- "Where Did Robinson Crusoe Go with Freddie on a Saturday Night?"
- "Would You Rather Be a Colonel with an Eagle on Your Shoulder or a Private with a Chicken on Your Knee?"
- "Plant a Watermelon on My Grave and Let the Juice Soak Through"
- "You Can't Have Your Kate and Edith Too"
- "If the Phone Doesn't Ring, It's Me"
- "I Didn't Come to Kiss the Bride, I Did That Long Ago"
- "Jesus Loves Me (But He Hates You)"
- "A Bowl of Chop Suey and You-Y"
- "When It's Toothpickin' Time in False Teeth Valley"

Crazy Christmas Carols

For people with:

- **Multiple personality disorder:** "We Three Queens Disoriented Are"
- **Narcissistic personality disorder:** "Hark the Herald Angels Sing about Me"
- **Manics:** "Deck the Halls and Walls and House and Lawn and Streets and Stores and Office and Town and Cars and Buses and Trucks and Trees and Fire Hydrants and . . ."
- **Paranoid:** "Santa Claus Is Coming to Get Me"
- **Personality disorder:** "You Better Watch Out, I'm Gonna Cry, I'm Gonna Pout, Maybe I'll Tell You Why."
- **Depression:** "Silent Night, All Is Dreary, All Is Flat, All Is Lonely . . ."
- **Obsessive/Compulsive disorder:** "Jingle Bell, Jingle Bell, Jingle Bell Rock, Jingle Bell, Jingle Bell, Jingle Bell Rock, Jingle . . ."
- **Self-destructive personality:** "Thoughts of Roasting on an Open Fire"

Misheard Song Lyrics

There are lots of Web sites and books on misheard song lyrics. These are some of the funnier ones, a few chosen by the *Sacramento Bee's* "Smile" and "Required Reading" sections, and Web sites such as TheChicagoLoop.net/lyrics and KissThisGuy.com.

- "The girl with kaleideoscope eyes" was heard as "The girl with colitis goes by."
- "She's got a ticket to ride" was heard as "She's got a tic in her eye."
- "Oh beautiful, for spacious skies" was heard as "Oh beautiful, for spaceship skies."
- "Oh tannenbaum, oh tannenbaum" was heard as "Oh atom bomb, oh atom bomb."
- "Lead on, oh king eternal" was heard as "Lead on, oh kinky turtle."
- "You are lost and gone forever, dreadful sorry, Clementine" was heard as "You have lost your gum forever, dreadful sorry, Clementine."
- "He is tramping out the vineyards where the grapes of wrath are stored" was heard as "He is tramping out the vintage where the great giraffes are stored."
- "There's a bad moon on the rise" was heard as "There's a bathroom on the right."
- "See the blazing yule before us" was heard as "See the grazing mule before us."
- "Paperback writer" was heard as "Paid for my Chrysler."
- "The answer, my friend, is blowing in the wind" was heard as "The ants are my friends, they're blowing in the wind."

A musical greeting card that played "Silent Night" was tossed into a latrine in Jamaica. Afterward, someone sitting on the toilet heard the song and thought he was the victim of a voodoo curse. He called the police, who found the card.

If you knew that a woman was pregnant and had syphilis, and she had eight kids already, three of whom were deaf, two blind, and one mentally retarded, would you recommend that she terminate the pregnancy? If you said yes, you just aborted Beethoven.

WORDS
Perfect Anagrams

An anagram is a word or phrase that you can make by changing the order of
the letters in another word or phrase, like stain can be made from the word
satin. Here are some anagrams that are more interesting than that one:

- President Clinton of the USA: To copulate, he finds interns
- Mother-in-law: Woman Hitler
- Elvis Aron Presley: Royal Pelvis Sneer
- Desperation: A rope finds it
- Slot machines: Cash lot in 'em
- Dormitory: Dirty room
- Snooze alarms: Alas, no more Zs

Eschew Obfuscation

Here's how Little Miss Muffet would have sounded if written with a
thesaurus:

> *Lilliputian damsel Muffet*
> *Was resting upon a squatty seating apparatus*
> *Ingesting the lacteal substances in her possession*
> *At this point arrived an arachnid . . .*

What a Difference a Comma Makes!

See the difference a little punctuation can make. . . .

> *Dear John:*
> *I want a man who knows what love is all about. You are generous,*
> *kind, thoughtful. People who are not like you admit to being useless*
> *and inferior. You have ruined me for other men. I yearn for you. I*
> *have no feelings whatsoever when we're apart. I can be forever*
> *happy—will you let me be yours?*
> *Truly, Gloria*

Here's the letter when punctuated differently:

> *Dear John:*
> *I want a man who knows what love is. All about you are generous,*
> *kind, thoughtful people who are not like you. Admit to being useless*
> *and inferior. You have ruined me. For other men, I yearn. For you, I*
> *have no feelings whatsoever. When we're apart, I can be forever*
> *happy. Will you let me be?*
> *Yours truly, Gloria*

Verbiage for the Verbose

A book called *Verbiage for the Verbose* offers some well-known phrases and translates them. Can you figure out what these are?

1. Nonattendance causes the cardiac organ to become more affectionate.
2. A heart of the hot season late part of the day's sleeping thought.
3. Battling using a gum protruberance and the hard part of a fingernail.

Answers: (1) Absence makes the heart grow fonder. (2) A Midsummer's Night Dream. (3) Fight tooth and nail.

The Absolutely Worst Analogies

The *Washington Post* had a contest asking people to write the worst possible analogies they could think of....

- The hailstones leaped from the pavement, just like maggots when you fry them in hot grease.
- McBride fell twelve stories, hitting the pavement like a Hefty bag.
- Her hair glistened in the rain like nose hair after a sneeze.
- His thoughts tumbled in his head, making and breaking alliances like underpants in a dryer without Cling Free.
- John and Mary had never met. They were like two hummingbirds who had also never met.

New Buzz Words for Today's Times

- **Jabber-walky:** People who walk around talking to others on their cell phones.
- **Lewinsky:** Oral sex. (Monica's father has objected to the public use of this term, but if he's not around, go for it.)
- **Nato:** No action, talk only.
- **Sitcom:** Single income, two children, oppressive mortgage.
- **Squirt the bird:** Transmit a signal to a satellite.
- **Starter marriage:** Short-lived early marriage.

- **Eye candy:** An attractive, but not necessarily intelligent, woman.
- **Swiped out:** ATM or credit cards that can't be used because the magnetic strip is worn away.
- **Stress puppy:** Someone who seems to thrive on being stressed out.
- **Fanny bumper:** A very crowded party.
- **Nostril shot:** Unflattering movie shot, as in one with more nostril than nose.

Pizza Lingo

Here's some pizza slang from a former "Dominoid," that is, someone who worked for Domino's Pizza. This first appeared in a fascinating newsletter called *Maledicta (The International Journal of Verbal Aggression)*, and was incorporated into an article in the *St. Paul Pioneer Press*:

- **Flyers and fungus:** Pepperoni (called flyers because they look a bit like Frisbees) and mushrooms
- **Alpo or sausages:** Toppings with sausages
- **Blood pie or hemorrhage:** Extra sauce
- **Green slime:** Green peppers
- **Screamers and squealers:** Mushrooms and bacon

And here are a couple of names for customers:
- **Placer:** A person who puts a hair or a dead fly or something disgusting or dangerous on their pizza slice and then tries to get the slice for free or a second one discounted
- **Republican:** Someone who orders GOP—green peppers, onions, and pepperoni

Restaurant Slang

- **Duke:** A tough customer, à la John Wayne (he was known as the "Duke"), who thinks he knows everything
- **Gummer:** An older person who takes a long time to get through a meal because he doesn't have teeth to bite into the food
- **Julia Child:** A customer who analyzes the meal (like the famous chef Julia Child), and who wants to know what's in all the dishes before she orders anything
- **Leona:** A difficult customer, or someone like the notoriously difficult real-estate-tycoon-felon Leona Helmsley
- **Lungs:** A smoker

SOURCE: *Tricks of the Trade*

How to Be Obnoxious in French

- ℮ You've put on weight. *Tu as gross.*
- ℮ Haven't the police found you yet? *La police, ne t'a pas encore trouve?*
- ℮ Would you stop spitting on me while you're talking? *Voulez-vous cesser de me cracher dessus pendant que vous parlez?*
- ℮ You have a chive on your tooth. *Vous avez de la ciboulette sur votre dent.*
- ℮ Your children are very attractive. Are they adopted? *Vos enfants sont tres beaux. Ils son adoptes?*
- ℮ This room's a bit of a dive but it has some nice mold. *Ca fait an peu boui-boui, mais il ya de la jolie moisissure.*

And finally, when asked if you have anything to declare upon leaving France, say:
- ℮ I like Spain better. *Je prefere l'Espagne.*

SOURCE: HTTP://YOYO.CC.MONASH.EDU.AU /~MONGOOSE /FRENCH /PHRASES.HTML

"Instead of learning a foreign language, I grew hair under my arms."
—Sue Mollinsky

Cockney and British Slang

In Cockney, people use an expression that rhymes with what they're really trying to say. Here are some popular expressions right now.

- ℮ Britney Spears: A beer
- ℮ Brad Pitt: A shit
- ℮ Mork & Mindy: Windy
- ℮ Jackson Pollock: Bollock (testicles)
- ℮ Winona Ryder: Cider

And a few words and expressions:

- ℮ Mumblers: A girl in tight shorts with moving "lips"
- ℮ Up on blocks: Menstruating
- ℮ Pictures of the queen: Paper money

SOURCE: LONDONSLANG.COM

In cockney slang, the rhyming equivalent for going to the bathroom is "taking a Donald Trump."

The word *toilet* used to mean "grooming," which is why "toilet water" isn't water from the bowl.

Smart-Ass Additions to Signs

The Toilet Papers printed some signs and what people had added below them:

- To "Please do not cross the yellow lines" someone added "It takes forever to untangle them again."
- To "Please do not throw matches into the urinals" someone added "The crabs have learned to vault."
- To "Mr. Chan will be cremated on Monday, April 3, at 2 p.m." someone added "Can you put him on low? I can't make it until 3."
- "Jesus died for your sins" someone added "There you go, I didn't even know he was sick."

The English word *loo* derives from the fact that British hotels once wrote the number "100" on bathroom doors so other people wouldn't know they were going to the bathroom; "100" looked like "loo," and that's how the word developed.

SOURCE: FUNTRIVIA.COM

Silly Names

Adolph Oliver Nipples
Amanda B. Reckonedwith
Annie Enormous Fanny
Buster Hyman
Helen A. Handbasket
Rufus Leaking
Sam Which
Seymour Butts
Stan Dup
Sue d'Bastards
Tyrone Shoelaces
Wanda Party
Wendy Shoofitz
Will Uyashadup
Yuri Tarded

Alicia Gottlaid
Anita Fixx
Bee Verhunt
Dee Flower
Robin Cradles
Sal M'nella
Sara Doctor Inahouse
Stan Back
Stu Pott
Titus A. Drum
Van Tasstic
Wendy Lottery
Will N. Testament
Will Yewmarrieemee

SOURCES: *The Ultimate List of Stupid Names* BY MICHAEL DARE, ON THE INTERNET AND HTTP://HOME.EARTHLINK.NET /~DARE2B /STUPIDNAMES.HTML

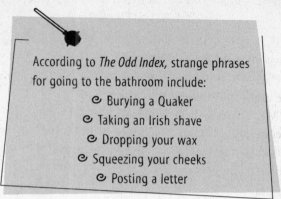

According to *The Odd Index,* strange phrases
for going to the bathroom include:

- Burying a Quaker
- Taking an Irish shave
- Dropping your wax
- Squeezing your cheeks
- Posting a letter

FOR PEOPLE WITH SMARTS
Here's What the World's Smartest Woman Says . . .

Marilyn vos Savant, listed in the *Guinness Book of World Records* Hall of Fame
as having the highest IQ in the world—228—has a column called "Ask
Marilyn" in *Parade* magazine. Some of these questions and answers have been
included in her book *Ask Marilyn:*

- **What are the worst things we teach our kids?** That knowing science is nice but not necessary, and that knowing about sex is necessary but not nice.
- **Why don't psychics ever win lotteries?** They do, because they have the same chance as anyone else of winning a lottery. The question should be why don't they always win the lottery?
- **Is it true that no two snowflakes are alike?** Probably, but no people . . . parakeets and . . . pickles are exactly alike either. So why is it such a big deal for snowflakes?
- **How can you tell if you're awake or dreaming?** If you wonder if you're dreaming, you're dreaming.

"My definition of an intellectual is someone
who can listen to the *William Tell Overture*
without thinking of the Lone Ranger."
—Billy Connolly

Could You Have Passed the Eighth Grade a Century Ago?

Here are a few sample questions from a test given in Salina, Kansas:

- Give nine rules for the use of capital letters.
- Define verse, stanza, and paragraph.
- What are the principal parts of a verb?
- A wagon box is 2 feet deep, 10 feet long, and 3 feet wide. How many bushels of wheat will it hold?
- Find the interest of $512.60 for 8 months and 18 days at 7 percent.
- What is the cost of a square farm at $15 per acre, the distance around which is 640 rods?
- Give two rules for spelling words with final "e." Name two exceptions under each rule.
- Name and describe the following: Monrovia, Odessa, Manitoba, Hecla, Yukon, St. Helena, Juan Fernandez, Aspinwall, and Orinoco.

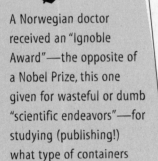

A Norwegian doctor received an "Ignoble Award"—the opposite of a Nobel Prize, this one given for wasteful or dumb "scientific endeavors"—for studying (publishing!) what type of containers his patients chose when submitting urine samples.

Silly Latin

- *Gramen artificiosum odi.* I hate Astroturf.
- *Ex post fucto.* Lost in the mail.
- *Veni vidi velcro.* I came, I saw, I stuck around.
- **Rigor morris.** The cat is dead.
- *Log floggit cum palma folliculus.* If you don't stop it, you'll go blind.
- *Domino vobiscum.* The pizza guy's here.
- *Erectionus finalum.* Anna Nicole Smith is here, Gramps.
- *Veni, veni, veni.* I came, I came, I came.
- *Sharpei diem.* Seize the Wrinkled Dog.
- *Bodicus mutilatimus, unemploymi forevercus.* Better take the nose ring out before the job interview.
- *Minutus cantorum, minutus balorum, minutus carborata descendum pantorum.* A little song, a little dance, a little seltzer down your pants.

The major expert on flatulence, Dr. Michael Levitt, jokingly called "Dr. Fart," has authored or co-authored 275 articles on flatulence in medical journals.

Not-So-Fuzzy Math

- 2,000 pounds of Chinese soup: won ton
- Half of a large intestine: 1 semicolon
- Basic unit of laryngitis: hoarsepower
- 365.25 days of drinking low-calorie beer: 1 lite year
- Ethics required not to be a lawyer: 1 scruple
- Lawnmowing required to buy a cheap car: 500 yards
- Salt to take with a politician's statement: 1 grain
- 2,000 pounds of midgets: 1 short ton

Intellectual Graffiti

- Oedipus was a motherfucker.
- Charybdis sucks.
- Luther eats worms.
- Shakespeare eats bacon.
- Melville eats blubber.
- Kubla Kahn.
- Immanuel Kant.
- Neitzsche is pietzsche
- Help stamp out and eradicate superfluous redundancy.
- If God had wanted us to have the metric system, Jesus would have had ten apostles.
- Some nights it all seems so feudal.
- Be suspicious of all native-born Esperanto speakers.
- Santa's elves are just a bunch of subordinate clauses.

Dumb Questions People Ask Librarians

- Do you have a list of all the books I've ever read?
- Which outlets in the library are best for my hairdryer?
- Why were so many Civil War battles fought on national park sites?
- I need to find out Ibid's first name for my bibliography.

Trick Quiz

1. What month(s) has twenty-eight days?
2. If a doctor gives you three pills and tells you to take one pill every half-hour, how long would it be before all the pills had been taken?
3. If you go to bed at 8:00 at night and wind the alarm so it will go off at 9:00 the next morning, how many hours of sleep would you get before being awakened by the alarm?
4. If a farmer had 17 sheep and all but 9 died, how many live sheep were left?

(See the next page for answers.)

Answers: 1. All of them. 2. 1 hour. If you take one at 1 and another at 1:30 and another at 2 they will be taken up in one hour. 3. 1—a wind-up clock knows no difference between the morning and afternoon. 4. 9 live sheep.

Sexy Shakespeare

Reinhold Aman, who produces fascinating books and articles about cursing and politically incorrect statements and writing, wrote an article in his *Maledicta Monitor* titled "Penile Shakespeare."

A survey by Scott Paper Company found that people with advanced degrees were more likely to read on the toilet than those who had not gone on to college. One could easily pooh-pooh this study on the basis that less-educated people are less likely to read in general, but . . .

e He said that Shakespeare wrote a few plays about penis size: *Much Ado about Nothing* (three inches), *As You Like It* (six inches), and *A Midsummer Night's Dream* (nine inches).

e *The Tempest* is about a woman with PMS.

e *Measure for Measure* is about two men comparing their penises.

e *All's Well That Ends Well* is about simultaneous climaxing.

e *The Comedy of Errors* is about a man trying to copulate with a woman wearing panty hose.

IN THE NEWS
Outrageous Headlines from *The Weekly World News*

e "Lobster Pinches Socialite's Boob in Ritzy Restaurant"

e "Your Dead Pet's Ghost May Be Peeing on Your Carpet"

e "Heartless Doc Rejoins Siamese Twins" (allegedly, after their parent's check bounced for the surgery that separated them earlier)

e "Aliens Dead in UFO Wreck—Because They Weren't Wearing Seat Belts"

e "Cannibals Order Pizza—Then Eat the Deliveryman"

e "Carve a Turkey—The O. J. Way"

e "How to Tell if Your Dog Worships Satan"

e "Mom Delivers Her Own Baby Using a Pizza Cutter"

e "New Remote-Control Device Gives Women Orgasms—Up to 80 Yards Away"

e "Time Warp Tot Hasn't Aged a Day in 89 Years"

e "Jon Benet Ramsey's Killer Was Skyjacker D. B. Cooper"

How They'd Headline the Apocalypse

- Wall Street Journal: "World to End Tomorrow: Markets Will Close Early"
- USA Today: "That's It!"
- Washington Post: "World to End Tomorrow: Women & Minorities Hardest Hit"
- New York Post: "See Gossip about World Ending Tomorrow on p. 6"
- New York Times: "World to End Tomorrow: Story & Analysis on D14"
- GQ: "What the Well-Dressed Man Is Wearing for the End of the World"
- National Review: "Why Democrats Are Responsible for the End of the World"
- New Republic: "Why Republicans Are to Blame for the End of the World"
- American Lawyer: "The End of the World: Class-Action Suit Gold Mine?"
- People: "Best and Worst Dressed for the End of the World"
- Esquire: "Last Chance to Find Out If Kevin Spacey Is Gay before the End of the World"

Newspaper Headlines That Sounded Dirty But Weren't

- "Gators to Face Seminoles with Peters Out"
- "Governor's Penis Busy" (should have had a space between "pen" and "is")
- "Clinton Places Dick in Gore's Hands"
- "Starr Aghast at First Lady Sex Position"
- "Textron Inc., Makes Offer to Screw Company Stockholders"
- "Married Priests in Catholic Church a Long Time Coming"
- "Never Withhold Herpes Infection from Loved One"
- "Messiah Climaxes in Chorus of Hallelujahs"
- "Queen Mary Having Bottom Scraped"

New Scientist's headline that many would like to see: "Pope Joan-Paula I Approves New Contraceptive."

Actual Newspaper Headlines

- "After Cutting the Ribbon, Her Majesty then Pissed over the Bridge" (about Queen Victoria)
- "Diaper Market Bottoms Out"
- "Queen Mary Having Bottom Scraped"
- "Police Station Toilet Stolen: Cops Have Nothing to Go On"
- "Flaming Toilet Seat Causes Evacuation in High School"

> Bathroom books you *don't* want to read:
> *The Zen of Bowel Movements: A Spiritual Approach to Constipation* (Rock Rose,1995)
> *The Urine Dance of the Zuni Indians of New Mexico* (1885)
> *Golden Fountain: The Complete Guide to Urine Therapy* (Coen Van Der Kroon, 1996)

These Stories Were Really in the News!

If you want to read the crazy things that are going on out there, go on the Internet and surf to ThisIsTrue.com, NewsoftheWeird.com, Fark.com, ObscureStore.com, or BizarreNews.com, which link you to stories like the following.

A woman hired a private investigator to find out who was making **collect obscene calls to her.** The police found out, and then told her that the easiest way to stop them would be for her to stop accepting the phone charges when he called.

The 1982 National Father's Day Association awarded a man its Father of the Year Award—at about the same time the state awarded him jail time for not paying child support.

How could Eve have given Adam an apple? Evolutionary scientists have recently completed a study that seems to show that all female DNA currently in modern humans can be traced to a single woman who lived in Africa 143,000 years ago. They have named this woman "Mitochondrial Eve."

Her male counterpart, however, did not show up until 84,000 years later. He is believed to have formed gradually over centuries. At least their "relationship" was unmarred by domestic arguments, and she didn't have to deal with a bunch of friends frowning on the **84,000-year age difference,** telling her that because she was so much older it would never work out.

An apartment house in England had a major problem because their toilets faced east and they had a number of Muslim tenants. Not wanting to offend Allah, the tenants solved the problem by sitting sideways.

It's not only regular citizens who have a monopoly on accidents. At a county jail in Asheville, North Carolina, a few years ago, a prisoner who was an avid Monopoly player was having stomach problems. An X-ray revealed that **he had swallowed several houses and hotels** used in the game, probably in an attempt to get himself in the hospital. After the doctor treated his problem, he sent the man back to the sheriff with this note: "Go directly to jail. Do not pass Go. Do not collect $200."

This'll Kill 'Em
In the Riviera town of Le Lavandou, **dying isn't just a bad idea, it's against the law.** Faced with a severe lack of cemetery space, the town sprang into action with a brilliant solution. They passed a law stating: "It is forbidden without a cemetery plot to die on the territory of the commune." Obviously, the law provides no penalty for those who break the law by dying. What can they do to them? Shoot them?

A man decided to kill himself by **setting himself on fire,** and then changed his mind when he started burning. So he threw himself into a lake, forgetting that he couldn't swim, and drowned.

One more sign that Britannia will never rule the waves again: Some British Royal Navy recruits are no longer firing live shells during training, but just *pretending* to fire them while shouting "Bang." Humiliated sailors forced to do this described it as a "sad joke," like "playing cowboys and Indians in the school ground."

Odd Animal Encounters
A bed and breakfast in North Yorkshire wants you to have a cow. Worse still, they want you to cuddle her. The owner of the **Cattle Ready to Be**

Cuddled, Bill Ward of Dunsley Hall Hotel, came up with this idea when he thought his guests might want to get "hands-on with nature." He even gives his guests a tape of mooing cows to help them sleep at night after a full day of cow cuddling.

East Bradford, Pennsylvania, authorities are puzzled over finding a series of mutilated goats that were beheaded, their hooves restrained with duct tape, and their carcasses filled to bursting with **baked beans!** So far, no one knows beans about this bizarre episode.

Dumb People

In an almost too-dumb-to-believe story, an Illinois head-shrinker was reported to the authorities for his bizarre therapy, which included convincing a patient that she had **hundreds of different personalities.**

One of them supposedly liked to bake an unorthodox meatloaf, made of **Jeffrey Dahmer–type ingredients,** for thousands of guests. The woman only realized that either she or her psychiatrist was nuts when she figured out that "no way could I be eating two thousand people a year" (at least not without any leftovers around in the refrigerator).

A woman needed to go to the bathroom desperately and so she stopped at a pub. It was filled with smoke and the owner told her the place was on fire and they were waiting for the fire trucks. She begged to go anyway. (They refused her.)

A woman in Bogota, Colombia, thought she had found a clever way of sneaking a gun to her friend in prison: by **stuffing it up her butt.** Not surprisingly, she was in agony, but she couldn't admit what caused it. So she said **she was pregnant.**

She was taken to a hospital, and only after three days in which no baby emerged, and she got tired of hearing "push, push," did she admit the cause of her pain was in her other end, the result of her bum smuggling plan. Lucky for her she didn't go off half-cocked.

What's in a Name?

It must be hard enough being named "Jack" and having all these a-holes trying to make jokes about, "You don't know Jack" or "jacking off." Now they've got another problem.

A co-pilot named Jack happened to meet a friend on a corporate jet who heartily greeted him by calling out "Hi, Jack!" This was overheard by someone in the control tower who thought he heard the word *hijack*.

If that seems silly to you, remember that if these guys were rocket scientists, they'd be working for NASA and not La Guardia. They called out a swarm of local and county police, a Sheriff's Department SWAT team, the FBI, and other federal authorities, and surrounded the plane.

To prevent this type of fiasco from happening again, a law could be passed making all Jacks call themselves "John" at an airport. After all, it's a lot less scary for passengers sitting in a plane to look out the window and see a team of plumbers than a phalanx of police surrounding their plane.

Ian Lewis was a family-obsessed man from Lancashire, England, who spent thirty years of his life meticulously researching his family history and **constructing a four-hundred-year genealogy.** He interviewed more than two thousand relatives for this massive project, and when he was finally finished, he presented his results to his family.

That's when they admitted to him that he had been adopted! When he was one month old, he changed families and names and went to live elsewhere. Ian belatedly learned that his real name was David Thornton. So, starting from this, he is now researching his *other* family history.

The Truth about Spontaneous Human Combustion

Lots of people get all fired up on the subject of supposed spontaneous fires. For years, the tabloids have been full of stories of people minding their own damned business who burn up one day with no apparent explanation. Or was there one? Is this normal, paranormal, or just a lot of hot air?

To find out, **the FBI** decided to investigate one of the most famous cases, a woman in St. Petersburg, Florida, who was found **burnt to a crisp** in her easy chair fifty years ago. Spontaneous human combustion, for sure, everyone said.

But the FBI suspected that a burning cigarette ignited her clothes, turning the obese woman's fat into a human candle. It was thought that she might not have noticed what was happening because she was so zonked on her sleeping medication.

The California Criminalistics Institute performed an experiment by **wrapping a pig carcass in cotton** and then setting it on fire. The pig simmered and spluttered for hours until it was entirely consumed. This proved something, but because pigs don't take sleeping medication, or drink themselves into a stupor, maybe all it proves is that people who are fat pigs should be careful around fires.

Best Personal Ads

From "If You Like Piña Coladas . . . the humor and weirdness of personal ads":

> *"BLAH BLAH BLAH Professional, blah blah blah, white male, blah blah blah, 32, blah blah blah, nice looking, blah blah blah, seeks blah blah blah, fun, blah blah blah, energetic, blah blah blah, creative, blah blah blah, female."*

Another unusual personal was this recent ad in *The New York Review of Books*:

> *PRETTY WOMAN, 53, will exchange sexual favors and affection for routine dog walking. Large poodle likes Maine, Mozart, and mysteries. Owner/food source likes same, plus hiking, biking, and kayaking. Both are blonde.*

Worst Ad in a Newspaper

Sumitoma, a Japanese steel company, came out with a pipe called Sumitomo High Toughness and took out a two-page spread in popular business newspapers saying: "SHT—FROM SUMITOMA."

And as if that weren't bad enough, another read: "SUMITOMA BRINGS SHT to the U.S."

For Rent?

The Best Newspaper Real Estate Ad

> *2 BDRM house: with fireplace, garage, work shop & large yard. $220 per month. No children, no pets, no smokers, no drinkers, no drugs, no gays, & no freethinkers; no Buddhists, no Baptists, no Moonies, no Junies, no Communists, sympathizers, room deodorizers, nor tranquilizers; no creeps, no punks, no fools, no losers, no onions, & hold the mayo. In fact, never mind . . . I'm going to sell the property & move to Denver or India or someplace. (And no musicians!)*

If you have any questions as to whether advertising in toilets isn't the next thing, a study found that 62 percent of people remembered the exact message in a bathroom ad—as compared to 16 percent of people remembering advertisements they saw on a billboard.

The Second Best Newspaper Real Estate Ad

> *Free 1 can of pork & beans with purchase of 3 br 2 bath home.*

# Money

HOW TO GAMBLE AND WIN
How to Win Super Lotteries

Think you're going to win one of those super lottery jackpots? According to a professor of statistics at California State University, if you bought fifty lottery tickets a week, you would win a typical super jackpot once every 30,000 years. You're three times more likely to be **killed by an airplane falling on you** than to win a super lottery. Furthermore, if every time you drove one mile you bought a ticket, you would have to drive the distance of 165 roundtrips to the moon before you won.

Not So Fast

If you do win, though, *Bottom Line* suggests you immediately:

- Sign the back of your ticket.
- Photocopy the front and back of the ticket and put it in a **safe deposit box.**
- Type up a separate statement of authenticity and have your signature on it notarized.
- **Don't spend the entire pot** because you may have won the jackpot with others and have to share it.
- Remember that the **tax could be as high as 40 percent,** another reason not to run out and spend the entire sum immediately.
- Get an unlisted phone number—right away.

Improving Your Chances of Receiving More $$$

Bottom Line also included suggestions on how to get a bigger jackpot by choosing numbers others won't, so the amount you win will be bigger because you won't have to split it with anyone.

- Choose several numbers higher than thirty-one. People who play birthdays and anniversaries can't choose those numbers.
- **Multiples of seven** are good because suspicious people don't choose those.
- Numbers that form patterns on a card, say a vertical or horizontal line on your betting card, should be avoided because they're popular.

Slot Machines

Bottom Line says that the machines with the **highest payoffs** are located three or four in from a busy aisle, where the most people will see and hear the payoffs. The worst slot machines are those nearest the entrance to a casino showroom, because many people waiting to get into a show (or buy tickets) play to pass the time, regardless of the payoff.

Other slot machines with bad payoffs include those at airports, hotels, and cruise ships because they've also got a captive audience who'll play regardless of the odds.

There's no report yet on the newest slot machines: 25-cent slots attached to stationery bicycles in Atlantic City—so your wallet can get thinner while you do.

And finally, an Australian psychology magazine analyzed **people who talk to slot machines.** They found that women were more likely to do so than men, that what they said made no sense, and that talking to a slot machine did not alter in any way hitting the jackpot—or not hitting it.

No one could figure out why areas with heavy gambling had a higher number of adult diaper purchases—and it wasn't that winners became so excited that they literally peed in their pants. It turns out that some compulsive gamblers wear diapers so they don't have to leave a slot machine or table to go to the bathroom if they are winning or waiting for a particular machine to pay off.

Keno

The odds of hitting all fifteen numbers on a fifteen-spot ticket is one in almost five hundred *billion*. (Which is only slightly higher than the chance of **O. J. Simpson** finding "the real killer.")

Is It Safer to Play the Stock Market or in a Casino?

Marilyn vos Savant, the woman alleged to have the highest IQ in the world, says stocks might be the safer bet because the company you're investing in is working to make the stock go *up*. At a casino, they want you to *lose*. She also explains that when you're playing in a casino, you're betting *against* the house, but when you play Wall Street, you're betting *with* the house.

Lotteries are a tax on people
who are bad at math.

Great Sweepstake Advice

You've heard the joke about the man who complains to God that he's never won the lottery and begs Him for help to win the next one. "Make it easier for me," says God. "Buy a ticket for a change." That's an obvious tip. Here are some that are not as apparent and you usually don't hear.

- ℮ Look for the same contest in different issues of the same magazine or newspaper. Some sweeps use different P.O. boxes in order to figure out which one pulls best.
- ℮ Look to see if it says only one person in a family can enter, and if not, **you can legally increase your chances** by entering several times.
- ℮ **Enter local contests** instead of national ones because they have fewer people entering them so you have a better chance of winning.
- ℮ **Crumple the form.** Some people have found that doing this gives the paper more volume, and makes it stand out from other entries. The same is true if you fold the paper into an accordion, which makes it more likely to stick to the hands of someone picking it up.
- ℮ If the contest says to write down your phone number, remember to **include your area code.** This is a common mistake that disqualifies many winners.

SOURCE: *Retirement Secrets: What They Don't Want You to Know*

> Look for contests with short entry periods, which also limits the number of people you'll compete with.

How to Win Radio Contests

Stations that run contests regularly often announce them at the same time each day or each week. So figure out when to listen and call them then.

In addition, when you call the station, you frequently get a recording saying that the lines are busy and to try later. Ignore it and don't hang up. Calls are sometimes answered from these lines.

WORK
 ## Reasons to Go to Work Naked

- Your boss is always yelling, "I wanna see your ass in here by 8:00!"
- People stop stealing your pens after they've seen where you keep them.
- Get out of all those gifts you have to buy by saying, "I'd love to chip in, but I left my wallet in my pants."
- Diverts attention from the fact that you also came to work drunk.
- Gives "bad hair day" a whole new meaning.
- No one ever steals your chair.

 ## Office Sayings

- "This office is like a cactus plant except our pricks are inside."
- "Give a man food and he can eat for a day. Give a man a job and he can only eat for thirty minutes on break."
- "A cubicle is just a padded cell with a door."
- "I'd like to quit my job but I need the sleep."
- "I'm just working here until a good fast food job opens up."
- "I pretend to work. They pretend to pay me."

WANT TO CATCH UP ON EXTRA WORK?
Do what *Men's Health* reported that one busy entrepreneur does. He keeps the toilet tank top clear and goes to the bathroom seated backward, facing the top of the tank. Then he works while he's seated on the john.

- "If work is so terrific, why do they have to pay you to do it?"
- "I thought I wanted a career. Turns out I just wanted paychecks."
- "I always give 100 percent at work: 12 percent on Monday, 23 percent on Tuesday, 40 percent on Wednesday, 20 percent on Thursday, and 5 percent on Friday."

 ## Names for Office Cubicles

- Tomb of the Unknown Bureaucrat
- Slack in the Box
- Yuppie Terrarium
- Luxury Manhattan Apartmen
- International Porn Downloading Headquarters

New Office Buzzwords

- **Floor whore:** Salesman who pounces on people who come to the store or lot.
- **Booth bunny:** Pretty woman who stands at a convention exhibit and knows nothing about the product.
- **Assmosis:** The process of becoming successful by kissing up to the boss.
- **Uninstalled or deinstalled:** Fired.
- **Xerox subsidy:** Swiping free photocopies from the workplace.
- **Working for the mouse:** Working for Disney.
- **Dilberted:** Exploited and oppressed by your boss.
- **Flight risk:** Employee suspected of planning to leave the company or department.
- **Flexecutive:** Worker whose hours and place of work are flexible due to the new technology.
- **Work judo:** Getting someone else to do your work without looking as if you're doing it.
- **Pitch the bitch:** Making a presentation to a female.

Office Talk That Sounds Dirty . . . but Isn't

- "I need to whip it out by five!"
- "Put it in my box before I leave."
- "If I have to lick one more, I'll gag!"
- "Hmmm . . . I think it's out of fluid."
- "It's an entry-level position."
- "When do you think you'll be getting off oday?"

Five Ways to Squirrel Away Money

These are from Charles A. Jaffe, Personal Finance columnist of the *Boston Globe*:

1. **Keep all change.** "Pay in paper money, round to the next dollar, pocket the change, and don't spend it." Then, each time you reach $20, deposit it in a savings account.
2. **Cut a dollar a day** from your spending and put that aside. After you're comfortable with that, take another dollar away.
3. **Continue paying bills** even when they stop. For example, if you've paid off your car loan, continue putting that same monthly payment aside.
4. **Put windfalls into the bank,** because unexpected money is often spent frivolously.
5. **Try to put off purchases.** If you lived without it yesterday, chances are you can live without it today.

JOB INTERVIEWS

 ## What Those Job Descriptions Really Mean

- **Some overtime required:** Some time each night and some time each weekend.
- **Career-minded:** Female applicants must be childless (and remain that way).
- **No phone calls please:** We've filled the job with the boss's nephew. This request for résumés is just a legal formality.
- **Must have an eye for detail:** We have no quality control.

Résumés of Famous Historical Figures

- JULIUS CAESAR: My last job involved a lot of office politics and back stabbing. I'd like to get away from all that.

- LADY GODIVA: I look forward to working for a company where the dress is casual.

- JOSEPH GUILLOTINE: I can give your company a head start on the competition

- **Relaxed environment:** All our employees are on drugs.
- **Go-getter:** Job involves "Go get me this, go get me that."
- **Opportunities for advancement:** After three years you get to run the fry machine.
- **Energetic self-starter:** You'll be working on commission.
- **Entry-level position:** We will pay you the lowest wages allowed by law.
- **Experience required:** We do not know the first thing about any of this.

- **Fast learner:** You will get no training from us.
- **Good organizational skills:** You'll be handling the filing.
- **Make an investment in your future:** This is a franchise or a pyramid scheme.
- **Much client contact:** You handle the phone or make client "cold calls."
- **Quick problem-solver:** You will work on projects months behind schedule.

"Tired of working for only $9.75 per hour? We offer profit sharing. Flexible hours. Starting pay: $7 to $9 per hour."
—Actual classified ad

When you go in for a job interview, be sure to ask if they ever press charges.

Jobs: The Good, the Bad, and the Ugly

Best Jobs

- **Porn czar:** The position of Obscenity and Pornography Complaints Ombudsman was recently available in Utah, and paid $75,000 for six months. Although part of the job consisted of (getting paid to) go through nudie magazines and adult videos, the job was filled by a Mormon virgin who had never seen a porn movie before. The position may be available again.
- **Virgin deflowerer:** Some wag once said that the only virgin in her house was the olive oil. But in some places, there are a lot of virgins around, more than they want. For example, in Guam, there are men who supposedly work full time deflowering young virgins—*and get paid to do it*, because virgins there are not allowed to marry.

Worst Jobs

- Proctologist in a nursing home
- Kamikaze pilot
- Sperm scraper at peep shows, porn theaters, and so on
- Bomb squad technician
- Gravedigger on the graveyard shift
- (They left out such fun jobs as chicken sexers, armpit sniffers, and rat tattooers—who mark lab rats.)

SOURCE: PLAYBOY.COM

> **GETTING TO THE BOTTOM OF THE PROBLEM**
> A mysterious odor that caused employees to become nauseated and dizzy turned out to be the result of too many urinal cakes in the men's room.

Most Stressful Job

Not police, as you would think, but it was firefighters who had the most stress and anxiety according to one study. That study also showed that musical instrument repairmen have the least stressful job.

Most Dangerous Job

Probably President of the United States of America, because his risk of being killed is 175 times greater than that of a law enforcement officer. As for the danger of an occupation more people occupy, it's fishing. (You learned that when you saw *The Perfect Storm*, right?) It came in slightly ahead of logging and twice as high as airline pilot, which came in third.

SEE "FISHING," PAGE 122.

BOSSES

Differences Between You and Your Boss

- When you take office supplies, you're **pilfering**. When your boss takes office supplies, he's **requisitioning**.
- When you pad your expense accounts, you're **embezzling**. When your boss pads her expense accounts, she's **meticulous**.
- When you sit and do nothing, you're **loafing**. When your boss sits and does nothing, he's **thinking**.
- When you fall asleep at work, you're **snoozing**. When your boss falls asleep at work, she's **power napping**.
- When you take a long time, you're **slow**. When your boss takes a long time, she's **thorough**.
- When you make a mistake, you're an **idiot**. When your boss makes a mistake, he's **only human**.
- When you do something without being told, you're **overstepping your authority**. When your boss does something without being told, that's **initiative**.

> When you take a long lunch with friends, you're goofing off. When your boss takes a long lunch with friends, he's entertaining potential clients.

- When you take a stand, you're being **bull-headed**. When your boss takes a stand, she's being **firm**.
- When you please your boss, you're **apple-polishing**. When your boss pleases his boss, he's being **cooperative**.
- When you're out of the office, you're **wandering around**. When your boss is out of the office, she's **on business**.

What Bosses Mean When They Say . . .

- **Reorganization:** We're going to fire half of the department.
- **We're thinking that:** We lied.
- **Projections:** Lies.
- **Forward-looking expectations:** Complete and utter lies.
- **Performance bonus:** Bribe for not distributing those photos from the Christmas party.
- **Unexpected developments:** We lost your pension money playing the stock market.
- **Under consideration:** Never heard of it.
- **Under active consideration:** We're searching the files for it.
- **We're making a survey:** We need more time to think of an answer.

RAISES AND RECOMMENDATIONS
How to Get a Raise

In asking for a raise, you need to remember only one thing: timing. Ask for a raise when you're about to get one. If you're getting a routine raise, and you don't think it will be high enough, that's the best time to ask for more because they're already putting out money anyway.

- According to a McGill University study, the best time to ask the boss for a raise is in **January**, because that's the beginning of a new fiscal year and the purse springs are looser.
- The best day to ask for a raise is **Thursday**.
- The best time is **morning**. That's when office people are the most positive. Besides which, bosses don't want to feel bad all day because they turned you down.
- *The Practical Guide to Practically Everything* stresses that you should not be shy about claiming credit for work you've done. The farther down the ladder you are, the more you'll have to be sure your boss knows about your accomplishments. But don't compare yourself to a better paid coworker because it can backfire. Your boss may start to think that you're not worth as much as your coworker.

Honestly Described Management Styles

- Managing by hiding in the washroom
- Managing by saying, "Is that so?"
- Managing by walking faster than the employees
- Managing by staring out of the window
- Managing by Post-its
- Managing by knowing nothing

What Those Letters of Recommendation Really Mean

Wording is everything. (You've never heard of a car color called "Lemon Yellow," have you?) Now, the politest way to fire someone may be to say something like, "I really don't know how we're going to get along without you. But starting Monday, we're going to try."

What happens if someone asks for a letter of recommendation? Nowadays, if anyone says something negative about an employee—even if it's true, in fact, *especially* if it's true, they can be sued. So here's what you could truthfully write about someone you'd rather not recommend—and someone could write about you.

- **For the chronically absent:** A man like him is hard to find. It seemed her career was just taking off.
- **For an employee with no ambition:** He could not care less about the number of hours he had to put in. You would indeed be fortunate to get this person to work for you.
- **For a bad employee:** I would urge you to waste no time in making this candidate an offer of employment. All in all, I cannot say enough good things about this candidate or recommend him too highly.
- **For a stupid employee:** There is nothing you can teach a man like him. I most enthusiastically recommend this candidate with no qualifications whatsoever.
- **For a lying employee:** He was an unbelievable worker.

Finding out What Your Former Boss Thinks of You

If you're unemployed and searching for a new job, even before you start interviewing, have a friend call your former boss and make believe he's a prospective employer checking you out. That way, you can find out what your boss says about you—and more importantly, *how* he says it.

What's the difference between the pope and your boss? The pope only expects you to kiss his ring.

OTHER MONEY MATTERS
Unique Ways to Collect a Debt

They've come up with an unusual way to collect a debt in India: send one of their eunuchs after the deadbeat. **Indian eunuchs**—and there are several hundred thousand of them—are notorious for acting obnoxiously. They show up at weddings and birth celebrations, take over, swarm around everyone, and demand money to go away. If they're not paid promptly, they go around fondling the guests, acting provocatively, and worst of all, **flashing the crowd.** This sight is sufficiently disgusting that guests quickly pay them to keep everything covered.

These pariahs have generally found it difficult to find acceptable means of employment other than scaring newlyweds. Now a firm, accurately named **"Unique Recoveries,"** employs a team of these freaks and sends them to the houses of deadbeats. You've heard of strippers in America who jump out of a cake? Everyone wants these people to get back *into* the cake. Those confronted with a genuine eunuch will pay anything—even their debt—to get these "women" *not* to take it off.

Another way of collecting (or stealing) money is to show the deadbeat (or victim) a poisonous snake. This method is currently being used in Nicaragua, India, and the United States. Just showing the person a portion of the snake (which may be kept in a bag) is so effective, that one woman passed out when the "collector" showed her only a tiny portion of the snake's face.

> "People are still willing to do an honest day's work. The trouble is they want a week's pay for it."
> —Joey Adams

Wacky Questions People Ask the IRS

The IRS has a telephone service, and over the years they've collected some strange and silly questions from confused taxpayers:

- In Virginia they got a phone call from a taxpayer asking, "Is there any legal way I can cheat?"
- In Salt Lake City, a man called to ask if the cost of the clothes his wife wore to work were deductible. They told him no—some uniforms are deductible, but not regular work clothes—and he argued that if she didn't work, **she wouldn't have to wear clothes.**
- A woman called the Richmond office and asked, "My daughter just married a man I can't stand and we had to pay for the wedding. Is this cost deductible as a casualty loss?"

Tax Time

The Witchita IRS office received an angry phone call from a man who said, "I just got a letter from you all and I demand to know what it's all about." The IRS employee asked, "Would you read the letter to me, please?" The man said, "Wait a moment. I have to open it first."

ℭ One irate woman called the Indianapolis office and demanded **to talk to the computer.**

ℭ Another woman called the Indianapolis office, became flustered, and instead of asking to speak to a tax preparer, asked for "Preparation X."

ℭ **A goldfish dealer** wanted to deduct the expenses of burying one of his fish. He asked if he should keep the dead fish in case he was audited.

ℭ There's a general misunderstanding that burial expenses are always deductible. When one woman was advised that they were not, she said that if she had known that, she wouldn't have buried her husband.

ℭ Many people ask if they can claim their **dogs as "dependents."**

ℭ A taxpayer handed an IRS teller 25 cents. When asked what it was for, he responded, seemingly serious, "Isn't it true that you can pay your taxes a quarter at a time?"

ℭ An immigrant, who wasn't familiar with the American tax structure and had two dependents, called the IRS to ask where she should go to collect her $1,000 for each child.

People: Manipulating Them for Fun and Profit

HOW TO GET WHAT YOU WANT BY USING CHEAP TRICKS

How can you do what you're not supposed to do? Get what you're not supposed to get? By using cheap psychological tricks. Here are a few from the psychological literature, compiled in an interesting book titled, what else, *Cheap Psychological Tricks:*

Want to Cut in Line?

Whether it's a movie, airport, car line, or whatever, it's easier to get people to let you cut in *nearer* the front than further back in the line. As people get closer, they become more optimistic about getting in and won't see you as a threat. Plus, they're probably in a better mood.

Some people, when cutting in line, don't ask the person if they can cut in front of them, but instead ask the person in *back* of where they want to be if they can get in *back* of them. This is ridiculous, of course, because nobody cares if someone gets behind them, but that's exactly why it works. And the person in back of them (now in back of you) who's been cut in on is usually too astounded and confused to protest.

> Are you worried about people walking in on you when you're on a public toilet? You really might have something to worry about on an airplane. For safety reasons, they have a lever on the outside of the door that enables someone to open it from the outside.

Want to Squeeze a Secret out of Someone?

℮ If you beg them to tell you, they'll realize how important what they knows is, and it gives them the upper hand, which they'll enjoy too much to give up. **Act indifferent** and uninterested in the secret and they may want to share it—so you know how good their secret is.

- Ask about gossip item and then **say nothing.** Many people are uncomfortable by silences and will fill it in with what you want to know. Staring at someone while waiting may also add to their discomfort.
- **Turning gossip into a game** may entice someone to play along with you, while also subtly letting their guard down enough to tell you what you want to know. For example, you might say something like, "Let me guess why she's leaving her husband." Or, "Come on, give me a hint why he's going to jail."
- **Tell a secret about yourself** (or someone else). They may feel obliged to reciprocate.

WANT TO FIND OUT WHAT SOMEONE'S *REALLY* THINKING?
Stop listening to his words and start looking into his eyes. Pupils expand when people are positive about something; they shrink when they're turned off. If you see a car you'd like to buy, your pupils expand. But if you see someone on the street you'd rather avoid, back they go. It's a trick a lot of poker players use successfully.

Other Tips

Reaching Real People on the Phone
If you don't want to get stuck in voicemail hell with robots talking to you instead of people, the minute you hear a prerecorded announcement hit zero—and just keep hitting it. Most of the time you will be connected to a real person.

Using a Restaurant Bathroom
Richard Smith's *Guide to Getting Even!* jokingly suggests that if a restaurant won't let you use the bathroom when you're not eating there, smile and tell them you didn't use their bathroom when you *did* eat there the last time, so they owe you one.

Dealing with People Who Don't Split Checks
If you go out with people who never reach for the check, Smith suggests you take the check and actually split it in two, hand them the lower part and say, "Let's split it." Alternately, put the check on the table, lean down, and blow the check over to their side.

Want to keep a seat empty next to you on a train or bus or at the movies? Smile and nod at people as they approach your seat.

How to Get out of a Traffic Ticket

Officer, I was trying to keep up with the other traffic.

Yes, I know there are no other cars around. That's how far ahead of me they are.

When one driver leaves his car for a few minutes, say, to stop in a store, he always **leaves the windshield wipers turned to a fast wipe** so a policeman can't put a ticket in them. (This works best when it's raining.)

A twenty-three-year-old woman in British Columbia led a group of cops on a high-speed chase. After she got caught, she revealed that she had been masturbating while they chased her at 120-miles-per-hour. She claimed that she suffered from a "sexual speed fetish" and, according to *Real Sex*, told them that "I only come when I smell the aroma of hot tires."

Some recommend (seemingly accidentally) sniffling and sneezing on your driver's license, because the officer then doesn't want to touch the license—**unless he's wearing gloves.** This works better if you're a woman. Although if you're a man, he might *really* want to get away.

Nice Try, But Here's Your Ticket

"I just washed my car but forgot the towels. I didn't want to get all those water sports on the car—and needed it to dry real quick."

A forty-two-year-old, obviously intoxicated driver said to the officer: "Please give me a break. I'm drunk."

CAN YOU CRY AND KVETCH YOUR WAY OUT OF TICKETS?

A lot of people cry, which may work—but again, only for women. Some policemen, though, say that even if it is a woman who's crying, it increases her chances of getting a ticket because the officer is uncomfortable and wants to get away as quickly as possible—without hearing any excuses.

Getting Warmer . . .

Because policemen love donuts, someone got out of a ticket by saying that her mother had called to tell her that the **"hot donuts"** sign had just gone up at the local Krispy Kreme.

Someone who was stopped for speeding told the policeman that **his gold-fish needed fresh water.** (This worked because he kept a plastic bag with a fish in the backseat.)

Bet You Never Thought of This!

A teacher suspended for drunk driving was reinstated when she argued that she wasn't drunk but disoriented as a result of silicon poisoning. She claimed her breast implant had burst while she was driving.

Gastrointestinal problems or feminine hygiene problems are commonly used, which sometimes also work. Some policemen, however, follow the person home or to a rest stop and have a ticket waiting for them when they get out of the bathroom or wherever.

SOURCES: CARCONNECTION.COM, APB NEWS, *Bizarre Magazine*

HOW TO PICK SOMEONE UP
Lines That Should Work—and Won't Offend

- "My name is Chance. Do I have one?"
- "Can I borrow a quarter? I promised I'd call my mother when I found the woman I was going to marry."
- "I make more money than you can spend."
- "Can you call 911 for me? I think my heart stopped beating when I saw you."
- "Hi, I'm Mr. Right. Were you looking for me?"
- Take the ice cube out of your drink, smash it on the bar, and say, "Now that I've broken the ice, let's talk."
- "I'm writing a phone book. Can I have your number?"
- "Is there a rainbow, because you're the treasure I've been searching for."
- "Inheriting $80 million doesn't mean much when you have a weak heart."

"Some man tried to convince me to have sex by saying he would only put it in for a minute. What am I, a microwave?"
—Beverly Mickins

- "Hello. I'm a thief and I'd like to steal your heart."
- "Do you believe in love at first sight or should I walk by again?"
- "I seem to have misplaced my phone number. Can we switch houses?"

Slightly Dirtier Lines—but Go for It!

- "If I told you that you had a terrific body, would you hold it against me?"
- "What's a nice girl like you doing in a dirty mind like mine?"
- "Those are some nice jeans you have on. You think I can talk you out of them?"
- "I'd really like to see how you look when I'm naked."
- "Your dress would look great in a crumpled heap on my bedroom floor."
- "Hi. My name is milk. Can I be your mustache?"
- "Fuck me if I'm wrong, but is your name Helga?"
- "My name isn't Elmo but you can tickle me anytime you want to."
- "I'd like to tickle your belly button—from the inside out."
- "Do you wash your pants in Windex . . . because I can see myself in them."

Lines Almost Guaranteed to Fail

- "Nice legs, what time do they open?"
- Looking down at your crotch, say "Well, it's not going to suck itself."
- "I wish you were a door so I could bang you all day long."
- "You've got 206 bones in your body. Want one more?"
- "Can I buy you a drink or do you just want the money?"
- "My name is _____. Remember that because you'll be screaming it later."

Serious Advice from the Expert

Ross Jeffries, said to be the real-life model for Frank T. J. MacKey in the movie *Magnolia*, is the author of a book titled *How to Get the Woman You Desire into Bed*. A *New York Post* story chose these as Jeffries's most promising techniques:

- **Pretend you're gay:** Say, "If I weren't gay I'd be all over you because you're beautiful. . . . Do you have a brother? Do you have a boyfriend I can steal from your lovely clutches?" Once she's relaxed because she thinks you won't hit on her and you've established that she has no boyfriend, you come in for the kill: "I have a confession. I'm not really gay. I just had to talk to you—you're so beautiful."

⌘ **Eavesdrop:** Without her knowing it, eavesdrop on her, so when you talk to her, she thinks you understand her. Try to give her back any phrases or ideas you've heard from her.

The Commandments of Pick-Ups

R. Don Steele, Jeffries's competitor and enemy (Jeffries is suing him), is the author of *How to Date Young Women*. He offers these as commandments in his "Steele Balls" dating theory. The first time you meet her:

⌘ Thou shalt not stare at her body.

⌘ Thou shalt not mention your ex or your children.

⌘ Thou shalt not look at other females.

⌘ Thou shalt not mention sex.

⌘ Thou shalt not touch except to shake hands.

Contract for a New Girlfriend

There are some men who would like future girlfriends to agree to something like the following:

Whenever my friends and I get together for a girlie chat—and whenever I talk to your friends—I will tell them that you are better hung than a large-balled Himalayan yak. After sex (which I will never refer to as "making love"), I will not expect you to cuddle me for hours till your arm goes dead. In bed, I will be happy to try any novel sexual position you fancy, especially ones where I do all the work and you just lie there, grinning. I will ruthlessly interrogate my attractive female friends and inform you if any of them have the slightest bisexual tendencies, then I'll invite them around for dinner and hide their car keys so they have to stay the night.

HOW TO HANDLE TELEMARKETERS

The single best way to get rid of a telemarketer: When you find out what company she works for, tell her that you work for the same company. Many of them are not allowed to sell to their employees. If you've got some time to spare, however, here are some ways to have fun with telemarketers.

Ask him to marry you. After he gives you his spiel, ask him if he will marry you. Then explain to him that you've asked because you're not going to give out your credit card number to a complete stranger.

Try to embarrass her. After she introduce herself, say in a sexy, husky voice, "What are you wearing?"

Repeat what he says. Make believe you're hard of hearing and ask him to repeat everything he says a few times. Shout it back to him and keep getting it wrong.

Use call waiting. Tell her you're interested in what she has to say but that you have to put her on hold for a moment while you finish another call. Then put the phone down and leave it there. Or, put her on a speaker phone, and let her listen to you eat dinner. Better yet, put your toddler on the phone.

Confuse her. When you realize she's trying to sell you something, ask, "Is this the Chinese restaurant I just called? Thanks for calling back. I'd like to place my order now." Then give her an order for Chinese food.

> ### HOW TO BORE A TELEMARKETER
> When he asks how you are, tell him you're glad he asked because no one seems to care about your hemorrhoids, your bum knee, or whatever. Describe each problem in great detail until he hangs up on you in disgust.

Do a Vegas act. Because you've got a captive audience, this is a good time to sing loud show tunes as if you were Ethel Merman. Don't hang up until he hangs up first.

Promise to call back. Ask for her phone number and say you'd like to wait until *she's* eating and then you'll call her. Or ask for her home phone number, and when she says you can't call her at home, ask, "Why not? You just called me at *my* home.

SOURCE: *How to Get Rid of a Telemarketer*

HOW TO GET REVENGE
Revenge Against Men by Jilted Women

Sweet Revenge and *The Woman's Book of Revenge* offer some bizarre but probably effective ideas on how to get back at people who deserve it:

One woman who was left by her husband for a younger woman removed the license plates from his luxury car every few weeks. Every time it happened, he had to go down to the Department of Motor Vehicles and wait in long lines to get new ones!

Another case: The romance started off wonderfully. Her husband even proposed to her dressed as Richard Gere in *An Officer and a Gentleman*. But, wrote the *National Enquirer*, this vacuum cleaner salesman was so obsessed with his job that he totally neglected her after they were married. So, to get his attention, she:

- **Put itching powder in his boxer shorts**
- Smeared a thin layer of cat food over the radiator to make the place smell funny
- Crushed **laxatives** into his instant coffee
- Scrubbed the toilet with his toothbrush
- Cut all the buttons off his favorite suit

P.S. They are now divorced.

Other Ways to Get Revenge

Of course you won't do these (my lawyer told me to write that), but here are some other ways nasty, miserable people (not you) have gotten revenge.

- Replace **hemorrhoid cream** with Vick's Vapo-Rub.
- Put a beef bouillon cube in the victim's shower head.
- **Rub fish on someone's car.** This attracts birds—and also their droppings.
- Put a small marble or a BB inside the car door, so the driver goes slightly bonkers trying to figure out the cause of the sound.
- Have his pants shortened by three inches.
- Take her dress to the cleaners and have it taken in at the waist just a bit **so that she thinks she's getting fat.**

When Jerry Lewis became angry with his agent, he got his revenge by having his agent's photograph imprinted on toilet paper.

- Save his hair from his comb or brush and put it on his pillow while he's sleeping so that he'll worry that he is losing his hair.
- Shake a can of soda or beer before giving it to your victim.
- Separate a coworker's office chair and fill it with **frozen shrimp,** which, as it melts, will prove most fragrant.
- *Stuff* prints cool stuff, such as suggesting a way to drive someone in your office crazy. If the person has a recent version of Word, when she's not around, go to her AutoCorrect function (under Tools), which corrects spelling mistakes as you type. Change it so that whenever she types a common word like *the,* it switches to *vulva,* or some startling word like that.

SOURCES: *Sweet Revenge, The Woman's Book of Revenge*

Take That!

A woman suspected her spouse was having an affair after he began cruelly telling her she had lost her looks and insisted she leave the house they had lived in for fifteen years. She did, but before she left, she sewed miniature shrimp into the hems of all the curtains in the house. The other woman who moved into the house was never able to get rid of that smell, and finally moved away—taking the curtains with her to the new place.

More Fun Ways to Get Even

Richard Smith's *Guide to Getting Even!* jokingly suggests the following:

- **Noisy upstairs neighbors:** Attach speakers to your ceiling and insert a repeating patriotic tape or "The Best of the Mormon Tabernacle Choir" in it. Set the control at full volume. Go away for the summer.
- **Neighbor's dog:** Your neighbor's little dog relieves himself on your lawn? Install a lawn sprinkler and wait until the dog is right above one of the sprinklers, turn it on, and watch the dog fly. Or get a slingshot, wait until the droppings harden, and then return the dog's droppings to the owner.

HOW TO TELL IF SOMEONE'S LYING

The eyes have it. Research shows that it's the upper part of the face—the eyes, eyebrows, and forehead—that tend to give people away. But most people focus on the *lower* half while talking to others because we look at people's lips to help us understand what they're saying. Besides, people tend to be uncomfortable if you look them in the eye too long (especially if they're lying)!

What else should you watch for if you're trying to tell if someone is lying? Paul Ekman, one of the best-known experts in this area, says that you should look for discrepancies between what the person is saying and what is happening. For example, someone may be *saying* yes, but shaking his head in a slight no at the same time. Ekman also suggests you look for microexpressions that betray the person, for example, a very brief look of fear when he says that something didn't scare him.

> **HOW CAN A WOMAN TELL IF A MAN IS LYING TO HER?**
> His lips are moving. No, no, besides the standard verbal and nonverbal cues already mentioned above, one study found that men who were lying to women usually looked longer and deeper into their eyes than when they were telling the truth.

What are some common things people say when they're lying? According to Dr. Alan Hirsch, of the Rush-Presbyterian-St. Luke's Medical Center in Chicago, who's another well-known expert on lying, people are more likely to make mistakes, verbal gaffes, and use stilted speech. They often expand contractions, saying things like "did not" instead of "didn't," or they use qualifiers and explanatory words, like "sometimes" or "generally."

Any other ways to tell if someone's stretching the truth? One study showed that liars tend to speak at a slightly higher pitch when they're lying than they do when they're not. And another study found that they tend to use their hands less than when they tell the truth. So if someone normally gesticulates a lot, and suddenly stops, he or she may be saying volumes.

Who's the best lie detector? Not lie detector "experts"—because their machinery only equips them to spot lies about 50 percent of the time—but brain-damaged people. Those who can't comprehend speech are able to spot liars three-quarters of the time.

SOURCES: *Reuters, Bottom Lne, Discovery Health, National Enquirer, Cheap Psychological Tricks*

How to Keep Someone from Lying to You

A private investigator for twenty-five years, who preferred not to be named, made these suggestions:

- ☙ Sit in a higher chair, which is a subtle form of **intimidation.**
- ☙ Challenge the liar by asking for tiny details.
- ☙ **Invade the person's personal space** by getting very close, making him or her uncomfortable.
- ☙ Make believe you didn't hear correctly or you didn't understand what was being said and ask the person to repeat it. This makes it easy for the liar to change the story and tell you the truth. It also helps you catch slips and inconsistencies with which you can confront the liar.

SOURCE: WEENO.COM

"I'm a very nonviolent person."
—Serial killer Ted Bundy, after he was arrested in Florida

President Pinocchio

There were twenty-three minutes during former President Clinton's testimony on the **Monica Lewinsky** case that were a total fabrication. And the only people watching more carefully than that creep Kenneth Starr were the experts in lying, who were sure he was showing the **"Pinocchio Effect."**

When you lie, Dr. Alan Hirsch explains your blood pressure rises. This increases the blood flow to the tissues in your nose and also to your sexual organs. (That's why people often have to breathe through their mouths when they're aroused.) As a result, the inside of your nose may swell and itch slightly, leading you to scratch or rub your nose.

During that twenty-three-minute stretch of untruthful testimony, Clinton scratched his nose **almost every four minutes**—but never once during the sixteen minutes that he was truthful.

So if he wasn't turned on—which is likely considering the circumstances—then it is pretty good proof that he did indeed have sexual relations with Miss Lewinsky.

SEE "PRESIDENTIAL PENISES," PAGE 237.

"I genuinely do not believe in divorce."
—Eight(?)-times-married movie star
Elizabeth Taylor

Interesting People, Places, and Things

THE ROYAL FAMILY: WHAT THEY DON'T WANT YOU TO KNOW

Princess Di, Fergie, Andrew, and Charles

Princess Di's former private secretary, P. D. Jephson, told a number of tantalizingly terrible tidbits about her in his tell-all tome, *Shadows of a Princess: An Intimate Account by her Private Secretary*:

When Di wanted to get rid of people on her staff, she sometimes started a totally false rumor about them and then used that as an excuse to fire them. She might spread some gossip that a particular lady-in-waiting was really waiting for something else, like one more man for the night—and then **she would fire her because she was a "tramp."**

In fact, one woman she hated (other than Camilla) was the single nanny employed by Princess Charles after their separation to take care of her sons and future King, Will and Harry. Di went up to the nanny at a party and said, "So sorry to hear about the baby," as if she had been pregnant and aborted it. There was no basis for this statement and the woman sued the previously Teflon Di.

The death of Princess Di evoked some good sentiments but some **very bad poetry.** One publisher put out a book of more than a thousand poems people wrote, which contained such doggerel as: "She touched our heart, she filled a void/Her sudden death, has left us annoyed."

The *New York Times* ran a classified ad offering the toilet, bathtub, and sink that had once been owned by Princess Margaret in her former house in the Caribbean. "I have a lot of Irish customers who'd love to sit on her throne," said Des O'Brien, the owner of Langan's, who spotted the ad.

SOURCE: NEAL TRAVIS,
New York Post

The death of Di certainly didn't evoke very good sentiments in the queen. Although she has plenty of memorials for her dogs who died, she refused to erect a statue or memorial for her famous thorn-in-her-side daughter-in-law.

Di's own brother may not have treated her much better. The place where Diana was buried was previously used as **a pet cemetery,** and they had to remove the graves of dogs to make room for her body.

Princess Di once said that she didn't like Corgis, the Queen's favorite dog, because "They get the blame for all the farts."

Another person Di had bad relations with at the time of her death was **Fergie.** Although they had once been best friends, Fergie, the former wife of Prince Andrew, had borrowed a pair of shoes from Di. Di apparently had a wart problem and passed it on to Fergie through the shoes. When Fergie indiscreetly said something in public about her wart problem and how she had gotten it, Di never talked to her again.

Fergie's husband, **Prince Andrew,** is no bargain either. He has often been described as a "boor," starting as a child, when he would tie together the shoelaces of royal guardsmen who couldn't retaliate. Or he would drive his pedal car right through the favored pet dogs, scattering them. Or pour bubble bath into the stately Windsor Castle swimming pool, according to *Fergie Confidential.*

According to People Entertainment Almanac, under "the vulgar subject of money," it seems that Charles (who, like his mother, doesn't carry money around) is given a £5 note to put in the collection plate each week—but first his valet sprays, irons, and neatly folds it.

As an adult, Andrew wasn't much more refined. Once at dinner at Windsor Castle, he asked a young girl what she did for a living. When she said she was a secretary, he said, loudly so that everyone could hear him, "How terribly uninteresting. Is that the best you can find to do?"

Speaking of class, or lack thereof, **Prince Charles** has a tattoo.

The Queen Mother

The *Guardian,* a liberal English newspaper, ran a joking quiz titled, "How Much Do You Love the Queen Mother?" In this funny multiple choice questionnaire—in which they bluntly asked if her title was **"World's Oldest Parasite"**—they asked readers to state what they thought the centenarian has contributed to Britain. Possible answers included:

- "She has kept the gin industry going."
- "No one has done more for Great Britain, although I can't think of anything off the top of my head."
- "Nothing. She has kept the people servile, and perpetuated the class system that is the canker of society."

It may seem as if this says everything, but Christopher Hitchens, writing in *Vanity Fair,* added a few other choice facts she'd probably not want others to know:

- The Queen mother drinks **a bottle of gin a day.** ("Hence, perhaps, the radiant and perpetual smile, to say nothing of the waving.")
- She wears a colostomy bag.
- She has a £6 million bank overdraft and no one wants to ask her to pay up.
- In the middle of the morning, she has called down to the palace kitchen for a drink, saying, "Will one of you queens please bring this old queen a large gin and tonic."

The Queen Mother had her hip replacement done twice, the second time when she was ninety-seven. For this second surgery, she chose the same doctor as for the first. Only by then, **her male doctor had become a female doctor.**

The Queen

The world's richest woman receives £16 million a year—on which, until fairly recently, she didn't have to pay taxes. In addition, the state picks up an additional £40 million annually to maintain her royal palaces, plus £10 million for her private planes, *and £3* million for her private train. Yet the Queen is so notoriously frugal that she goes around turning out lights at Buckingham Palace.

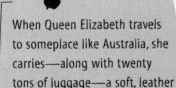

When Queen Elizabeth travels to someplace like Australia, she carries—along with twenty tons of luggage—a soft, leather white toilet seat. (But some say that it's really Prince Charles who carries his own toilet seat when he goes away.)

When the Queen went to Italy, Buckingham Palace let it be known that she was not to be served garlic, spaghetti, or "messy" tomato sauces. After all, it's hard to eat long strands of spaghetti daintily, as befits the queen, or greet others after a garlic-packed meal.

Two of the largest gems in Queen Elizabeth's crown are paste. The big red ruby right in the center is **a cheap imitation** with a tiny red ruby in the center. The seemingly gargantuan sapphire on the top is just two smaller much cheaper sapphires glued together.

Recently, Queen Elizabeth **personally wrung the neck of a pheasant** to put it out of its misery after one of her hunting dogs nearly killed it. On another occasion, she picked up a rabbit her dog had killed and gave it to the kitchen staff, saying, "We can eat this."

SURPRISING TRUE STORIES ABOUT FAMOUS PEOPLE IN HISTORY

Nuns claim the last words of **Mother Teresa** were, "Jesus, I love you. Jesus, I love you." Her doctor said her last words were, "I can't breathe."

Remember all those great stories about **Christopher Columbus** they taught you in school? Here's a shocker they didn't tell you, but was revealed in the *Best of the World's Worst* book.

When Christopher Columbus met the Arawak natives in the Caribbean island of Hispaniola (now Haiti and the Dominican Republic), he instituted a rule whereby everyone older than fourteen had to come up with a certain amount of goods (i.e., goodies). And if they didn't, they could have **both their hands cut off!**

When Chris found out there wasn't a heck of a lot of gold or other valuables there for him to extort under pain of amputation, he simply "shipped those who had not previously fled or bled to death to Spain, where they were sold in the slave markets of Seville."

Stick your tongue out and go yikes: As much as you'd like to forget, you probably still remember **Elian Gonzales,** the young Cuban boy whose mother died when they tried to sail to America on a raft, resulting in a tedious custody battle and endless news about his Cuban and American families.

One interesting story got little play. When Elian's Cuban grandmother came to visit him, she asked him to stick out his tongue—and then she bit it. She also unzipped her grandson's pants and **tried to examine his genitals** to see whether they'd grown!

✎

Ted Turner, best known for owning CNN (and marrying Jane Fonda), once fired his own son, Teddy, when his company merged with Time Warner. "You're toast," he told his son. He was also quoted as saying it was "good for the company" for his son to leave.

✎

Everyone is taught that the **Taj Mahal** was erected in India by a man who was broken-hearted over his beloved wife. The truth is that this love-besotted builder had a harem containing thousands of women—and he also had a sexual relationship with one of his own daughters!

Well, with so much love in his heart, he had to be a kind man. Yeah, sure. After building the Taj Mahal, the ungrateful bastard had the chief architect and the other top artisans put to death lest they create anything to rival the Taj. The best stone masons had their working hands amputated, and those who did the delicate inlay work were blinded.

> A scam perpetrated by guides near the Taj Mahal is to direct tourists to places where the food is deliberately tainted so the diner will get the runs. When it happens, the guide takes him or her to a doctor, who collects money for the guide.

✎

The famous writer **D. H. Lawrence** supposedly turned his favorite horse into a duffel bag after it died.

✎

Even people who had bad things to say about **Mussolini** said that at least he made the trains run on time. In fact, he didn't. Someone examined the arrival and departure times of Italian trains from 1922–1945 and found that they were no better than before—or since.

✎

Joseph Hazelwood, **former captain of the oil tanker Exxon Valdez,** and best known for being so drunk that he caused one of the greatest environmental disasters in history, got hired by the New York Maritime College to teach students how to stand watch.

✎

According to the *Bathroom Trivia Book,* **John J. Audabon,** whose name is associated with the beauty of birds, killed as many as a hundred birds a day so he could look at them closely as models for his paintings. (He found that stuffed birds lost their color.)

By analyzing Beethoven's hair, a historian concluded, "his deafness, illness, and death were almost certainly the result of lead poisoning." And while this may have come from his overindulgence in adulterated wine, it more likely came from **chewing on the lead pencils** with which he wrote his music," believes Russell Martin, who wrote a book on this.

The worst part is that as Beethoven became more and more deaf, "He would rest the pencil that was killing him on the piano to feel the vibrations of each note through his teeth." Then, of course, he would chew on it.

Two women were talking about a woman they knew who had just had Siamese twins. "Do you know that it happens only once in thirty million times?" said one. "Really," said the other. "When did she have time to do her housework?"
—*The Comedy Quote Dictionary*

Fascinating Facts about the Original Siamese Twins

- Cheng and Eng were first spotted together in 1824 by someone who saw them swimming and thought they were some kind of **strange sea monster.**
- Their names meant "left" and "right."
- **The two dreamed the same dreams.**
- One was a heavy drunk but the other a teetotaler who wasn't affected by the alcohol the other drank.
- They never fought but their wives did, and they had to build separate houses and divide the time they spent with their spouses.
- The two lived a nice long life, dying at sixty-three when the average person made it to only thirty-nine.
- **They fathered twenty-two basically normal children**—although two were deaf and mute).
- More than one thousand people have descended from them, including a president of the Union Pacific railroad and a major general in the U.S. Air Force.
- Someone wrote "Ask Bizarre" of *Bizarre* magazine asking **how the**

two brothers made love. They replied that the brothers were able to lie side by side rather than chest to chest so one didn't have to participate or watch the other do it. They probably used the missionary position—and forget about doggie style, which would have required the non-participating partner to get into that same humiliating

If they had been born today, the original Siamese twins could easily have been separated because they were joined only by a small band of scar tissue with one vein running through it.

stance. In whatever position they used, the brothers usually placed a blanket between them so the other couldn't see (or feel) what was going on. And the two had **separate nervous systems** so one couldn't have experienced pleasure when the other came; the participating brother just had to enjoy it enough for the two of them.

PSYCHICS
Psychic Meditations

- "I almost had a psychic girlfriend but she left me before we met."—Steven Wright
- "All those who believe in telekinesis, raise my hand."—Steven Wright
- Why do people who laugh at gypsy fortune tellers take economists seriously?
- "I called a psychic hotline and we spoke for six hours. She didn't realize that I wasn't going to pay my bill."—Michael Aronin
- Help wanted: Telepath. You know where to apply.
- Why do psychics have to ask you for your name?

"Rumpology" and Psychic Dogs

Sylvester Stallone's mother, Jacqueline, is a psychic who practices what she calls **"rumpology,"** or reading people's futures from their backsides. She says the crack corresponds to the hemispheres in the brain. Jacqueline also believes her dog is psychic.

She was quoted by Roy Rivenberg in the *Los Angeles Times* as saying that her "dogs have been invited to start a **psychic dog hotline,** in which callers would pay to have their fortunes told by the canines. But, she said, 'I'm not going to use them for nonsense.'"

Nonsense or not, some believe in canine clairvoyance; others think that it's just a tall tale (tail?). Jacqueline's dog did better than all the political analysts of the time: He "predicted" that **George Bush** would win the election by a couple of hundred votes. Although the actual number was closer to six hundred (and many people believe he really lost by thousands), make no bones about it, this dog did better than any of the humans did at predicting the election. SEE "OUT OF THIS WORLD," PAGE 46.

Hilarious Predictions That Didn't Come True

The gossip tabloids—such as the *Enquirer, Star,* and *Globe*—are generally more accurate in most of their stories than given credit for, except for one area in which they are consistently wrong: their annual psychic prediction issues. Here are some of the predictions made within the last five years by their not-so-top-notch psychics:

Television and Radio Personalities

> David Letterman did his own psychic schtick on his show one night and predicted, "At some point this year Michael Jackson will do something weird."

- **Martha Stewart** will develop a temporary but bizarre Tourette's syndrome–like condition that will cause her to swear uncontrollably and gobble food like a slob.
- **Bryant Gumbel** will join a religious cult that preaches polygamy, and he will marry five different women.
- **Jay Leno** will be axed as the host of *The Tonight Show* and replaced by **Kathie Lee Gifford**—and she will choose Frank as her sidekick.
- **Regis Philbin** will quit showbiz and go off to medical school. (This was predicted just before *Who Wants to Be a Millionaire?* started. Shows how much they know.)
- **Ellen Degeneres** will relocate to Beirut, claiming that she really is Lebanese and was misunderstood.
- **Johnny Carson** will come out of retirement to co-host *Good Morning America.*
- **Howard Stern** will play Rhett Butler to **Pamela Anderson Lee**'s Scarlett in a successful rock musical version of *Gone with the Wind.*
- **Barbara Walters** will cut back on her news anchor duties and teach part time at a girl's high school. (Another prediction about Barbara from another psychic at a different paper has her starting a *Playboy*-type magazine for the over sixty set and being the first nude centerfold in it.)

Movie and Political Personalities

- **Brad Pitt** will donate a kidney to **Mother Teresa** after a computer says he's a perfect match.
- **Patrick Swayze** will turn his back on showbiz to go live the simple life of a desert tribesman in Saudi Arabia.
- **Paul Newman** will learn hypnotism and will mesmerize **Larry King,** making him cluck like a chicken on the air for five hours until the trance ends.
- **Sylvester Stallone** will challenge ex-boxing champion **Mike Tyson** to a charity match and knock him out. (Another psychic has him fascinated with Alcatraz, buying it and turning it into a theme park called "Rockyland.")

> A psychic predicted that Hilary Clinton will visit her doctor with menopausal symptoms and discover that she's pregnant.

Signs You're Visiting a Fake Psychic

- She predicts lotto numbers for you after they've been announced.
- When you're not looking, he calls the psychic phone line.
- When you show her your palm, she slaps you five.
- He can predict tomorrow's weather forecast.
- She tells you you're going to die, but not when.
- He needs pliers to bend spoons.
- She shakes her crystal ball and predicts that it will snow.

REDNECKS AND TRAILER TRASH
 ## Are You a Redneck?

True or false?
- A spread eagle is an extinct bird.
- Kotex is a radio station in Cincinnati.
- Semen is a term for sailors.
- A condom is a large apartment complex.
- An orgasm is a person who accompanies a church choir.
- A diaphragm is a drawing in geometry.
- An erection is when Japanese people vote.
- Pornography is the business of making records.
- Genitals are people of non-Jewish origin.

You Know You're Trailer Trash When . . .

- **You watch** *Jerry Springer* because it's your only chance to see your extended family.
- You let your twelve-year-old daughter smoke at the dinner table **in front of her kids.**
- The Halloween pumpkin on your front porch has more teeth than your spouse.
- You think a woman who is "out of your league" bowls on a different night.
- Your wife's hair-do was once ruined by a ceiling fan.
- You think loading the dishwasher means **getting your wife drunk.**

How to Tell If a Redneck Has Been Working on a Computer

- The monitor is up on blocks.
- The six front keys have rotted out.
- The numeric key pad only goes up to six.
- There's a gun rack mounted on the CPU.
- There's a Skoal can in the CD-ROM drive.
- The mouse is referred to as a "critter."

Southern Wit and Wisdom

- "I'll slap you so hard your clothes will be outta style."
- "Well butter my butt and call me a biscuit."
- "He fell out of the ugly tree and hit every branch on the way down."

- "My cow died last night so I don't need your bull."
- "He's busier than a cat covering crap on a marble floor."
- "If things get any better, I'll have to hire someone to help me enjoy them."

And how hot is it?
- "It's so hot, the flashers are describing their trench coats."
- "It's so hot, the trees are whistling for dogs."
- "It's so hot, the squirrels are fanning their nuts."

If the Olympics were held in Arkansas, doves released during the opening ceremonies would be shot by the crowd, and afterward, they would be sold at the concession stand.

NOW THEY'VE THOUGHT OF EVERYTHING
Museums You Might Want to Skip

Sandra Gurvis has about American museums in a book titled *The Cockroach Hall of Fame and 101 Other Off-the-Wall Museums.* Here are a few of them:

- **Combat Cockroach Hall of Fame (Plano, TX):** This museum includes "roach art" with failed samples of presidential aspirant Roach Perot, Marilyn MonRoach, and various others dressed as roaches. Got a problem with that?

- **The Potato Museum (Albuquerque, NM):** This one contains Victorian postcards with sayings such as: "Like the potato is true, I am fairly mashed on you." No mention of Dan Quayle anyplace.

GOING TO POT
In Munich, there's a chamber pot museum with over two thousand chamberpots, including a musical one, and one from World War II with Hitler's face painted on the bottom.

- **The Center for the History of Foot Care and Foot Ware (Philadelphia, PA):** Eat your heart out, Imelda Marcos.
- **The Mutter Museum (Philadelphia, PA):** It's at the College of Physicians and it contains things you can't live without seeing, like a tumor from former President Grover Cleveland's jaw, bladder stones removed from a Supreme Court justice, John Wilkes Booth's thorax, and worse, if that's even possible. It's actually available for weddings and bar mitzvahs!
- **Frog Fantasies Museum (Eureka Springs, AR):** There's enough here to make you croak. The owner, who doesn't toady up to the idea of eating frogs legs, started this museum when she put some money in a gumball machine "and out came a you-know-what."

> **THE BULL HALL OF FAME (PLAIN CITY, OH)**
> No bull! This place includes a catalog with information you don't see in people's social registers, such as "scrotal circumference."

- **The Hair Museum (Independence, MO):** Lots of artifacts here, but the owner "bristles at the suggestion of selling any of them."
- **Banana Museum (Auburn, WA):** This museum is for those who find this fruit a-peeling.
- **American Sanitary Plumbing Museum (Worcester, MA):** This place flushes out lots of facts about toilets through the ages.
- **Museum of Death (Hollywood, CA):** This includes execution devices, serial killer artwork, morgue photos, celebrity-pet death exhibits, paintings by Dr. Death, and lots of other killer exhibits.
- **Drug Enforcement Administration Museum (Arlington, VA):** This museum contains all kinds of things for dopers.

Weird Clubs and Cults

- Committee for Immediate Nuclear War
- National Society for Prevention of Cruelty to Mushroooms
- The Institute of Totally Useless Skills
- The American Guild of English Handbell Ringers
- Club of the Friends of Ancient Smooth Irons
- Order of Manly Men

SOURCE: THE ODD INDEX

The Toilet That Has It All!

Japan is so crowded that often the only privacy to be found is in the john. That might explain why the Japanese want the visits to be such a pleasant experience, and they demand so much more of their toilets than we do. We're happy if toilets flush and don't use up too much water. But the Japanese have developed **toilets into works of art.**

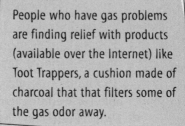

People who have gas problems are finding relief with products (available over the Internet) like Toot Trappers, a cushion made of charcoal that that filters some of the gas odor away.

At first glance, their high-tech toilets look more or less like normal American toilets. Until you see that there's a control pad, like **something from one of James Bond's cars,** with buttons for anything and everything.

There's a button for men to lift the seat and lid, and one for women that lifts only the lid. Another button activates a mini-bidet, which looks like a little toothbrush-shaped squirt gun that **sprays warm water to clean the nether regions.** There's even a button that activates a blow dryer to dry the rump afterward.

As if that wasn't enough, the seats are heated. There's also a digital clock so you can monitor how long you have to sit. But why? There's even a noisemaker that makes a flushing sound to cover any **unpleasant and embarrassing noises** you may make.

Because explanations are in Japanese, trying to figure out what all these buttons do to and for your rear can be, well, a bummer.

The *Washington Post* reported a horrifying gaffe by an American diplomat at a dinner party who just wanted to flush the damned toilet. He could not figure out which button did that and started pushing buttons at random. Inadvertently activating the bidet, he sprayed water all over the bathroom and the mirror. He ended up on his hands and knees, in his tuxedo, frantically trying to clean up the bathroom with wads of toilet paper.

Someone has developed a deodorant for your derriere. It costs $8.50 a bottle, is available in citrus and jasmine-scented versions, and is called Nature's Simple Solution.

As if these toilets don't seem to do enough, the Japanese company that's responsible for these Bondian toilets, Toto, is working on other models, such as one that will **analyze urine automatically and send a computer printout of the results to your doctor,** wherever he or she is. Oh great. Just what a doctor's dying to read—an analysis of someone's urine—while he's teeing off on the seventh hole.

CARS
Secrets for Car Owners

Bottom Line Personal is great because they excerpt items down to a few interesting lines, making *Reader's Digest* look like *War and Peace*. Here are a few worthwhile hints for car owners from the experts at *Bottom Line Secrets*.

Determining Whether an Odometer Has Been Tampered With
- Be especially wary of cars that have been driven a lot, like those owned by rental car companies or those leased by companies or individuals.
- Look at the service records of the car and see if it makes sense compared with how many miles they claim the car was driven.
- You can also try to find the car's previous owner through the Department of Motor Vehicles. If you can't do either, don't buy the car.
- At Carfax.com you can learn about the history of a car (accident record, odometer reading, title history, and so on) by entering its vehicle identification number on the site. Reports are not free, but you could ask the used car dealer if he subscribes and have him run the report before you agree to buy the car.

Deciding Whether to Report an Accident
You don't always know whether to report an accident, because if you do, your insurance rates may go up. But if you don't, and you're sued, you may not be covered for failing to give notice. An insurance expert suggests that you report an accident whenever it involves another person—even if you're sure it wasn't your fault.

Choosing the Safest Car Color
Generally, light-colored, single-tone cars have fewer accidents than darker cars, presumably because it's easier for other cars to spot them. Black is one of the least safe colors, probably because they're not as likely to be seen as other cars.

Registering Your Car
It may be best to register your car in the name of the primary driver. If you own it jointly with your spouse, and either of you are involved in an accident, in most states the person suing you may go after both of your incomes and assets.

Finding Cheap Insurance

Find out if your insurance company gives a discount if you take a defensive driving course. Some companies do and its worth it to take the course.

Determining If Are You Being Followed

Make four right turns so that you end up back where you were. If that car is still behind you, you're not paranoid, you really do have enemies.

GETTING RID OF THE DEALER'S DECAL

Take a hair dryer, set it to low, and hold it over the decal until the glue melts a bit and you're able to peel it off easily. (Better still, tell the dealer in advance that you don't want a decal, and that if they want you to advertise for them, they can pay you a monthly fee to do it.)

Making It Hard to Be Towed

If you have reason to believe you might be towed, park with your emergency brake set and the front wheels turned all the way to the left or to the right. That makes it harder for those bastards to tow you away. Itmay also slow down a thief trying to steal your car.

Five Worst Cars in the Past Fifty Years

Click and Clack, or Tom and Ray, hosts of *Car Talk* on NPR, put together a list (on their site Cartalk.com) of the worst cars of the millennium. Here are a few funny comments about them:

- **Yugo:** "At least it had heated rear windows so your hands would stay warm while you pushed."
- **Renault Le Car:** "It would put you in mortal danger if you had an accident with anything larger than a croissant."
- **Cadillac Cimarron:** "When we traded it in, my wife was upset because we didn't keep it long enough for her to buy a gun and shoot it."
- **Renault Dauphine:** "Truly unencumbered by the engineering process."
- **Volkswagon Bus:** "There was no heat, unless the auxiliary gas heater caught fire."

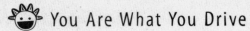 You Are What You Drive

Here's your car could reveal about your personality:

- **Buick Park Avenue:** "I'm older than thirty-four of the fifty states."
- **Cadillac Cimarron:** "I'm stupid enough to pay extra money for an uglified Chevrolet."
- **Cadillac El Eldorado:** "I am a very good Mary Kay salesperson."
- **Cadillac Seville:** "I am a pimp."
- **Dodge Dart:** "I teach third grade and I voted for both Bushes."
- **Dodge Daytona:** "I delivered pizza for four years to buy this car."
- **Ford Mustang:** "I slow down to 85 miles per hour in school zones."
- **Peugot 505 Diesel:** "I am on the EPA's ten most-wanted list."
- **Rolls Royce Silver Shadow:** "I think Pat Buchanan was too liberal."

"You know those signs that say 'Baby on Board.' Doesn't it make you want to hit the car harder?"
—Sue Kolinsky

What Car Initials Stand For

- **BMW:** Beautiful money waster.
- **CHEVROLET:** Can hear every valve rap on long extended trips.
- **FIAT:** Fix it again, Tony.
- **FORD:** Fix or repair daily.
  Found on road, dead.
  Fast only rolling downhill.
- **GM:** General maintenance.
- **GMC:** Got a mechanic coming?
- **HONDA:** Had one, never did again.
- **OLDSMOBILE:** Old ladies driving slow make others behind infuriatingly late every day.
  Overpriced leisurely driven sedan made of Buick's irregular leftover equipment.
- **SAAB:** Send another automobile back.
- **TOYOTA:** Too often Yankees overprice this auto.
- **VOLVO:** Very odd looking vehicular object.
- **VW:** Virtually worthless.

How to Tell Where a Driver Is From

- **New York:** One hand on the wheel, one hand on the horn.
- **California:** One hand on the wheel, one hand cradling a cell phone in the lap.
- **Chicago:** One hand on the wheel, one finger out the window.
- **Boston:** Both hands on the wheel, eyes shut, both feet on the brake, quivering in terror.
- **Italy:** Both hands in the air, gesturing, both feet on the accelerator, head turned to talk to someone in the back seat.
- **Montana:** One hand on the wheel, one hand on a gun.

Sassy Bumper Stickers

- Honk if you want to see my finger.
- Keep honking. I'm reloading.
- Honk if you love peace and quiet.
- Honk if you love cheeses.
- *Sona si latine loqueris.* (Honk if you speak Latin.)
- If that phone were up your butt, maybe you would drive a little better.
- I drive way too fast to worry about cholesterol.
- Hit me—I need the money.
- DAMM—Drunks Against Mad Mothers.
- Stupidity is not a handicap. Park somewhere else.
- Hang up and drive.
- If you can read this, I've lost my trailer.
- Horn broken. Watch for finger.
- So many pedestrians. So little time.
- He who hesitates is not only lost but also miles from the next exit.
- [Seen upside down] If you can read this, please flip me over.
- Remember folks: Stop lights timed for 35 miles per hour are also timed for 70 miles per hour.

> **BUMPER STICKERS TO DISCOURAGE TAILGATERS**
>
> - If you're not a hemorrhoid, get off my ass.
> - If you can read this, I can slam on my brakes and sue you.
> - Sorry for driving so close in front of you.

Vanity License Plates

Some think that former President Clinton should have had vanity plates saying: RU 4 69? Actually, some people have plates that are almost as bad (good?) and here are some of the best from a Web site that collects them:

- 9IN PNS: 9-inch penis—oddly, on a car driven by a woman.
- DRG DLR: Drug dealer—parked outside a pharmacy.
- 2P C ME: To pee, see me—a urologist's license plate.
- 1 ON ICE: One on ice—a mortician's license plate.
- GON LOCO: Gone loco—seen leaving a mental hospital.
- FU OJ: Fuck you, O. J.
- PAID2ARGU: Paid to argue—a lawyer's license plate.
- 2Q2BSTR8: To cute to be straight.
- C U N QRT: See you in court—an attorney's plate.
- 1 HNG LO: One hung low.
- FUHQUE: This one slipped past a sleeping censor at the license plate bureau.
- EZ 4U 2NV: Easy for you to envy—a great car.
- H2O GATE: Watergate—the corvette of G. Gordon Liddy, who arranged the Watergate burglary that ultimately brought the Nixon scandal to light.

SOURCE: WWW.CHAOS.UMD.EDU/MISC/ORIGPLATES.HTML

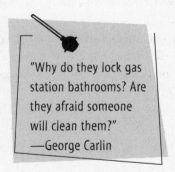

"Why do they lock gas station bathrooms? Are they afraid someone will clean them?"
—George Carlin

Love and Marriage

GENDER WARS
Are You Male or Female?

- At a doctor's office, the doctor tells you to: cough, or scoot down a little more?
- When playing sports, you need athletic support with: one cup, or two cups?
- When you're feeling insecure, you say to your best friend: nothing, or "Do I look fat?"
- You've slept with several hundred people. You are: "a legend" or "a tramp"?
- Multiple orgasms are something you: give, or get?

SOURCE: JULIE LOGAN AND ARTHUR HOWARD

Breaking Up a Cat Fight

Says Steve Wilkos, the head of security of the *Jerry Springer Show,* when men fight on the show they really want the fight to be broken up—especially the loser.

This isn't true with women. "They often struggle to get the last lick in—**one more hair pull, kick, scratch, whatever,**" he noted. "And once women go at it, they don't care how bad they look, or what their hair looks like, or whether their makeup is running, or whatever. One woman was so intent on pulling the hair of her opponent that she ended up pulling her own hair instead."

SOURCE: *Jerry Springer's Wildest Shows Ever*

And They Say Chivalry Is Dead . . .

Here are some cutting remarks with which you can zing your lady friends:

- "Who lit the fuse on your tampon?"
- "I hate it when broads like you try to get sexist."
- "So you're a feminist. I think that's precious."
- "What I really want is a meaningful overnight relationship."
- "Don't worry. It only seems kinky the first time."
- "If you think the way to my heart is through my stomach—you're aiming too high."

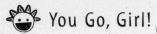 You Go, Girl!

And here are the comebacks:

- "Sorry buddy, but a hard-on doesn't count as personal growth."
- "You have the right to remain silent, so please shut up."
- "Save your breath. You'll need it to blow up your dates."
- "Please tell your pants it's not polite to point."
- "So many men—so many reasons not to sleep with any of you."
- "If they put a man on the moon, why can't they put all of you there?"
- "Well, this date was a total waste of makeup."

How to Insult Your Wife

- "My wife told me I should be more affectionate. So I got myself a girlfriend too."
- "The difference between a girlfriend and a wife is about forty pounds."
- "Love is the delusion that one woman differs from another."

"The main excitement in some women's lives is spotting women who are fatter than they are."
—Helen Rowland

- "When a man steals your wife, there's no better revenge than to let him keep her."
- "I married Miss Right. I just didn't know her first name was Always."
- "Losing a wife can be hard. In my case, it was almost impossible."
- "Just think, if it weren't for marriage, men would go through life thinking they had no faults at all."
- "A man said his credit card was stolen but he decided not to report it because the thief was spending less than his wife did."
- "There are two theories about arguing with a woman. Neither one works."
- "The most effective way to remember your wife's birthday is to forget it once."
- "Happiness is seeing your ex-wife on a milk carton."
- "I haven't spoken to my wife in eighteen months—I don't like to interrupt her."

After a company established that women talk to each other about men when they go to the ladies room, the club built double cubicles without doors so women could gossip about their dates sitting side by side.

How to Insult Your Husband

- "The trouble with some women is they get all excited about nothing—and then marry him."
- "No husband has ever been shot while doing the dishes."
- "The reason I got rid of my husband was the cat was allergic."
- "The best reason to divorce a man is a health reason—you're sick of him."
- "All men are idiots and I married their king."
- "If my husband said something in the woods and there was no one around to hear him, would he still be wrong?"

WOMEN
 ## Words to the Wise

- All men are animals. Some just make better pets.
- Men's brains are like the prison system. Not enough cells per man.
- There are easier things in life than finding a good man . . . nailing Jell-O to a tree, for one.
- To attract a man, wear a perfume called "new car interior."
- If men had periods, they'd brag about the size of their tampons.
- When God made man, she was only kidding.
- Few women admit their age, few men act it.
- Men are all the same—they just have different faces so you can tell them apart.

> Almost 20 percent of women admit that they've used the men's room rather than wait in a long line for the ladies room.

- Don't imagine you can change a man—unless he's in diapers.
- A sense of humor doesn't mean that you tell him jokes—it means you laugh at his.
- A man's idea of a serious commitment is usually, "Oh, all right, I'll stay the night."
- Go for younger men. You might as well. They never mature anyway.
- The best way to a man's heart is to saw his sternum open.
- The best way to get a man to do something is to suggest he's too old for it.
- A bachelor is someone who missed his opportunity to make some woman miserable.

- Men are like fine wine. They all start out like grapes and it's our job to stomp on them and keep them in the dark until they mature into something we'd like to have dinner with.
- Scientists have just discovered something that can do the work of five men—a woman.
- Women sleep with men who, if they were women, they wouldn't even have bothered to have lunch with.

Feminese

WHAT SHE SAYS	WHAT SHE MEANS
We need . . .	I want . . .
We need to talk.	I need to complain.
Sure. Go ahead.	I don't want you to.
You're so manly.	You need a shave and you sweat a lot.
I'm not emotional.	I'm having my period.
Be romantic. Turn out the lights.	I have cellulite.
This kitchen is so inconvenient.	I want a new house.
I want new curtains.	. . . along with carpeting, furniture, and wallpaper.
I heard a noise.	I noticed you were almost asleep.
Do you love me?	I'm going to ask for something expensive.
How much do you love me?	I did something today that's going to upset you.

Women's T-Shirts

- If you want breakfast in bed, sleep in the kitchen.
- My idea of housework is to sweep the room with a glance.
- Us blondes aren't bumb.
- I married my husband for better or worse. He couldn't do better and I couldn't do worse.
- Dinner is ready when the smoke alarm goes off.
- Guys have feelings too, but like, who cares?
- If a woman's place is in the home, why am I always in this car?
- Women should put pictures of missing husbands on beer cans.
- Put "eat chocolate" at the top of your list of things to do each day so you're sure to get one thing done.
- If it has tires or testicles, you're going to have trouble with it.
- Coffee, chocolate, men . . . some things are just better rich.
- Don't treat me any differently than you would the queen.
- Make yourself at home. Clean my kitchen.

MARRIAGE
The Married List

- If **Oprah Winfrey** married **Deepak Chopra**, she'd be Oprah Chopra.
- If **Sondra Locke** married **Elliot Ness**, then divorced him to marry Herman Munster, she'd become Sondra Locke Ness Munster.
- If **Dolly Parton** married **Salvador Dali**, she'd be Dolly Dali.
- If **Liv Ulmann** married **Judge Lance Ito**, then divorced him to marry **Jerry Mathers**, she'd be Liv Ito Beaver.
- And **Michael Caine** once suggested that if **Tuesday Weld** married **Frederick March III**, she'd be Tuesday March III.

Things You Don't Want to Overhear as You Walk Down the Aisle

- "She looks even better than she did in *Hustler*."
- "I heard her father wasn't the only one giving something away lately."
- "Dead man walking. Dead man walking."
- "Isn't it amazing what those Danish surgeons can do?"
- "Wonder what the priest is going to do on Saturday nights now?"
- "Why is the entire football team in tears?"
- "She's much prettier than the girl who gave him that rash."
- "When do we get to object to this thing?"

 ## What Never to Say to Your Pregnant Wife

- "Can't you ask the doctor to induce labor? The twenty-fifth is the Superbowl."
- "Maybe we should name the baby after my secretary, Tiffany."
- "Got milk?"
- "Are your ankles supposed to look like that?"
- "Get your own ice cream, Buddha."
- "Fred at the office passed a stone the size of a pea. Boy, that's gotta hurt."

Four Kinds of Marital Sex

- **House sex:** When you've just gotten married and you have sex in every room of the house.
- **Bedroom sex:** After you've been married for a while, you have sex only in the bedroom.
- **Hall sex:** When you've been married for many years and you just pass each other in the hall and say, "Screw you."
- **Courtroom sex:** When your wife and her lawyer screw you in divorce court.

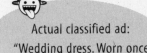

Actual classified ad: "Wedding dress. Worn once by mistake."

Quotes on Love and Marriage

Henny Youngman on Marriage

- "You know what I did before I married? Anything I wanted to."
- "My wife dresses to kill. She cooks the same way."
- "I brought my wife a new car. She called and said, 'There's water in the carburetor.' I said, 'Where's the car?' She said, 'In the lake.'"
- "For my anniversary my wife asked me to take her to a place she had never been before—so I took her to the kitchen."

- "Any husband who says, 'My wife and I are completely equal partners' is talking either about a law firm or a hand of bridge." —Bill Cosby
- "I was married by a judge. I should have asked for a jury." —George Burns
- "My mother buried three husbands—and two of them were just napping."—Rita Rudner

"My husband and I are either going to buy a dog or have a child. We can't decide whether to ruin our carpet or ruin our lives." —Rita Rudner

- "My wife and I were happy for twenty years. Then we met." —Rodney Dangerfield
- "My wife made me join a bridge club. I jump off next Tuesday." —Rodney Dangerfield

BRAD PITT THINKS MARRIAGE IS A REAL GAS! When he was asked how he liked wedded life, he said that being married meant he could pass wind and eat ice cream in bed.

FAMILY VALUES

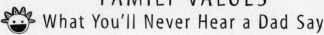

What You'll Never Hear a Dad Say

- "What do you mean you want to play football? Figure skating isn't enough for you?"
- "Your mother and I are going away for the weekend. You might want to invite some friends over and throw a party."
- "No son of mine is going to live under this roof without an earring. Now quit complaining and let's go to the mall."
- "What do you want to go and get a job for? I make enough money for you to spend."

Take My Kids . . . Please

- Children and husbands are best if they're someone else's.
- School days are the best days of your life—provided your children are old enough to go.
- If I wanted to hear the patter of little feet, I'd have put shoes on my cat.
- Who are these kids and why are they calling me mom?
- Hug your kids at home—belt them in the car.
- The kids drive me crazy, I drive them everywhere.

"I like children—
if they're properly cooked."
—W. C. Fields

Rodney Dangerfield on Childhood

- "I was so poor growing up. If I hadn't been born a boy, I'd have nothing to play with."

- "I could tell that my parents hated me. My bath toys were a toaster and a radio."

- "I'm so ugly, my father carries around the picture of the kid who came with his wallet."

- "I was such an ugly kid that when I played in the sandbox, the cat kept covering me up."

Real Books You Don't Want to Leave Out for Your Children to Find

Flatulence runs in families because relatives tend to harbor the same kinds of intestinal parasites and may eat the same kinds of foods.

- *Solo Explorations in Male Masturbation*
- *The Bottom Book to The Deviant's Dictionary*
- *Anal Pleasure and Health*
- *Peeping . . . and Getting Away with It*

 Things You Never Hear in Church

- "It's my turn to sit in the front pew."
- "I was so interested in what you were saying that I didn't notice that your sermon went twenty-five minutes overtime."
- "I find witnessing much more enjoyable than golf."
- "Because we're all here, let's start the service early."

 Death to All Fanatics!

- Just remember: God wants spiritual fruits, not religious nuts.
- Opportunity only knocks once; if you hear a second knock it's probably a Jehovah's witness.
- Jesus loves you—the rest of us think you're an idiot.
- People who want to share their religious views with you almost never want you to share yours with them.
- If God, who created the entire universe with all of its glories, decided to deliver a message to humanity, he would not use a person on cable television with a bad haircut as his messenger.
- Televangelists are the pro wrestlers of religion.

Who were the most constipated men in the Bible? Balaam, who had trouble with his ass; Moses, who took two tablets and had to run down the hill; David, who sat on the throne for forty years; and Titus who . . . well, just say his name out loud!

Good God! Sacrilegious Musings

- When an agnostic dies, instead of going to the Great Beyond, does he go to the Great Perhaps?
- Because Unitarians don't accept Jesus as the son of God, do they start their prayers with "To whom it may concern"?
- Can atheists get insurance for acts of God?
- If going to church makes you Christian, does going to a car dealer make you a car?
- "Sir, what did you think of my book?"—Norman Mailer, when asked what he'd say to Jesus if he met him
- "Like many classics, it's not that well written."—Norman Mailer, on the New Testament
- "The trouble with born-again Christians is that they are an even bigger pain the second time around."—Herb Caen
- "Religion is when you kill each other to see who has the better imaginary friend."—Steven Wright
- "Atheism is a non-prophet organization."—George Carlin

Legal Loonyism

COURTROOM ANTICS
Odor in the Court!

Lawyers are reviled for being windbags, and usually the hot air comes from their mouths. However, some lawyers are additionally castigated for not just being windbags, but for breaking wind in open court.

A legal case involving excessive afflatus was that of a check-out clerk, Anthony Taper, who sued a coworker for $100,000 for the pain and suffering of enduring the coworker's **endless farting.** The court was unimpressed and dismissed this stinker of a case.

Another woman, Paula Levins, claimed that her employer "constructively dismissed" her by forcing her to endure the flatulence of a male coworker sharing her office, despite her repeated complaints about his **noxious activities.** She claimed his gas, on more than one occasion, caused her to become "physically sick."

One time she entered the office and "an awful smell hit me. I stood up and opened the window. As I left the room, he stuck his head out the window. I went to the bathroom and was sick for five minutes." On being ordered back into the scene of the **gaseous attack,** she refused and left her job. This case was settled out of court without further exchange of hot air. **SEE "HOW TO GET OUT OF JURY DUTY," PAGE 226.**

What a Windbag!

One lawyer less known for his skill in oral argument than for the volume and intensity of his emissions from a different orifice was a district attorney of Tuolumne County, California. His opponent on one case, Clark Head, even threatened an appeal on the conviction of a client, claiming this lawyer's gas warfare constituted "misconduct."

He claimed his opposing council farted "about a hundred times," and "even lifted his leg several times." He argued that the flatulent lawyer blasted out several juicy ones during closing arguments, not surprisingly, causing hilarity among the jury. The court viewed this objection as so much empty wind.

The Worst—And Best—Defenses

A Fool for a Killer

Handsome law student and mass murderer of women, Ted Bundy, insisted on being his own lawyer during portions of his trials for murder. During one of the sessions, he charmed the jury by calling his girlfriend to the witness stand and proposed to her. She accepted.

But he literally killed himself during another portion of the trial. A woman who had managed to escape from him before he had a chance to murder her was called to the witness stand. Bundy then disastrously asked her what she recalled of the man who had almost murdered her.

She started listing the physical characteristics of Bundy, standing right in front of her. "What I noticed most was he had a very prominent nose, a straight bridge that almost came to a point, not quite, thin lips," she continued.

Instead of quitting while he was obviously behind, Bundy foolishly charged ahead. "Do you see that man in the courtroom?" She then pointed dramatically to the lawyer, Bundy.

Objection, Your Honor

When all else fails, object. There was such overwhelming evidence against mass killer **Charles Manson** during his trial that there wasn't much a lawyer could do to help him. So Manson hired a lawyer who was known to upset the proceedings with repeated objections. The lawyer even objected once to the court asking a witness his name—saying it was hearsay because the man first heard it from his mother!

Lousy Defenses

A lawyer argued that **his client was too fat** to have fit in the back of a getaway truck, and therefore couldn't have committed the crime. Fat chance a jury would believe that one. He was convicted.

During closing arguments in a Canadian murder case, a lawyer said that his client couldn't have conspired to kill another man because the lawyer thought his client was useless: "No one would hire him to cut the grass. Why would someone hire him to kill someone?" He was also convicted.

What's the difference between a lawyer and a vulture?
The lawyer gets frequent-flyer miles.

Some Lawyers Give the Rest a Bad Name

Although the law firm of "Dewey Cheatem & Howe" is a joke, a law firm in Jamaica had the name **"Lawless & Linch,"** which confirms many people's opinions of lawyers. Here are a few incidents that won't help.

Real Sex told the story of a woman who sued a man for **videotaping them having sex** together without her knowledge and then showing the tape to his frat brothers. The man's lawyer lost the case—and then showed the tape to sixteen people at his firm. The resulting litigation over *that* ended up costing the law firm more than half a million dollars.

How does an attorney sleep? First he lies on one side, then he lies on the other.

What do you throw to a drowning lawyer? His partner.

One lawyer, while working on a government contract, wrote a definition of the words *and/or* that was three hundred words in length.

A Kansas lawyer received nearly $35,000 in worker's compensation because he claimed he hurt his shoulder reaching into the backseat of his car for his briefcase.

Alan Dershowitz may be one of the greatest lawyers in the country, and he may have been correct that it was his strategy that won a major case against the cigarette industry. But, even though he had nothing in writing, he wanted 1 percent of $34 million received by the lawyers for his work on the case, which was only 118 hours. *News of the Weird* figured out that this works out to **$288,000 per hour!**

King's Ransom

The twenty-three lawyers who formed Rodney King's legal team charged the city of Los Angeles $4.4 million—or $600,000 more than the $3.8 million King received in his judgment against the city. Not only that, but the thirteen thousand hours they billed (at about $350 an hour) included the time the lawyers spent on talk shows, attending King's birthday party, taking him to movie and theater premieres, and so on.

SOURCE: *News of the Ridiculous and Sublime*

LAWSUITS

A man once sued himself for trying to raid his own trust fund. Here are some other oddities that have made it to court.

Suing for Sex

In a now-famous case, **a phone sex operator** claimed she got RSI (repetitive stress syndrome) because she had to masturbate for hours each day when she talked to her clients on the phone. (Didn't anyone tell her they all fake it?)

Someone sued **Kenny Rogers** because a Frisbee he tossed during a concert struck a chandelier. The glass fell on the plaintiff, who claimed that this lead to his depriving his wife of "services, love, and guidance."

HOLD THE PEANUT BUTTER

A woman sued a pharmacy because she got pregnant despite using contraceptive jelly she bought there. But she ate the jelly on a piece of toast. "The woman is a complete idiot," said a lawyer, who asked not to be named.

A couple hit by a train while they were making love on the track sued the train company.

A woman taking a CPR training course sued the organization conducting the course, saying she got herpes when she gave **mouth-to-mouth resuscitation to the mannequin!**

A man sued his girlfriend for making obnoxious noises during sex—a case chosen to be heard on Playboy's *Sex Court* show. The judge ruled that she should shut up.

A honeymooning couple—who were both lawyers and perhaps thought this would pay for their honeymoon—sued Holiday Inn for $10,000, **claiming that their sex life was harmed** when an employee walked in on them on their wedding night.

Suing for Harassment

Has sexual harassment gone too far? People laughed when **a six-year-old boy was accused of sexual harassment** for kissing a six-year-old girl. But how about the mother who got a temporary restraining order to keep a three-year-old boy away from her three-year-old girl in the neighborhood sandbox?

What's the difference between a tick and a lawyer? A tick falls off of you when you die.

Then there was the waiter at T.G.I. Friday's in Florida who was on the receiving end of what most men dream about: female employees touching him and **grabbing his genitals.** He claimed harassment and lost wages and was awarded $125,500 for his "suffering," because when he objected to the fondling, the others called him "disparaging names for homosexuals."

Suing for Embarrassment

A lawyer sued the Yellow Pages Company in California for $100,000, alleging libel when they accidentally listed her under "Reptiles."

A woman sued (and received $12,000) after a local disc jockey opened the stall door while she was seated on the john and put a microphone in front of her so listeners could hear her screams.

A gambler sued a casino for $50,000 after he got stuck on **a crazy-glued toilet seat.** It seems that after they pried him off, he had to walk through the entire casino with a towel draped over his ass.

A man who had **a penile implant** sued the manufacturer, saying he would be walking down the street and the device would suddenly erect for no reason.

> A man sued the city of San Diego for $5.4 million for the emotional distress he claimed he suffered when women entered the men's room while he was there.

Incredible Settlements from Odd Lawsuits

A man in Wisconsin was **publicly spanked by his boss** with a four-foot-long carpenter's level in a bizarre workplace initiation. He received $143,000.

A group of air passengers suffering emotionally during severe turbulence caused by a thunderstorm got together and sued, receiving $2.2 million. *Playboy,* calling it "Skyway Robbery," figured out that the cost of the twenty-eight scary seconds came to $78,571 per passenger.

Weird News told the story of the **"Mountain Man,"** an escaped murderer from Bulgaria, who spent twelve years burglarizing houses. While he was being arrested, a police dog bit off part of his foot. He received almost half a million dollars for the accident.

Ridiculous Lawsuits Kicked Out of Court

Not everyone who files a frivolous suit comes out ahead. A thirty-one-year-old man who was refused a $1.25 senior citizens' discount sued for **age discrimination.** He was fined $8,600 for "making a mockery of the system." Amen!

A man sued McDonald's, claiming they should have warned him of **the dangers of eating and driving** because he spilled one of their cold chocolate shakes on his lap while he was driving. He was also left out in the cold by the court.

A rock climber who was hit by lightning while climbing in a state national park sued the park services, claiming they should have warned him that he might be hit by lightning. His suit was also dismissed.

A Texas prisoner—serving fourteen years for robbery and assault—sued *Penthouse* magazine for $500,000 for publishing a "disappointing" layout of **Paula Jones.** Not only did the judge dismiss the lawsuit and fine the prisoner $250, but he wrote a funny Christmas poem about it. Here's part of it.

> *'Twas the night before Christmas and all through the prison*
> *Inmates were planning their new porno mission. . . .*
> *The minute his* Penthouse *issue arrived,*
> *The Minister ripped it open to see what was inside.*
> *But what to his wondering eyes should appear—*
> *Not Paula Jones' promised privates, but only her rear.*
> *Life has its disappointments. Some come out of the blue,*
> *But that doesn't mean a prisoner should sue.*

HOW TO GET OUT OF JURY DUTY

It's been said that when you put yourself in the hands of a jury, you're letting your future be decided by a bunch of people too dumb to get out of jury duty. Of course, *you're* going to be a good citizen, and not read this to get ideas . . . yeah, yeah. Anyway, these have worked for some people.

Act like you want to be on the jury. If you really want to get out of it, pretend you really want to be part of it. Someone calling himself "ratboy" on the Internet said that during voir dire, the defense attorney asked if anyone wanted to be on the jury. He was the only one to raise his hand. When asked why, he replied, "When I received the summons, I fully expected to take part in the process, and not find a way to cop out and shrink the duty." He was dismissed. He thinks the questioning lawyers believed, "There's just something fundamentally wrong with someone who wants to be on a jury, and lawyers don't want to deal with it."

Say you watch television. Say that you watch all the courtroom shows and are glad to be part of the process. Lawyers don't want people who have preconceived ideas of what goes on in a courtroom.

Be logical. It's been said that if you claim to be a student who is studying logic, you would not be seated on a jury because the lawyer with the weaker case doesn't want people who can think clearly. (That's logical.)

Be famous. David Letterman showed up for jury duty in his Connecticut hometown but the judge turned him down. He said Letterman was too opinionated to be deciding a case. But the lawyer on the prospective case said the real reason was that he was too famous and he feared he would be a distraction. "You want people paying attention to the witnesses, not a fellow juror," he said.

Be dead. There's a law in Oregon that prevents dead people from serving on a jury.

Be prejudiced. You are often asked during voir dire whether you have any prejudices toward certain groups of people. Say yes.

Say yes! One woman was rapidly dismissed from a case involving lawyers when she said to the questioning lawyer: "I'm sure you're an honest lawyer, but in my opinion, all the others are thieves."

> ## A Sure-Fire Way to Avoid Jury Duty
>
> **Have gas.** Let the court transcript reprinted in *The Other F-Word* tell the story.
>
> THE COURT: I have a communiqué from the jury ... for the last week and a half [Juror Number 4] has been passing gas like mad.... A couple of the [other jurors] asked if their seats can be moved, but there are only so many seats in the box and he is right in the middle.... The clerk will excuse Juror Number 4.
>
> **SEE "ODOR IN THE COURT!", PAGE 221.**

Similar statements admitting to prejudice against policemen may be effective. Because they often testify in cases, jurors may be asked if they think a policeman's testimony is likely to be more believable than the person on trial. Saying "yes," or "no, that it's less likely," will generally get people dismissed.

Be bored. Judges often ask prospective jurors if they've served on a jury before. If you say yes, they will probably ask what you thought of the experience. One woman got off a jury by saying she had been bored by the experience.

A jury consists of twelve people chosen to decide who has the better lawyer.

Be sure of guilt in advance. In one famous exchange, a judge asked a potential juror "When you heard about this case, did you form any opinion about the defendant's guilt or innocence?" The potential juror responded: "Not really. I just assumed that he had committed the crime."

George Carlin says you should tell the judge that you'd make a great juror because you "can spot guilty people just like *that*." But you have to be careful with something like this. There's a joke that when a judge asked if there was any reason why someone couldn't serve on a jury, one prospective juror leaped up. "I can tell from his shifty eyes, stupid grin, and cheap suit that that man is guilty." "Shut up and sit down," said the judge. "That's the defense attorney." And then there's the old joke about the Jewish woman who was turned down from jury duty—she insisted that *she* was guilty.

Say you've moved. This may or may not work, and it may or may not be legal (probably not), but it did work for one person. When he got a jury duty notice, he sent it back saying, "Moved, no forwarding address." He later got a postcard saying he was excused.

Beware: Acting crazy doesn't always work. Consider the following true story. There's a woman who referred to herself as "Commander," wore a red *Star Trek: The Next Generation* uniform, carried a "phaser" and "tricorder," and made it clear when questioned for jury duty that "I stand for *Star Trek* ideas." Not only did she earn an *Esquirer* Dubious Achievement Award (under the category "To Boldly Go Nuts Where No One Has Gone Before"), but a position as an alternate juror. And it wasn't just on a rinky dink traffic ticket either—but on James McDougal's Whitewater trial during the Clinton administration.

If all else fails, you may also get out of jury duty by:
- Not bathing before going to voir dire.
- Claiming that bright lights give you headaches.
- Asking them to repeat every question at least twice, and then saying something like, "I didn't realize my hearing was so bad."
- Answering questions with other questions.
- Telling them that you follow the news carefully.
- Having an IQ over room temperature.
- Walking in for jury selection while dragging your knuckles on the ground and drooling.

And if these fail, as someone who served on jury duty suggested, instead of trying to get out of jury duty, "Have some pride, and make yourself a useful citizen. Or move to Cuba, where justice is much more certain."

JUDGES
You Tell 'Em, Judge Judy!

- "I don't give a rat's behind what you're talking about."
- "I don't care if you were living with Queen Latifah."
- "Ma'am, you don't get reimbursed for stupidity. Your case is dismissed."
- "The only reason why you're here, sir, is because you are a loser."
- "Sir, I'm talking about your character, not about your stupidity."
- "Idiots don't get rewarded."
- "Sir, you were probably high on loopdee-loops."
- "Come on now, you don't live on Pluto do you?"
- "Honey, listen closely. Beauty fades, but dumb is forever."
- "You've got more excuses than a cat has lives."
- "You look a little neurotic."
- "Sir, on my best day you are not as smart as I am on my worst day."
- "You must be penalized for being so dumb."

SOURCE: TVTALKSHOWS.COM

Judge Not

It's not only lawyers who raise eyebrows with their behavior. According to sources, including the book *Legal Blunders:*

A Pennsylvania judge was caught by a hidden camera offering convicted men lighter sentences if they let him **shampoo their hair.**

> A Nebraska judge set bail at "a gazillion" dollars and signed legal forms as "Snow White" and "Adolph Hitler."

Another judge became so enraged when a defendant swore at him that he stepped down from the bench, took off his robe, and **chest-butted** the guy. Then he bit him on his nose, removing a quarter of an inch of it, before spitting in the man's face.

What Judges Are Really Saying

"**I think now might be a good time to take a short break.**" "I'm trying desperately to keep from falling asleep, pitching forward into the file folder, and having to get staples removed from my forehead."

"**I believe this is a question better determined by the jury.**" "Let's see if you can get twelve people to buy this load of crap."

"**Counsel, could you address the jurisdiction issue first?**" "Show me how I can unload this turkey on some other poor judge in another district."

CRIME
Frightening Facts about Crime

Here's something new to worry about: the guy next to you with a mobile phone. They now make fake ones that **fire real bullets.** Pressing the keypad triggers the firing mechanism. If you look at it, it looks just like a real phone. It's only when you hold one that you realize it's much heavier.

Here's another new one. Men are meeting beautiful women in bars who take them out to their pickup trucks to have sex. The women suggest they get out in the snow and rub themselves with it to get sexually aroused. Then the women drive off with the men's wallets.

According to a survey of more than one thousand women conducted by *Glamour* magazine, nine out of ten women think it's OK to murder an abusive husband. Furthermore, more than 80 percent think that women who kill an abusive mate shouldn't be convicted.

So far, **DNA analysis** has freed about one hundred people who were wrongly imprisoned for their crimes. And it has implicated even more. (What about all those people who were executed who *weren't* able to take these tests?) That's why some criminals are now trying to beat DNA evidence by forcing their victims to do such things as scrub themselves in a shower after they rape or attack them.

A Few More Scary Facts

"In New Orleans, if you go in to buy a pair of nylon stockings, they want to know your head size."
—Billie Holliday

- One out of every one thousand people in the Unted States is a murderer.
- There may be as many as one hundred serial killers out there—looking for a victim.
- **January 1** is the day you are most likely to be murdered.
- Every two hours a woman is killed by a stalking husband or stranger.
- You are more likely to be murdered than audited by the IRS.
- The most likely sign a **violently psychopathic man** will eventually kill is if he resorts to attempted strangling.
- **Ford Bronco sales** went up 25 percent after the O. J. chase.
- Two percent of kids in America who want to see their mother or father have to go to a prison to do so.

In Other Countries

In Japan, when people are sentenced to death, they can be executed any day, at any time, without being told when it will happen. So the condemned person lives with the constant fear that every time a guard comes near, or his door is opened to bring him food, it could be the death knell for him. (Another form of Japanese prison torture is for non-capital-offense prisoners to be put in cells too small for them to stretch out or stand up in.)

In India, fourteen women are executed by their husband's family every day, many because their dowries weren't high enough.

Is Your Car Likely to Be Stolen?

You've got a 50 percent chance of your car being stolen in your lifetime (and a 66 percent chance of getting it back). If you think because your car isn't new that it's less likely to be stolen, you're wrong.

One study showed that older cars were just as likely to be stolen as new ones—sometimes more so. In some places, according to insurance company statistics, up to 60 percent more older cars are taken. Why? First, because people who have older cars are more lax about their security, thinking no one would want them. Second, thieves like older cars because they can get more for the hard-to-obtain parts.

The FBI's Most-Wanted List

Here are some little-known facts about the list:

- **Only seven women have made the list.**
- Almost all who have appeared on the list have been caught—429 out of 458.
- Most have been captured an average of one thousand miles from the crime scene.
- Twenty-six have been found hiding in other countries.
- A few have made the list twice, like **James Earl Ray,** who made it the first time as the suspected assassin of Dr. Martin Luther King, and again after escaping from prison.
- The person who was on the list for the shortest amount of time was only on for two hours before being found hiding in an attic.
- **The Son of Sam** never made the list because his real name wasn't learned until after his capture.
- Being a high-profile case not only won't get a person on the FBI's Ten Most-Wanted List, but it may keep that person off it. When heiress **Patty Hearst** was indisputably the top fugitive in the United States (after she was filmed robbing a bank with her alleged captives

from the Symbionese Liberation Army), she wasn't put on the list. Because she had so much publicity, there was no need to introduce her to the public, which is the purpose of the list. On the other hand, not being known may also keep people off the list.

SOURCE: *New York Times*

Alan Dershowitz on Criminals

Here's what the world-famous attorney believes about criminals, their trials, and their lawyers, according to his book *The Best Defense*:

- Almost all criminal defendants are guilty.
- Criminal defendants and their lawyers don't want justice. They want acquittals or short sentences.
- The job of the defense attorney is **to prevent the whole truth from coming out.**
- Dershowitz doesn't feel guilty about helping a murderer go free, even though he may go out and kill again.
- The famed attorney once told a group of Yale Law School students that he would have defended **Adolph Hitler**—"And I would have won," he said.

The Most Often-Stolen Items and Other Frauds

Although thefts of batteries and cigarettes are high in supermarkets, they're nothing compared to baby formula. That's because formula is expensive, small, and needed by mothers—and also possibly **by cocaine users and dealers** who may cut the drug with it. And drug dealers aren't usually the type to worry too much about stealing something.

Shoplifting ... Hemorrhoid Cream?

A (supposedly) often-stolen item from drugstores (especially in certain cities) is hemorrhoid cream. The thieves may be regular customers embarrassed to ask for it. Or, like baby formula, it's being stolen by cocaine dealers and users, since hemorrhoid cream supposedly sooths and shrinks the swollen tissues in the brain that comes from doing too much coke.

Other frequently pilfered articles from drug stores are batteries, cosmetics, film, and sunglasses. As for the most often-stolen items from hotels, according to *USA Today*, towels are first, followed by soap, shampoo, bathrobes, and hangers. Some guests go much further than that, taking bed linens, or the tray holding the soap. The oddest item reported stolen was **a goldfish** from a hotel in Seattle, which temporarily provides them for customers who want a "pet" in their room.

"Negotiations in the Middle East are tough. Arafat wants Netanyahu to give the PLO the West Bank. Netanyahu wants Arafat to give that towel on his head back to the Tel Aviv Hilton."
—David Letterman

Novatel hotel chain in Australia and New Zealand did their own theft survey and found that women were more likely to steal than men. Furthermore, when men did steal, they "took 'blokey' things like wine openers and shoe-shine kits."

Another common fraud people try to perpetuate while in hotel rooms is attempting to **outsmart the mini-bar.** Some nosh on the candy and then stuff the empty wrapper with toilet paper before putting it back. Or they fill miniature vodka bottles with water and then replace them. These ploys rarely work because those who replenish the bars look for broken wrappers and seals. Besides, some mini-bars register even if you just *move* an item without opening it.

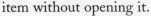

Ever wonder why some public places have such thin toilet paper? Not just to save money, but because the thinner it is, the less often they have to change it. In addition, the less comfortable it is, the less likely people are to steal it.

Finally, as for "literary" type thefts, in English libraries and bookstores, it's **the *Guinness Book of Records*** that has broken all records for theft.

But in America and Canada, some have reported that the *Bible* is the book most often stolen from libraries and bookstores—and *Sports Illustrated* the most popular magazine. So much for religion and good sportsmanship.

MURDER AND CORPORAL PUNISHMENT
Could You Be a Serial Killer?

1. Are you male?
2. Are you in your twenties?
3. Do you think you have superior intelligence?
4. Would you enjoy matching wits with the police?
5. Have you ever suffered from periodic or chronic headaches?
6. Did you have a head accident as a child?
7. Have you had violent episodes ever since?
8. Were you abused as a child?
9. Did you abuse small animals as a child?
10. Have you ever started a fire where you shouldn't?
11. Do you hate women?
12. Do you hate the type of person who has scorned you?

Ted Bundy's fiancée, a brunette with a part down the middle of her hair, changed her mind about marrying him—and many of his later victims had similar style hair.

13. Have you ever been forced to wear dresses?

*Many serial killers were. For example, **Charles Manson** was sent to elementary school in a dress by an uncle who thought it would help him learn how to fight like a man. **Henry Lee Lucas** (who supposedly killed two hundred people with Otis Toole) was sent by his aunt to school wearing skirts with his hair in curls. And **Otis Toole** had an older sister who dressed him in petticoats and lace.*

14. Would you mind hurting people who trust you?

*"Boston Strangler" **Albert DeSalvo** posed as a maintenance man and got women to believe he was there to help them. Ted Bundy put his arm in a sling and asked women for assistance before grabbing them and forcing them into his car.*

15. Are you oblivious to bad smells?

*Some killers, such as **John Wayne Gayce**, **Gary Heidnik**, and **Ira Einhorn** have kept their victims' bodies around afterward, seemingly oblivious to the foul stench.*

16. Do you like to move around a lot?

Serial killers often frequently move from place to place, sometimes to find more victims, sometimes to stay one step ahead of the police.

SOURCE: BASED ON "DEATH ROW SERIAL KILLER PROFILE," A WEB PAGE BASED ON THE BOOK *Death Row*, WHICH INCLUDES THE WARNING THAT THE QUIZ IS NOT MEANT TO BE INTERPRETED LITERALLY—WHICH IS ALSO TRUE FOR THIS QUIZ

Are You Likely to Go Postal?

1. Are you male?
2. Are you older than thirty-five?
3. Are you white?
4. Do you live alone?
5. Do you have many friends?
6. Do you own several guns?
7. Are you obsessed with guns or explosives?
8. Do you hold grudges?
9. Are you very upset with what's happening at work or in your private life?
10. Do you think some employees are scared of you?
11. Do you carry weapons to work?
12. Have you made threats at work?
13. Do you feel you're in trouble at work or school or in danger of being fired or disciplined?

"Every postal worker I've ever met has been friendly. Sure, some occasionally get freaked out and go on a shooting spree, but who doesn't?"
—Joel Stein, *Time*

SOURCE: *New York Post*

Death Row

Gear magazine uncovered some interesting facts on this grisly subject.

Because men get erections when they're hanged, gallows were designed with a place for the bodies to drop and be hidden, so women and even little children could share in the joy of watching an execution without being offended.

THE WORLD'S DUMBEST KILLER

After a woman pointed to a defendant in court saying he was the killer, he shouted, "I should have blown your fucking head off." There was total silence in the courtroom before he quickly added "If I'd been the one that was there." He was given thirty years.

In a five-year period in Texas, under the governorship of **George W. Bush,** one person was executed every two weeks. Bush has therefore overseen more executions than any governor since the death penalty was reinstated in 1976. The only person Bush pardoned was Henry Lee Lucas, who claimed to have killed as many as **six hundred people.**

There are more whites than blacks on death row.

Although appeals to save a condemned man can cost $1 million, here's how much it costs to actually execute him:

- Electric chair = 31 cents per death
- Cyanide for the gas chamber = $250 per death
- Chemicals for lethal injection = $700 per death

How much does it cost you, the taxpayers? According to CrimeMag.com, death row studies show that incarceration costs about $20,000 per year, per inmate.

- Death row inmates average 9.9 years awaiting execution.
- By the time someone is executed, taxpayers have shelled out about **$2 million in legal fees** for each death row inmate's defense.
- There are usually more executions around November—election season.

One bizarre fact about an execution: one hangman later became a U.S. president. **Grover Cleveland** was once a sheriff in New York, and in his capacity as such, had to hang two men who were convicted of murder.

> A British man was jailed for life after he murdered a male friend who yelled at him for not lifting the toilet seat.

Aw, These Final Requests Were Turned Down

Many prisoners have requested a final cigarette and have been refused, presumably not because the officials were afraid of the prisoner getting cancer.

A request to hold a Bible during an electrocution was denied a prisoner in 1986 because officials felt that the book would have presented **a possible fire hazard.**

One prisoner asked to be allowed to have sexual intercourse with "a sexy little boy."

Best Last Words

- "You're about to see a baked apple."—George Appel, right before he was executed in the electric chair

- "Let's rock 'n' roll."—David Stoker, who was executed for the murder of a convenience store clerk

- "I've always wanted to try everything once...."—Jesse Walter Bishop

# Politics

PRESIDENTIAL PENISES

John F. Kennedy, after being treated for gonorrhea, suffered throughout his life from acute post-gonococcal urethritis, an inflammation of his penis. As a result, he admitted once that he had a burning sensation whenever he urinated.

By the way, his lovemaking wasn't all that hot either. Although this handsome man has been assumed to have been a great lover—he certainly was a busy one—the many women who had him knew otherwise. According to the *Celebrity Sex Register,* "Said one, typically, 'Our lovemaking was so disastrous that for years I was convinced I was frigid . . . **he was terrible in bed.**'"

His choice in women was both indiscreet and surprising. Two secretaries at the White House, whom he made love with regularly, were called "Fiddle and Faddle" by others. One senator described them as "A couple of dogs . . . those two girls were the ugliest things I've ever seen."

Johnson's Johnson

Lyndon B. Johnson's fondness for his dick is understandable when you consider that "Johnson" is a Briticism for "wang."

- When he was young, LBJ liked to show off his penis, which he called "jumbo."

- When he was older, others apparently agreed, because LBJ's nickname was "Ball Nuts."

- He also liked to show it off—and intimidate others—by swimming naked in pools after he was president, and by suggesting to men he was swimming with that they do the same.

- LBJ once told a tailor, "I need some more goddamned ball room in these pants."

- LBJ once explained why we were in Vietnam to reporters by unzipping and saying "Here's why."

SEE "AMERICA'S MOST DISGUST-ING PRESIDENT," PAGE 240.

 In the famous painting of **George Washington** crossing the Delaware, Washington's pocket watch, draped over his thigh, looks to some dirty minds like his penis. It was close enough to disturb teacher's aides in Georgia, who went through more than two thousand copies of a fifth-grade textbook to alter the pictures.

Richard Nixon, who was hospitalized for phlebitis while he was president, liked to put on his hospital gown backward and walk up and down the hall with the front open. A former secret service agent said it would make "nurses stop in their tracks."

How Good Were Clinton's Lovers?

Clinton's Turn-Ons

Gennifer Flowers, an early, long-term former girlfriend of former President Clinton, revealed that to get him hot, she would tie him to the bedpost with silk scarves. But it was her oral activities that she (and he) was best known for. Indeed, it has often been said that she was so good at oral sex that "she could suck a tennis ball through a hose."

If **Monica Lewinsky** had been a *really* good lover, she would have swallowed the evidence of Clinton's crime. He could then simply have denied her claims that they had had oral sex, and would never have been impeached. **Gennifer Flowers** was probably better at her job than Monica.

Lots of women would have liked to have been lovers of the former president. (Lots of women were!) His sexual activities became such a joke that museum officials at Madame Tussaud's in Australia finally had to **sew up the fly on Bill Clinton's statue** because visitors kept sneaking into the exhibit and pulling the zipper down. They would also frequently sneak under the rope and pose for a picture on their knees, seeming to service the former president. (And by the way, Tussaud's in New York has had a problem with lipstick marks all over **Brad Pitt** too.)

Monica Lewinsky Jokes You May Have Missed

☞ "Monica is considering suing the president. She wants $1 million for pain and suffering and $2.50 for dry cleaning."—Jay Leno

Said Clinton to young Ms. Lewinsky
We mustn't leave clues like Kaczynski
Since you look such a mess
Use the hem of your dress
And wipe that stuff off your chinsky.

- "She's a young woman with both knees planted firmly on the ground."—Jay Leno
- "Monica Lewinsky says she's going to law school. And just when you thought she couldn't sink any lower."—David Letterman
- If she didn't spit, you must acquit.
- What's the most popular game in the White House? Swallow the leader.
- What did Ken Starr find in Monica Lewinsky's pocket? A wad of Bill's.
- What's the fluid capacity of Monica Lewinsky's mouth? One U.S. leader.
- Gas is so expensive, guys are now dating Monica Lewinsky just for her siphoning skills.

Willy's Willy

The best-known penis of any president—more than we want to know—is that of Bill Clinton. It was described (by someone who hated him) as circumcised, "rather short and thin, about five to five-and-a-half inches or less in length, and having a circumference of the approximate size of a quarter. . . ." And Paula Jones also said it was crooked (if you must know, it's to the left).

Going Down on Clinton versus *The Titanic*

Here are some of the differences between the movie and the intern affair:

THE TITANIC	CLINTON
Jack is a starving artist.	Bill is a bullshit artist.
In one part, Jack enjoys a good cigar.	Ditto for Bill.
During the ordeal, Rose's dress gets ruined.	Ditto for Monica.
Jack teaches Rose to spit.	Let's not go there.
Rose remembers Jack for the rest of her life	Monica doesn't remember Jack.
Rose goes down on a vessel full of seamen.	Monica . . . uh, never mind.
Jack surrenders to an icy death.	Bill goes home to Hillary (basically the same thing).

DISGUSTING PRESIDENTS
America's Most Disgusting President

The winner is Lyndon B. Johnson . . .

- **Johnson on the john:** If he was talking to someone in the White House and had to move his bowels, he might move the discussion to the bathroom and go right in front of them. (This would also be a terrific power play, because he could ask the person anything and they'd say yes just to get away.)
- LBJ made his secretary take dictation while he was on the john.
- Once, he had to go to the bathroom while driving and got out of his car with his secret service agent. He relieved himself, after which the agent complained angrily that he had just **urinated on him.** And Johnson casually said something like: "I'm the President of the United States. I'm allowed to."
- After he had gall-bladder surgery, LBJ lifted up his shirt to show reporters his raw, new surgical scar. (This led one columnist to remark: "Thank God he didn't have a prostate operation.")
- While he was on the road campaigning, before he was president, LBJ stayed at rooming houses. If they had a bathroom at the end of the hall, **he didn't bother to close the door when he was using the john** so other guests could see and hear him.

LBJ put a microphone and loud speaker in the bathroom of his house. Then he'd say, "Hi there, honey" while his female guests were on the toilet.

- LBJ stole furniture from the White House and flew it to his ranch. (Does this sound familiar?)
- Johnson used "colorful" language, for example, he'd say that he "didn't trust a man unless **I've got his pecker in my pocket.**" Or, he'd tell people, "I want you to kiss my ass and tell me it smells like roses."

Spitting Image

The armed forces hated **Bill Clinton,** partially because of his "Don't ask, don't tell" policy about gays in the military. Like all presidents, Clinton's photo hung in the Pentagon while he was the chief. But there was one major difference between him and the other presidents: The Pentagon had to assign a janitor to wash the glass each morning to remove the spit left there the day before.

WISHY WASHINGTON:
U.S. PRESIDENTS AS YOU'VE NEVER
SEEN THEM BEFORE

The public was duly impressed when **George H. W. Bush** parachuted out of a plane in 1997 at age seventy-five. But Bush was accompanied by nine army divers, two of whom held on to his harness. The jump was described by one official as being "about as dangerous as going on a merry-go-round."

Lyndon B. Johnson, who was fabulously wealthy, was so cheap that he carried a light bulb in his pocket and screwed it into empty sockets of rooms as he entered them. He removed the bulb and took it with him when he left.

George W. Bush's salary is $400,000, twice what Bill Clinton was paid. But do our presidents receive enough after taxes? The *Wall Street Journal* analyzed how much money earlier presidents made in terms of buying power and concluded that today's presidents are being shortchanged. For example, although George Washington received only $25,000 a year as president, in terms of buying power, that would equal about $550,000 today.

Harry Truman may have been elected president because the other candidate (Thomas Dewey) looked like "the little man on top of a wedding cake."

> "I may not know much, but I know chicken shit from chicken salad."
> —Lyndon B. Johnson

Many people know that the *S* in **Harry S. Truman** didn't stand for anything, but they don't know why his parents didn't give him a middle name. The reason was that both of his grandfathers had middle or first names beginning with *S*. Harry's mother was afraid that if she gave her son the name of either grandparent, the other one would have been insulted.

The United States once had **three different presidents in five weeks.** On March 3, 1841, Martin Van Buren's term came to an end and William Henry Harrison succeeded him. Only one month after the inauguration, Harrison died. His vice president, John Tyler, then became president.

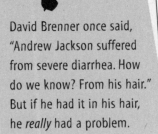

David Brenner once said, "Andrew Jackson suffered from severe diarrhea. How do we know? From his hair." But if he had it in his hair, he *really* had a problem.

And speaking of **Martin Van Buren,** if not for him, you would never have heard or used the term OK. OK stands for Old Kinderhook, which was his nickname, because he was born in Kinderhook. His followers started shouting "OK" to show their support for him.

Like french fries? You probably never would have heard of them if **Thomas Jefferson** hadn't served them at a White House dinner—horrifying John Adams, who thought he "was putting on airs."

Other Presidential Fun Facts

- **Rutherford B. Hayes** was called "His Fraudulency" because he was elected by just one electoral vote. (And what does that make George W. Bush?)
- Since the advent of television, the presidential candidate with the most hair has always won (except for Gerald Ford), according to Sy Sperling, head of the Hair Club for Men.
- **Abraham Lincoln** lost eight elections before winning in 1860.
- **FDR** and Eleanor once served the king and queen of England hot dogs for dinner.
- No American president was an only child.
- If a current retiring president has an average life span, his pension and staff may ultimately cost U.S. taxpayers more than $6 million.
- **Lincoln** was a very mystical president, seeking advice from deceased world leaders through a medium.
- **James Monroe** was only 5'4" and weighed less than one hundred pounds.
- President **George W. Bush** likes to eat bull testicles, or "calf fries," as they are called.

Presidential Putdowns

- "Bill Clinton's foreign policy experience stems mainly from having breakfast at the International House of Pancakes."—Patrick Buchanan
- "He doesn't dye his hair. He's just prematurely orange."—Gerald Ford, about Ronald Reagan

- "I think Nancy does most of his talking. You'll notice that she never drinks water when Ronnie speaks."—Robin Williams, about Ronald Reagan
- "I worship the quicksand he walks in."—Art Buchwald, about Richard Nixon
- "He looks as though he's been weaned on a pickle."—Alice Roosevelt Longworth, about Calvin Coolidge

After Jimmy Carter admitted that he had lusted in his heart after women, Shirley MacLaine said, "His lust is in his heart? I hope it's a little lower."

Presidential Lies

Al Haig, former Secretary of State to **Ronald Reagan,** once said that something his boss said wasn't a lie, it was "a terminological inexactitude." This isn't surprising considering Reagan himself once said, "Facts are stupid things."

Lyndon B. Johnson, when confronted with one of his many lies, asked, "Why must all those journalists be such sticklers for detail?"

Sure you can trust the government—just ask a Native American.

The most famous contemporary lie is, of course, "I did not have sexual relations with that woman, Miss Lewinsky." That led one wag to say later, "A man might forget where he parks ... but he never forgets **oral sex,** no matter how bad it is." SEE "PRESIDENTIAL PENISES," PAGE 237; AND "PRESIDENT PINOCCHIO," PAGE 191.

"Washington could not tell a lie; Nixon could not tell the truth; Reagan cannot tell the difference." —Mort Sahl

Television commentator Sam Donaldson once said of **Bill Clinton,** "The reason it's always so difficult for this president to tell the truth, the whole truth, and nothing but the truth, is because it's usually three different stories."

And here are some other doozies from our nation's highest office:
- "I will not send American boys to fight a war that Asian boys should be fighting."—Lyndon B. Johnson
- "Read my lips. No new taxes."—George H. W. Bush
- "I am not a crook."—Richard Nixon
- "When I was in England I experimented with marijuana a time or two. I didn't like it, I didn't inhale it, and never tried it again." —Bill Clinton
- Ronald Reagan told an Israeli prime minister that he had been one of the first photographers to take pictures of the victims at Nazi concentration camps. But Reagan never left America during the war.

Presidential Deaths

George Washington was so afraid of being buried alive that he told his secretary that he didn't want to be buried for three days after he died in order to be sure that he really had kicked the bucket.

Willliam McKinley always wore a red carnation in his lapel for luck, but took it off one day to give to a young girl in a crowd. He was shot moments later.

William Henry Harrison may have talked himself to death. He gave a two-hour inaugural speech outdoors when it was freezing. He didn't wear a coat or hat because he wanted to maintain his image as a tough guy and "Indian" fighter. He caught a cold, which turned into pneumonia, and he died one month after the inauguration.

The last words ever heard by **Abraham Lincoln** were, "You sock-dologizing old mantrap." Maybe that doesn't seem like a real thigh-slapper to you today, but the audience found it so hysterical that their laughter drowned out the sound of John Wilkes Booth's gunfire.

According to Salon.com, a few U.S. presidents may have been killed by their doctors:
- **George Washington**'s doctors were probably responsible for his death, by leeching his blood.
- **James Garfield**'s doctors probed his eventually fatal bullet wounds after superficially washing their instruments.
- **William McKinley**'s doctors didn't try to take the assassin's bullet out quickly enough.

Was Lincoln Racist?

Lerone Bennett Jr., executive editor of *Ebony*, has written a well-researched book called *Forced into Glory: Abraham Lincoln's White Dream*. This book, reviewed by *Time* but otherwise ignored by the uncomfortable mainstream press, argues that Lincoln was a racist because the "Great Emancipator":

The Pentagon has far more bathrooms than needed, because it was originally built in the 1940s, when Virginia had segregation laws on the books that required that there be separate bathrooms for blacks and whites.

- Frequently used the N-word
- **Loved black-faced minstrel shows**
- Liked demeaning, "darky" jokes
- **Supported the "Black Laws"** in Illinois, which took away the basic rights of African Americans
- Supported the Fugitive Slave Act, which forced the return of runaway slaves to their masters
- Wanted to keep as many slaves in bondage as he could until he could get support for his **ridiculous plan to end slavery:** shipping the black population back to Africa or South America

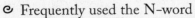

Speaking of racism, former President **George H. W. Bush** once referred to his grandchildren of Mexican descent as "the little brown ones." And presidential candidate George Wallace once said: "Sure I look like a white man, but my heart is as black as anyone here."

Another Lincoln Assassination

Although everyone knows that Lincoln was assassinated, few know that his dog was also killed. His beloved Fido was knifed to death by a drunk who became enraged when the dog got him dirty by jumping on him with muddy paws.

DUMB PRESIDENTS

Buck Wolf uncovered a great incoherent speech from a **Ronald Reagan** press conference:

The problem is the deficit is—or should I say—wait a minute, the spending, I should say, of gross national product, forgive me—the spending, I should say, of gross national product, forgive me—the spending is roughly 23 to 24 percent. So that it is in—it what is increasing while the revenues are staying proportionately the same and what would be the proper amount they should, that we should be taking from the private sector.

"What does an actor know about politics?"
—Ronald Reagan

℮ Lyndon Johnson once said about **Gerald Ford,** "He's a nice guy, but he played too much football with his helmet off."

Lyndon Johnson once said of Gerald Ford, "He's so dumb he can't even fart and chew gum at the same time." This was altered in many reports as, "He's so dumb, he can't even walk down the street and chew gum at the same time."

℮ **Richard Nixon,** our wiliest president of the last few decades, once said of football, "I never made the team. I wasn't smart enough to be quarterback."

℮ When **Ronald Reagan** was asked what kind of California governor he'd be, he replied with a straight face, "I don't know. I've never played a governor."

℮ When Richard Nixon was at Charles De Gaulle's funeral, he said, "This is a great day for France."

℮ **Gerald Ford** accidentally locked himself out of the White House.

℮ **George H. W. Bush** asked an official in Jordan: "How dead is the Dead Sea?"

℮ When **JFK** said his famous "Ich Bin Ein Berliner," he may have been saying, "I am a Berliner." But it also meant 'I am a donut.'"

℮ Stupidity isn't just a trait of modern presidents. **Andrew Jackson** believed that the world was flat.

"If Lincoln were alive today, he'd roll over in his grave."
—Gerald Ford

The World According to Dan

Vice presidents have also had their share of stupid statements—and Dan Quayle makes up for all of those who haven't. According to Corsinet.com's Brain Candy, a great source of quotes about and by just about everyone, John Cleese once said, "If life were fair, Dan Quayle would be making a living asking 'Do you want fries with that?'" Here are some equally intelligent remarks that have actually come out of the former vice president's mouth:

- "The Holocaust was an obscene period in our nation's history. I mean in this century's history. But we all lived in this century. I didn't live in this century."
- "Republicans understand the importance of **bondage between a mother and child.**"
- "It isn't the pollution that is harming the environment. It's the impurities in our air and water that is doing it."
- When Dan Quayle was campaigning, he stopped and shook hands with a woman. "I'm Dan Quayle" he said. "I'm your Secret Service agent," was her reply.

Bushisms

Here are a few Bushisms from before George W. became president:

- "We're just going to have a lot of work. . . . Redefining the role of the United States from enablers to keep the peace to enablers to keep the peace from peacekeepers is going to be an assignment."
- "Is our children learning?"
- Let's "tear down the terriers and bariffs."
- "Will the highways on the Internet become more few?"
- "Families is where wings take dream."
- He also complained that Gore's tax cut would require "numerous IRA agents."

POLITICIANS
Funny Putdowns by Politicians

Benjamin Franklin wrote a book called *Fart Proudly.*

- "She probably thinks Sinai is the plural of sinus."—Jonathan Aitken, about Prime Minister Margaret Thatcher
- "She's Attila the Hen."—Clement Freud, about Margaret Thatcher
- "He has devoted the best years of his life to preparing his impromptu speeches."—F. E. Smith, about Winston Churchill

Stupid Politicians

- "Those who died, their lives will never be the same again." —Senator Barbara Boxer, about the San Francisco earthquake
- "The Internet is a great way to get on the net."—Bob Dole
- "It is fitting that we pay tribute to Abraham Lincoln, who was born in a log cabin that he built with his own hands." —Pennsylvania Representative Dan Flood
- "The president doesn't want any yes-men and yes-women around him. When he says no, we all say no."—Elizabeth Dole
- A seventy-two-year-old candidate for mayor of Mesa, Arizona, told a racist joke about a black man, an Englishman, and a Frenchman—at a forum sponsored by Hispanic and African-American groups.
- Even indisputably articulate presidents aren't immune: Abraham Lincoln once said, "For those who like this sort of thing, this is the sort of thing they like."
- Democrats really are jackasses. Andrew Jackson's opponents called him a "jackass" and the cartoonists drew him as a donkey. And that's where it all came from.

Body and Soul

PRIVATE PARTS
What's the Hymen Doing Down There?

For virgins and men who want to change the status of these women, the hymen is a bloody nuisance. No one really knows why women have one anyway. Some nuts think it is just another **punishment from God** for Eve's hanky-panky with the apple and believe it serves some evolutionary purpose, such as keeping women monogamous by making the first penetration so painful that they'll be a bit cautious about going through the "ordeal."

Cecil Adams, in *The Straight Dope,* ridicules this notion by pointing out that hymens are **found in horses, whales, mole rats, hyenas,** and possibly other animals as well. And there's no evidence that it serves *any* purpose in these animals, because they'll screw anything whenever they can, regardless of impediments.

Incidentally, it isn't only the hymen that hangs around our body doing nothing. Organs such as the appendix are also completely useless, but manage to get passed on because (most of the time) they don't actually kill you.

There is also no particular purpose for the bellybutton after birth. But any woman who's gone through the breaking of her hymen will tell you that it's a lot more fun to pull lint out of her navel than to get rid of the hymen.

New Treatments Can Put Hemorrhoid Pain Behind You

It's been estimated that two out of three adults in the United States and Canada have this pain in the ass problem. Traditional treatments include:

℮ **Ointment,** which is only a temporary solution (some find it helpful to use facial tissues coated with moisturizing cream).

MORE HISTORICAL HEMORRHOIDS

There is a theory that part of the reason Napoleon lost at Waterloo was because his hemorrhoid pain prevented him from sitting on horseback to watch how the battle was going. (Other commentators blame a different asshole problem for his loss—namely, Wellington.)

- **Cutting,** which leaves extremely painful wounds.
- Tying the hemorrhoids with **rubber bands** to cut off their blood supply, which can cause gangrene, and works only with small hemorrhoids that most prefer to ignore if they can.
- **Injections** to reduce the inflammation.
- **Infrared laser treatment** for internal bleeding hemorrhoids.
- **Infrared photocoagulation,** which blocks the veins that feed blood to the hemorrhoids.

But now, there are two new forms of treatment:
The first is a finding by a surgery professor at Mt. Sinai that nitroglycerin ointment relieved hemorrhoid pain in almost all the people who tried it. Although it isn't commercially available yet, you can ask your doctor to write a prescription for it.

Second, there's a new technique, which leaves no wounds, doesn't require hospitalization, and is so quick that according to HealthScout.com, one doctor said the preparation for it took longer than the procedure itself! Quickly and painlessly, the doctor uses **a specialized staple gun** to simultaneously cut the swollen veins, seal the wound, and staple the hemorrhoid to a position further up the canal where there are no pain-sensitive tissues. It's too early to tell yet whether the result is permanent, and there have been some reports of problems later on down the line, so speak to your doctor before rushing into this.

Assholes of the world unite.
You have nothing to lose
but your veins.

Do Hemorrhoid Creams Really Reduce Eye Bags?

Periodically, some star gets publicity when she announces that she uses hemorrhoid cream on her eyes to reduce puffiness. The latest such pronouncement came from **Sandra Bullock,** who not only claimed that the butt-cream helped the lines around her eyes, but according to IMDB.com Celebrity News, it was "the most important tip I learned, in fact, in all my acting days that is the most astounding piece of information I've ever heard."

Where has this thirty-seven-year-old woman been? Even **Liberace** said he used to use it "as a temporary wrinkle remover." And **Conan O'Brian** told Howard Stern a few years ago that he also used it to get rid of the bags under his eyes.

To Pee or Not to Pee?

Here's a problem that's a real pisser. Men who are not free to pee. These piss-shy men can't use a public urinal with anyone nearby who can see or hear them, no matter how urgent the call of nature.

The condition, called **"bashful bladder," or "avoidance paruresis" (AP),** is estimated to affect as much as 7 percent of the population, or close to twenty million men. Women also occasionally suffer from AP and for some reason tend to have more severe cases than men.

> Stress can give you gas because if you eat too fast, it rushes a meal through your intestines so there's less time to digest it properly.

About one million people suffer so badly from avoidance paruresis that no matter what, when they gotta go outside the privacy of their own home, they can't. Their bladder (and neuroses) determines their itinerary. Like all problems in America, this one has its own support group, the International Paruresis Association. God knows what they do at their meetings. Actually we *do* know. And it ain't pretty.

Sufferers drink a whole lot of water, pair up with a "pee buddy," and go to public restrooms, urinating in increasingly difficult places. Their final goal is to go in a sports stadium—not *in* the stadium, of course, but in the restroom of one.

The guru of the group, Steven Soifer of the University of Maryland, was himself pee-shy for thirty-five years. He says that people with paruresis have developed all kinds of ways to cope. For example, **"peeing on the porcelain"** to reduce sound. Running the water. Talking to oneself ("Out damned pee!"). Or waiting until they've *really* got to go. He also believes that this fear of peeing is second only to public speaking.

This problem may seem insignificant, but people suffering from it often avoid vacations, sports events, and sometimes even employment outside their home. Some may not even leave their house at all because they can't be too far away from a private john.

This is not solely a psychological problem. When people are afraid (here, of urinating around others), there's an adrenaline reaction, causing the **sphincter muscle that controls urination to clinch** so tightly that nothing happens.

Supposedly, there's hope for some of these people with a new device called a **Stadium Pal.** Buck Wolf, who writes a funny, off-beat online column for ABCnews.go.com, described a condom-style catheter developed for the pee-shy and the lazy. The Stadium Pal can be hidden under loose pants with one end fitting over the penis. As the person urinates, it flows through eighteen inches of plastic tubing, ending up in a pouch that's hidden on the inner calf. The pouch can hold thirty-four ounces of water—or watered beer, which is more likely if it's being used at a stadium.

Of course, if someone is embarrassed to pee when they're not alone, they may not be able to do it when surrounded by cheering thousands. So these people will just have to develop their own twelve-step program: **twelve steps to the bathroom.**

FASCINATING TRIVIA ABOUT YOUR BODY

- When your face turns red from blushing, your stomach lining also turns redder.
- There's enough carbon in your body to fill 1,000 pencils, and there's enough phosphorus to fill 3,000 matches.
- **The thumb** is so important that it has a special section in the brain, independent of the section that controls the rest of your fingers.
- The amount of skin you shed each day is about the size of half an egg.
- Children don't develop kneecaps until they're two to six years old.

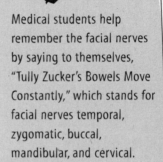

Medical students help remember the facial nerves by saying to themselves, "Tully Zucker's Bowels Move Constantly," which stands for facial nerves temporal, zygomatic, buccal, mandibular, and cervical.

Your Facial Hair

- A mustache can make your allergies worse. That's because it traps pollen, keeping it under your nose so you keep breathing it.
- Men's beards grow fastest when they anticipate sex.
- The stubble of a dry beard is as tough as copper wire of the same thickness.

- The sound from cracking your knuckles produced by a bubble of gas bursting.
- The bones in your feet make up one-quarter of all the bones in your body.
- People will die faster from lack of sleep than lack of food (ten days without sleep versus about a month without food).

Your Hair

A single strand can show:

- Whether you're on drugs—and which ones.
- Whether you live in an area with a lot of pollutants.
- Whether you live in an urban or a rural area.
- What you eat.
- Whether you work in certain places, like a gas station.
- To some degree, how smart you are (intelligent people have more zinc and copper in their hair).
- Whether you have ingested arsenic.

Your Nose

- **Allergies are nothing to sneeze at.** A Fort Worth, Texas, doctor says that people who have allergies at night should put hair spray on their hair before they go to sleep so the pollen that's floating around sticks to their hair instead of their nose.
- The average mattress will double its weight in ten years as a result of being filled with **dead dust mites**—which are the cause of a lot of allergies.
- One ragweed plant can release as many as one billion grains of pollen.
- Bacteria and fungi that grow inside air conditioning units cause Sick Car Syndrome. They can also cause allergies, asthma, headaches, and nausea.
- **Some people are allergic to their underwear**—if it's made of microfibers.

Are You an Average Male?

Men's Health does an annual survey to come up with "Mr. Average Guy." According to their latest findings, you're average if you take about 14 minutes to have sex, have sex 79 times a year (or 1.5 times a week), are married (in which case you have a 1 in 4.3 chance of cheating on your wife), are almost 5'10", gain about 1.1 pounds every year, weigh 175 pounds, and drink 3.3 cups of coffee and 1.2 alcoholic drinks each day.

"Does anybody really believe your health is more important than money? How many beautiful women say, 'Hey, should I sleep with Bill in the Porsche or Dave with low cholesterol?'"
—Nick Dipaolo

HEALTH AND DISEASES
Health Facts to Keep You Awake at Night

Your Tongue

Your tongue is the strongest muscle in your body. Your tongue is also the dirtiest part of your body—yes even dirtier than there—with more bacteria per square inch than any other area. (Are you still sure you want to kiss someone?)

We should bless people when they *hiccup*, not when they sneeze, writes Sam Uretsky. Everyone knows that we say *Gesundheit* when people sneeze because of what it's believed to do to the heart. But it turns out that hiccuping is linked to an altered heartbeat. A French hospital just found that each time you hiccup, your heart slows down a tiny bit.

Two hundred people a day, or the equivalent of a full jumbo jet, are killed by medical errors. (How many people would fly with those kinds of odds?)

The deadliest disease to ever appear in North America is **rabies encephalitis.** Only one person has ever been known to survive it, an American who was bitten by a rabid animal in 1970.

Worldwide, there have been more cases of AIDS among heterosexuals than homosexuals.

More than 2,500 left-handed people a year are killed because they used products that were supposed to be used by right-handed people.

Tuberculosis outlives its victims. A Baltimore mortician contracted TB while embalming someone who had the disease.

GETTING RID OF MOUTH AND BODY ODORS

Because a dry mouth often causes bad breath, fruits high in citric acid, such as oranges, are even better than mints for halitosis because the citrus stimulates saliva production. Have you heard that if a dog comes home with a skunk smell washing it in tomato juice will get rid of the stench? A tomato juice wash down also works for humans.

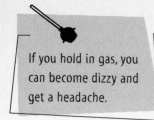

If you hold in gas, you can become dizzy and get a headache.

Hands-free kits for phones, which are supposed to be safer, can actually **increase levels of radiation transmitted to your brain.** One study found that these devices act as aerials, focusing three times as much radiation from the mobile telephone as without the aerial.

Small Symptoms That Could Be Signs of Doom

If you can't smell the difference between pizza and peanuts, you may get Alzheimer's. A two-year study found that none of the people with "mild memory problems" went on to get Alzheimer's if they could distinguish between the two scents. Here are some other things for all you hypochondriacs to worry about:

- If you **cough** it could be AIDS.
- If you get a **nosebleed,** or have severe diarrhea, you could have the Ebola virus. In three to fourteen days, all your organs will melt down, and you'll bleed through every hole in your body.
- A nosebleed could also be the first sign of leprosy or leukemia.
- **Stomach pain** could be caused by a parasite in the wall of your stomach.
- **Itchy skin** could also be an early sign of herpes, or worse, flesh-eating bacteria—which could kill you in days.
- **Sneezing** could be a symptom of the bubonic plague, which once wiped out one-third of the world.
- Having problems getting an erection? **Impotence** can be the first sign of heart disease.

SOUCE: *The Paranoid's Pocket Guide, I'm Afraid,* AND WIRELESS FLASH

Party Games for Senior Citizens

- Sag, You're It
- Pin the Toupee on the Bald Guy
- Twenty Questions Shouted in Your Good Ear
- Kick the Bucket
- Red Rover, Red Rover, the Nurse Says Bend Over
- Simon Says Something Incoherent
- Musical Recliners
- Spin the Bottle of Mylanta
- Hide and Go Pee

Cleanliness Is Next to Nothing

Of course you know how dirty doorknobs and drinking fountains and toilet flushers and money are, but here are some other places and objects you may not realize are *filthy*. Now, thanks to the *Paranoid's Guide, I'm Afraid, Maxim,* and *Stuff*, you have a whole new host of items to worry about.

Watch out for people with clammy hands. Bacteria thrives on moist surfaces.

Never eat in a restaurant. A beautifully arranged meal in a restaurant has had someone's hands all over it trying to make it look good. Restaurant menus have been touched by many dirty-handed customers before you. And after you read it, you're going to pick up your bread or eat something with your hands. For sure.

The dishcloth they use to "clean" where you're sitting (on which they'll also put the silverware that you'll put in your mouth) has been found to be contaminated almost 10 percent of the time. Self-service coffeepots and their handles, not to mention the washcloth used to "clean" the area, are all *bad*.

> Paranoid individuals sometimes fill their toilets up with cement, sand, or similar substances, because they think outside forces are out to get them and they want to prevent those forces from entering their homes through the plumbing.

Don't shop for food. Shopping cart handles, and the top basket, where parents often seat their children, are dirty.

Avoid going anyplace. The palms of tollbooth collectors probably harbor germs. Rails, posts on buses, and subways are nothing to write home about.

Don't go to see your doctor when you get sick. His stethoscope and pen are likely to be dirty as an indirect result of his contact with possibly (eccch!) *dying* patients.

Don't be admitted to a hospital. Those flowers can kill you, especially if your immune system is compromised, because the water in the vase contains microorganisms that may lead to infection.

In fact, never go outside at all. Escalator handrails and elevator buttons are likely to be contaminated. Vending, copy, and ATM buttons are full of you-know-what. The pen on the bank counter, not to mention the pen or pencil you frequently bite or suck on, could make you sick. Television remotes, especially in hotels, are as clean as the sheets. Movie theater seats are a mess, and they are where you're most likely to acquire lice.

Your home isn't so safe either. Your computer keyboard and mouse are filled with guk from all the times you didn't wash your hands before using them. (Have you ever?) Your dog or cat food bowls contain pet saliva and other contaminants.

The only safe place is your toilet. Most home bathrooms are cleaner than most home kitchens. As for public toilets, the joke goes that you can't get VD unless you sit down before the last person gets up.

After four years of a "Clean Your Hands" campaign at New York City train stations, *less* people washed their hands after using those bathrooms.

On a serious note, you can't catch VD from a toilet seat unless (perhaps) you rub your private parts exactly where the people before you did and they had to have something wrong with them there. That doesn't mean there isn't any bacteria on the seat. But as one science writer noted: "Simply sitting down on bacteria can't hurt anyone, except possibly the bacteria."

Fighting the Battle of the Bugs

Avoid germ-spreading words. Be wary of certain sounds in the English language (plosives and fricatives) that are real germ spreaders, such as *b*, *f*, *p*, *t*, *d*, and *s*. Avoid people who use those letters, and stand back from stutterers.

Avoid coughers and sneezers. If someone coughs, the air in front of her can move at speeds of up to 60 miles per hour—too fast for you to run from. It's even worse if someone sneezes near you because sneezes can travel through the air as fast as 100 miles per hour.

Bow. Don't shake hands, because you can catch everything (even warts) from a handshake. Do as the Japanese do and bow your head when you meet someone. (Unfortunately occasional concussions have led to death when two clean people cracked their heads as they bowed.)

Wear glasses. A large percentage of cold-causing viruses enter the body through the eyes, where they have access to your bloodstream.

Give up. You might as well give up the battle against bacteria. Remember: They're going to win in the end, because they're the ones who will ultimately eat you.

For people who have to blow their noses frequently, the Japanese have invented a "hay fever hat," which has a roll of toilet paper on top of it.

DEATH
A Few Weird Deaths in History

Alan Pinkerton, who started the famous Pinkerton agency, tripped and bit his tongue, then died of gangrene.

Famous writer Sherwood Anderson was at a cocktail party on a cruise ship when he accidentally **swallowed a toothpick** inside an hors d'ouevre.

Some idiot in the 1500s grew a beard that was almost nine feet long, which he kept wrapped around his body. It came undone while he was walking down a flight of steps, and he tripped and died.

The ancient (and very boring) Greek poet **Aeschylus** died after an eagle, thinking his bald head was a rock, dropped a tortoise on it to break the shell.

A Greek painter in the fifth century **laughed so hard** at a painting he did of an old lady that he burst a blood vessel and died.

> The average person spends over four years of his life in the bathroom.

The famous emperor of Rome, **Claudius I,** choked to death on a feather his doctor had put into his mouth to induce vomiting. (Some think the feather had poison on the end and that he was in fact murdered in this unique fashion.)

Fatal Things You May Encounter on a Normal Day

- **Bug zappers:** They can make you sick because electrocuted insects release bacteria and viruses that can end up on your body and in your stomach.
- **Vending machines:** Thirteen people a year are killed by vending machines falling on them.
- **Bread:** If you eat a slice of bread, it could be contaminated with ergot, similar to LSD, causing you to jump out of the window. (This is not a potential problem for people living on the ground floor.)
- **Microwaves:** If you use paper towels, napkins, or recycled waxed paper in your microwave, they can catch fire. They may contain tiny specks of metal, which can cause sparks that can burn down your house.

- **Speed bumps:** There's an actual group against them called Americans Against Traffic Calming. It turns out that these "sleeping policemen" or "dead cops" can slow you down permanently, causing injuries ranging from back pain to bumped heads. One woman went into a coma after she hit her head on the car ceiling while driving over a speed bump.
- **Potting soil:** It can be a breeding ground for a virulent form of Legionnaires' Disease.
- **Beauty parlors:** You can have a stroke if you're older and a technician jerks your head back to wash your hair.
- **Stationary bikes:** You could get jock itch if the person before you had it.
- **Perfumes:** When you approach someone wearing perfume, it can trigger asthma, migraines, and perhaps rheumatoid arthritis.
- **Bathing suits:** Wear them and you might get "seabathers eruption" from microscopic jelly that get trapped under your suit. Go naked and you'll not only be safer, but those around you will be happier. (It's the least you can do!)
- **Asteroids:** Almost 300 known asteroids are potentially hazardous to earth.
- **Alarm clocks, telephones, doorbells:** The sudden sounds can cause cardiac arrest if you have a heart-rhythm disorder.
- **Air conditioners:** Bacteria can grow in the water that's discharged by the unit, and mold can develop in the air ducts, which can lead to fatal allergic reactions.

Over four million Americans—many over sixty-five years old—are constipated all the time.

Death by Bra— and Penis

There have been at least three recorded cases of "death by bra." In two cases, women were struck by lightning in London's famed Hyde Park. The lightning was attracted to the metal underwires in their bras.

In another unusual incident, a nightclub in Massachusetts gave its patrons miniature plastic penises to put into their drinks as a joke. But no one was laughing after an inebriated customer choked to death after accidentally swallowing one.

How to Save Yourself in a Plunging Elevator

The chances that you'll be hurt in a plunging elevator have been calculated at one in twelve million. But if you do start falling, jumping up and down isn't going to do a whole lot for you because of gravity. As one person explained, in order for that to work: "We'd need the lift of airplane engines to jump while falling, and if we had that, we wouldn't need elevators." Here's what several experts suggest you *can* do so that you won't be that one in twelve million:

- Grab the rail.
- Stay low to ease the possible impact.
- Look for something to shield your head if you hit the ceiling when the elevator stops suddenly (and be prepared for a rough fall back to the floor).
- If possible, you could always do what **Sharon Stone** did. No, don't take off your panties. When she found herself in an out-of-control elevator, she slipped under her maid's service cart.

SOURCE: PORTIONS FROM *The Worst-Case Scenario Survival Handbook: Travel*,
USED WITH PERMISSION OF QUIRK PRODUCTIONS

How to Escape from Quicksand

Despite what you see in movies, quicksand holes are usually quite small and you can get out of them easily. As soon as you (God forbid) realize you're in quicksand, you can do a few things to save yourself, according to experts:

- Throw yourself out to your full length, and without making any unnecessary movements, swim or crawl out.
- **Try to run.** If you rapidly transfer your weight from one foot to the other, you won't sink.
- If you just want to wait until you get help, raise your legs slowly and lie on your back. If you do that, you can't sink in quicksand.
- And remember that if you **struggle frantically**, you'll sink faster.

SOURCE: PORTIONS FROM *The Worst-Case Scenario Survival Handbook*,
USED WITH PERMISSION OF QUIRK PRODUCTIONS

Simple Things That Could Kill You

- Hold that yawn. If it's too wide, it can break your jawbone.
- You can have a stroke if you blow your nose too hard.
- Stretching while yawning can dislocate your shoulder.
- If you sneeze too hard, you can fracture a rib.
- If you try not to sneeze, you can fracture a rib and rupture a blood vessel in your head or neck, and die.

How to Help Destroy the Earth

- Fart forty or more times a day.
- Spray your yard with DDT and not some wimpy pesticide.
- Wear polyester.
- Never wear anything twice.
- Use a few gallons of water each time you brush your teeth.
- Have thirty-seven children.
- Strangle a bald eagle.
- Own at least forty-three televi-

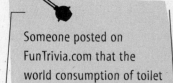

Someone posted on FunTrivia.com that the world consumption of toilet paper accounted for 72,000 acres of woodland a day.

sions per person per household and watch them all at once.

SOURCE: A MUCH LONGER VERSION OF THIS ORIGINALLY APPEARED IN *Ooze #3*, AN ONLINE 'ZINE, AND WAS WRITTEN BY PATTERSON, SCHMIDT & FITZGERALD. IT LATER APPEARED IN *Internet Insider*

 ## Realistic New Year's Resolutions

Supposedly, people only keep one in three New Year's resolutions. Here are some that you'll be sure to keep:

- I want to gain weight. Put on at least thirty pounds.
- Stop exercising. Waste of time.
- Read less.
- Watch more television. I've been missing some good stuff.
- Procrastinate more.
- Take up a new habit: smoking.
- Stop bringing lunch from home: I should eat out more.

 ## Famous Last Words

- So, you're a cannibal.
- Yeah, I made the deciding vote on the jury. What of it?
- It's probably just a rash.
- The odds of that happening are a million to one.
- I wonder where the mother bear is.
- These are the safe kinds of mushrooms.
- Gotti, schmotti. Get the hell off my lawn.
- "I eat guys like you for breakfast."—Jeff Dahmer
- "How's he going to read that magazine if he rolls it up like that?" —An insect
- "Let's have one more beer. It's an open ocean out there. What are we going to hit?"—Captain Hazelwood of the Exxon Valdez

HOW TO LIVE FOREVER
Could You (and Should You) Be Cloned?

Cloning involves taking a single cell and making an exact duplicate or a "genetic twin" either of the whole entity or parts. Now that you understand even less than before, here are some other questions you may have, answered:

Does anyone want to be cloned? Lots of people, especially self-centered ones, like celebrities. For example, Arnold Schwarzenegger said, "I'm extremely frustrated that there's only one of me around." (Others aren't.)

Haven't people been "cloned" for years? In a sense. For example, Liberace may have cloned his lover. After having plastic surgery at fifty-six, he had the same plastic surgeon transform the face of his seventeen-year-old male lover into a younger version of himself. (Jerry Seinfeld said of this: "I see some pitfalls in creating a living, breathing human blow-up doll in your likeness, so that you can then sodomize yourself as a young man.")

Rather than cloning new people in England, why don't they fix the teeth of the people they already have?

Could we clone just parts of us? Roseanne jokingly said, "Now that we have this technology for cloning, we should begin to biologically re-engineer the male for a larger penis and also breed him for more docility."

Could Jesus be cloned? First, he may not have had any DNA, for if he was the son of God, he could not be human. But if he did, *and* we came across a real relic, *and* we could get a usable sample—a big "if" because we haven't even been able to get DNA from well-preserved mummies—the baby would be "born in a different time and place and in a different world," and so might have a different destiny.

If you are cloned, would you be as great as you are now? Dr. Dean points out that what made someone like Einstein great was not just his genes. "Cloning him would create a big-brained, wild-haired baby who might grow up to be a drug addict." So a cloned you might *look* like you, but wouldn't *be* you. (And that could be a good thing!)

Will cloning help me live longer? Not necessarily. The most famous cloned animal in the world, the sheep Dolly, appears to be older than her chronological age. Her cells, when she was born, were the same age as the cells of the six-year-old ewe she was cloned from.

Will cloning make me healthier? It could. They may be able to take a young cell from a patient, make hundreds of thousands of cells from it, and give you something better than what you started with, say, a stronger immune system. Or, if something is wrong with your heart or your liver, they may be able to take a few healthy cells from there, grow new ones, and give you back a healthy heart or liver, which you wouldn't reject because they're from your own body.

Are any weird groups doing cloning now? There's a cult in Canada (associated with a cloning company) that claims a wealthy American couple saved some of their daughter's cells and has offered them $500,000 to clone their ten-month-old daughter, who died in an accident. This group believes that life on earth was created by extraterrestials using DNA engineering and that Jesus was the product of cloning. Founded by a former sports writer from France, the cult has set up a company in the Bahamas to produce babies for homosexual couples who don't want to go through the messy process of including a woman in their reproduction plans.

What's the hardest part of cloning humans? Getting women pregnant with a donor cell. The women have to be willing to have the inevitable miscarriages, so a lot of women will have to be paid a lot of money if there are to be babies born. And then there are the moral objections.

Why would anyone object to cloning? Some say "it threatens human uniqueness," that it's "playing God," and that it "devalues human life" because the person is just an "echo" of the original. (Others argue that the person isn't a "carbon copy" because identical twins are also genetically the same.)

SOURCES: MSNBC.COM, *New York Post*, DR. DEAN

Can You Clone Your Dog or Cat?

Soon you'll have designer dogs and copy cats. One couple has already spent more than $2 million trying to clone their mutt to whom they were obviously very attached. They've even set up a Web site for their little "Missy" called "Missiplicity," and soon all of Missy's little Missies won't miss the chance to visit it, because more than seven hundred of her embryos have been planted in dogs.

At first, it'll cost about $150,000 for each animal, but "in three years, the price to clone a dog or a cat will be under $20,000, less than a new car," promises the *Globe*. Companies like Genetic Savings & Clone and Operation Copy Cat have already been set up to clone animals, and tissues of animals are currently being stored—for about $500—until the donor can clone the animals later.

How to Copyright Your DNA

If you think there's no reason to copyright your DNA, just remember that **your cells don't belong to you** (unless you copyright them), and there are biotech companies that have made a fortune from other people's cells.

According to the *Christian Science Monitor*, **to make a "poor man's copyright,"** get today's newspaper and take a photo of yourself next to it (with the date clearly visible) with your tongue out, licking a stamp. The cheek cells on your tongue contain DNA that will stick to the glue.

When it dries, your cells and their DNA will be fixed. Put this stamp in an envelope and use another stamp to mail the photo and the licked stamp to yourself. But don't open it. You never know; you just might need it one day. OK, you probably won't.

Be a Good Egg

The *National Enquirer* reported on the case of a woman who turned her husband's ashes into **an hour-glass egg timer.** He totally approved of this egg-centric memento because the lousy eggs she cooked for him had been a private yolk (sorry) between them.

So, if like this man, you choose to have your ashes converted into a three-minute egg timer, those you leave behind will still be able to cook something up after you're gone.

I Want My Mummy!

An entrepreneur is charging a king's ransom to mummify people and their pampered pets. **For a mere $60,000,** they'll wrap you in twenty-seven layers of gauze, using the same process that will be utilized for customers such as Mohammed Al-Fayed (billionaire and father of Dodi Al-Fayed, the late playboy boyfriend of the late Princess Di) who has also signed up for the process.

The same treatment could also be given to your beloved dog or cat, who could be mummified in their favorite position. He or she will come complete with a bronze mummy case, a death mask, and the promise of a quiet little pet that eats little and won't rip up your furniture.

THE LAST WORD:
BATHROOM-WALL PHILOSOPHY
Graffiti

- To all you virgins: Thanks for nothing.
- Necrophilia means never having to say . . . anything.
- My mind is like a steel trap—rusty and illegal in thirty-seven states.
- No matter how good she looks, some other guy is sick and tired of her shit.
- How would the Lone Ranger handle this?
- The meek shall inherit the earth—after we're through with it.
- Drain bramaged.
- The world's full of apathy, but I don't care.
- Prejudiced people are all alike.
- Guns don't kill people, postal workers do.
- Look out for #1. Don't step in #2.
- Anyone can pee on the floor—be a hero and go on the ceiling.

Sign found underneath a toilet seat in a ladies room: "Thank God—A Man."

Schizophrenic Slogans

- I used to be schizophrenic but we're OK now.
- Allow me to introduce myselves.
- You're just jealous because the voices are talking to me.
- Out of my mind. Back in five minutes.
- It's been lovely but I have to scream now.
- "Why is it that when we talk to God we're said to be praying but when God talks to us we're schizophrenic?"—Lily Thomlin

T-Shirts

- Upon the advice of my attorney, my shirt bears no message at this time.
- Nobody knows I'm Elvis.
- The fact is familiar, but I can't quite remember my name.
- Wrinkled was not one of the things I wanted to be when I grew up.
- I'm having an out-of-money experience.
- "I got kicked out of Riverdance for using my arms."—Steven Wright

- I want to be a millionaire. (That's my final answer.)
- So many men, so few who can afford me.
- My mother is a travel agent for guilt trips.
- Liberal arts major. Will think for money.
- Gravity. It's not just a cool idea, it's the law.
- Wanted: meaningful overnight relationship.
- I'd rather be sad in a Rolls-Royce than happy on a bicycle.
- I'm so broke, if you rob me, it'll be for practice.
- Actually, I am a rocket scientist.
- If stress burned calories, I'd be a size 5.
- You have the right to remain silent; anything you say will be misquoted and then used against you.

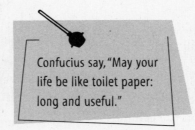

Confucius say, "May your life be like toilet paper: long and useful."

Bibliography

Alvrez, Alicia. *Ladies' Room Reader: The Ultimate Women's Trivia Book*. Berkeley, California: Conari Press, 2001.

America, Millard. *How to Get Rid of a Telemarketer*. Deluth, Minnesota: Bad Dog Press, 1995.

Bell, Simon, Richard Curtis, and Helen Fielding. *Who's Had Who*. New York: Warner Books, 1990.

Bernstein, Peter and Christopher Ma. *The Practical Guide to Practically Everything*. New York: Random House, 1995.

Bottom Line Editors. *Bottom Line Personal Book of Bests*. New York: St. Martin's Griffin, 1997.

Boyles, Denis. *A Man's Life*. New York: HarperPerennial, 1996.

Boyles, Denis, Alan Rose, and Alan Wellikoff. *The Modern Man's Guide to Life*. New York: Harper & Row, 1987.

Buffington, Perry W. *Cheap Psychological Tricks*. Atlanta, Georgia: Peachtree, 1996.

Cader Books. *1998 People Entertainment Almanac*. New York: People Books, 1997.

———. *That's Funny! A Compendium of Over 1,000 Great Jokes from Today's Hottest Comedian*. Kansas City: Andrews McMeel, 1996.

———. *That's Really Funny! Over 1,000 More Great Jokes from Today's Hottest Comedian*. Kansas City: Andrews McMeel, 2000.

———. *Celebrities: Jokes, Quotes, and Anecdotes 2001 Calendar*. Kansas City: Andrews McMeel, 2000.

Caine, Michael. *Michael Caine's Almanac of Amazing Facts*. New York: St. Martin's, 1984.

Cooper, Paulette. *277 Secrets Your Cat Wants You to Know*. Berkeley, California: Ten Speed Press, 1997.

———. *277 Secrets Your Dog Wants You to Know*. Berkeley, California: Ten Speed Press, 1999.

———. *277 Secrets Your Snake (and Lizard) Wants You To Know*. Berkeley, California: Ten Speed Press, 1999.

Dershowitz, Alan. M. *The Best Defense*. New York: Random House, 1983.

Dunn, Jerry. *Tricks of the Trade.* Boston, Massachusetts: Houghton Mifflin Company, 1991.

Feldman, David. *Imponderables: The Solution to the Mysteries of Everyday Life.* New York: William Morrow, 1986.

Flynn, Mike. *The Best Book of Bizarre but True Stories Ever!* London, England: Carlton Books, 1999.

Gallagher, Christine and Chris Gallagher. *The Woman's Book of Revenge: Tips on Getting Even When "Mr. Right" Turns Out to Be All Wrong.* New York: Carol Publishing Group, 1998.

Givens, Bill. *Film Flubs.* New York: Carol Publishing Group, 1990.

Garbage, Greta. *That's Disgusting: An Adult Guide to What's Gross, Tasteless, Rude, Crude, and Lewd.* Berkeley, California: Ten Speed Press, 1999.

———. *That's Disgusting Too: The 200 Most Disgusting Sites on the Internet.* Berkeley, California: Ten Speed Press, 1999.

Griffin, Gary. *Penis Size and Enlargement: Facts, Fallacies, and Proven Methods.* Aptos, California: Hourglass Book Publishing, 1999.

Gross, Leonard. *How Much Is Too Much: The Effects of Social Drinking.* New York: Ballentine Books, 1983.

Guinness Publishing. *Guinness World Records 2000 Millenium Edition.* New York: Bantam Books, 1999.

Gurvis, Sandra. *The Cockroach Hall of Fame: And 101 Other Off-the-Wall Museums.* New York: Citadel, 1994.

Hadleigh, Boze. *In or Out : Gay and Straight Celebrities Talk About Themselves and Each Other.* New York: Barricade Books, 2000.

Harvey, Edmund, H., Jr. *Reader's Digest Book of Facts.* Pleasantville, New York: Reader's Digest Association, 1987.

Kohut, John J. and Roland Sweet. *Real Sex: Titillating but True Tales of Bizarre Fetishes, Strange Compulsions and Just Plain Weird Stuff.* New York: Plume, 2000.

Krantz, Les. *America by the Numbers: Facts and Figures from the Weighty to the Way-Out.* Boston: Houghton Mifflin, 1993.

Lee, Stan. *The Best of the World's Worst: World Class Blunders, Screw-Ups, Oddballs, Misfits, and Rotten Ideas.* Santa Monica, California: General Publishing Group, 1994.

Louis David. *2201 Fascinating Facts.* New York: The Ridge Press, 1983,

Mingo, Jack and John Javna. *The Whole Pop Catalog.* New York: Avon Books, 1991.

Mooney, Shane. *Useless Sexual Trivia: Tastefully Prurient Facts About Everyone's Favorite Subject.* New York: Fireside, 2000.

Moser, Margaret, Michael Bertin, and Bill Crawford. *Movie Stars Do the Dumbest Things*. Los Angeles: Renaissance Books, 1999.

Munshower, Suzanne. *Simply Sophisticated: What Every Worldly Person Needs to Know*. Fort Worth, Texas: The Summit Group, 1994.

Muse, Melinda. *I'm Afraid, You're Afraid: 448 Things to Fear and Why*. New York: Hyperion, 2000.

Petras, Ros and Kathryn Petras. *The 176 Stupidest Things Ever Done*. New York: Main Street Press, 1996.

———. *Stupid Celebrities: Over 500 of the Most Idiotic Things Ever Said by Famous People*. Kansas City: Andrews McMeel, 1998.

Pezzi, Kevin, M.D. *Fascinating Health Secrets*. Gaylord: MI: Transcope, 1996.

Piven, Joshua and David Borgenicht. *The Worst-Scenario Survival Handbook*. San Francisco: Chronicle, 1999.

———. *The Worst-Scenario Survival Handbook: Travel*. San Francisco: Chronicle, 2001.

Pollack, Merrill. *How to Cope*. New York: Charter Books, 1963.

Poundstone, William. *Bigger Secrets*. Boston: Houghton Mifflin, 1986.

Prevention Magazine editors. *The Doctor's Book of Home Remedies: Thousands of Tips and Techniques Anyone Can Use to Heal Everyday Health Problems*. Emmaus, Pennsylvania: Rodale Press, Inc., 1990.

Prevost, Ruffin. *Internet Insider*. New York: McGraw-Hill, 1995.

Roberts, Nora. *Sweet Revenge*. New York: Bantam Books, 1997.

Rovin, Jeff. *The Signet Book of Movie Lists*. New York: New American Library, 1979.

Sealy, Shirley. *Celebrity Sex Register*. New York: Simon & Schuster, a Fireside Book, 1982.

Seltzer, Barry and Erwin Saltzer. *The Other 'F' Word*. Bearsville, New York: Prism Publishing, 1999.

Shepard, Alan and Deke Slayton. *Moon Shot: The Inside Story of America's Race to the Moon*. Atlanta, Georgia: Turner Publishing, Inc., 1994.

Smith, Ronald L. *The Comedy Quote Dictionary: The Best Jokes, One-Liners, and Epigrams from the Funniest Comedians, Writers, and Humorists of the 20th Century*. New York: Doubleday, 1992.

Slover, Tanya. *The Instant Genius: An Indispensable Handbook for Know-It-Alls*. Los Angeles: General Publishing Group, 1998.

The Bathroom Sports Almanac. Saddle River, New Jersey: Red-Letter Press, 1995.

The Bathroom Trivia Book: Nuggets of Knowledge for America's Favorite Reading Room. Saddle River, New Jersey: Red-Letter Press, 1986.

Tuttle, Cameron. *The Paranoid's Pocket Guide.* San Francisco: Chronicle Books, 1997.

Ulmer, James. *James Ulmer's Hollywood Hot List: The Complete Guide to Star Ranking.* New York: Griffin Trade Paperback, 2000.

Voorhees, Don. *Thoughts for the Throne: The Ultimate Bathroom Book of Useless Information.* New York: Carol Publishing, 1995.

vos Savant, Marilyn. *Ask Marilyn: The Best of "Ask Marilyn" Letters Published in Parade Magazine from 1986 to 1992.* New York: St. Martin's, 1992.

Wallechinsky, David, Irving Wallace, and Amy Wallace. *The Book of Lists.* New York: William Morrow and Company, 1977.

Wallechinsky, David, and Amy Wallace. *The Book of Lists: The '90's Edition.* Boston: Little Brown & Co., 1993.

Weber, Ken. *Toilet Papers: Wit, Wisdom & Wickedly Funny Stuff for Reading in the John.* Ontario, Canada: Stoddart Publishing Company Ltd., 1999.

Welch, Leslee. *The Complete Book of Sexual Trivia.* New York: Citadel Press, 1992.

ADDITIONAL SOURCES

Attribution for most items is given in the body of the articles, or at the bottom, but for the items below, a couple of sentences came from the following sources:

Bad (and Good) Hair Days of the Stars *(Movie Stars Say the Dumbest Thing)*; Rufus de Vane King story *(Bland Ambition)*; Academy Awards: Betty Middler and dog winning award stories *(The Hollywood Walk of Shame, The Wolf Files, ABCnews.com, Buck Wolf)*; Smoking (Ann Landers); How to Get Drunk Without Drinking *(The Best of the World's Worst)*; Hip Hip Hooray! Cheerleading Today *(Time)*; Animal Sex Facts (useless-sex.com); Computer Commandments (Juan M. posted this shorter version on the Internet); Hilarious (Real) Song Titles *(The Book of Lists* and the Country Music Hall of Fame in Nashville, reprinted in the *National Enquirer)*; Tongue Twisters (HealthScout.com and *Book of Lists)*; Worst Analogies (Gary F. Hevel, Paul Sabourin, Chuck Smith, Russell Beland); Intellectual Graffiti *(Esquire)*; How to Win Radio Contests *(Retirement Secrets: What They Don't Want You to Know)*; Office jokes about pressing charges (from "Deep Thoughts" by Jack Handy); Five Worst Cars (reprinted in the *New York Times)*; Real Books Your Don't Want to Leave Out for Your Children to Find *(Bizarre* magazine); Ridiculous Lawsuits Kicked Out of Court *(Whiplash: America's Most Frivolous Lawsuits)*; Dershowitz *(Sacramento Bee)*; The Most Often-Stolen Items from Drugstores *(Do Pharmacists Sell Farms?)*; Frightening Facts about Crime *(Esquire)*; Politicians *(White House Confidential: The Little Book of Weird)*; George Washington pocket watch story (Ali's World of the Infinitely Weird); LBJ peeing on secret service story *(Uncle John's 2nd Bathroom Book)*; Presidential Lies *(Wall Street Journal)*; Quote about president forgetting sex (Lenny Clarke); Your Hair *(Weekly World News)*.